F

F

days with your under-fives

HARPER
thorsons

HARPER
thorsons

an imprint of
HarperCollins*Publishers*
77–85 Fulham Palace Road
London W6 8JB

www.harpercollins.co.uk

10 9 8 7 6 5 4 3 2 1

Text © Julia Deering 2014

Julia Deering asserts her moral right to be
identified as the author of this work.

A catalogue record for this book is
available from the British Library.

PB ISBN: 978-0-00-751240-9
UK EB ISBN: 978-0-00-751241-6

Printed and bound in Great Britain by
Clays Ltd, St Ives plc

MIX
Paper from
responsible sources
FSC **FSC® C007454**
www.fsc.org

FSC™ is a non-profit international organisation established
to promote the responsible management of the world's forests.
Products carrying the FSC label are independently certified to
assure consumers that they come from forests that are managed
to meet the social, economic and ecological needs of present
and future generations, and other controlled sources.

Find out more about HarperCollins and the environment at
www.harpercollins.co.uk/green

Contents

Introduction

What should a four-year-old know?

'I was on a parenting bulletin board recently and read a post by a mother who was worried that her four-and-a-half-year-old did not know enough. "What should a four-year-old know?" she asked. Most of the answers left me not only saddened but pretty soundly annoyed. One mom posted a laundry list of all of the things her son knew. Counting to 100, planets, how to write his first and last name, and on and on. Others chimed in with how much more their children already knew, some who were only three. A few posted URLs to lists of what each age should know. The fewest yet said that each child develops at his own pace and not to worry.'

Written by a preschool teacher in the US

As both a parent and also an Early Years educator myself, I think I would have felt pretty annoyed by those mums' postings. Maybe you have a toddler or a preschooler, perhaps your child or children are older now, or maybe you're about to be spending some time with a young child, but whatever your situation, think of that child at four years old. What do *you* think they should know?

Here in the UK, the question 'What should a four-year-old know?' is being answered on a slightly larger scale than on a parenting bulletin board, as the current Government and its advisors are suggesting reforms to our education system that will focus on getting four-year-olds 'school ready'. That means a bigger emphasis on them knowing basic reading, writing and arithmetic before they even start in Reception. There's even talk of a new baseline test for five-year-olds in England – adding a competitive twist to the whole thing; just as the mums were doing on that preschool bulletin board. So, reading, writing and arithmetic – that's what the Department for Education think our four-year-olds should know.

Many Early Years experts, teachers, nursery staff and parents – myself included – are fighting back with a counter opinion. What *we* think four-year-olds really need to know is that they each have a brilliant talent; one that will absolutely get them 'school-ready', but not by achieving certain levels in the 3Rs. Instead, this talent will help them gain the skills they *really* need to start school. These include social and emotional skills to get along with others, curiosity about the world, practical skills, the ability to listen and understand instructions from grown ups, independence with personal care and the ability to spend time happily engaged with objects or in an activity without their parents.

And the talent? Well, it was my daughter, aged six, who put it very clearly. 'Mummy,' she told me, 'you know, all children have a talent.' When I asked her what that talent was, she replied – very matter of fact – 'All children can *play*. That's their talent.'

And I believe *that's* what a four-year-old should know; that they can *play*.

In her response to those parents on that bulletin board, the US preschool teacher also recognised the talent of a four-year-old. She knew it had little to do with reading, writing and arithmetic levels and all to do with their brilliant skills at *play*. Here are a couple of things she felt a four-year-old should know:

'He should know his own interests and be encouraged to follow them. If he could care less about learning his numbers, his parents should realize

*he'll learn them accidentally soon enough and let him immerse himself
instead in rocket ships, drawing dinosaurs or playing in the mud.*

*'She should know that the world is magical and that so is she. She
should know that she's wonderful, brilliant, creative, compassionate and
marvellous. She should know that it's just as worthy to spend the day
outside making daisy chains, mud pies and fairy houses as it is to practise
phonics. Scratch that – way more worthy.'*

This happy talent of children – play – can actually be seen from
birth. When they're not sleeping or feeling sleepy, feeding or feeling
too hungry, or feeling colicky or uncomfortable because they need
a nappy change, babies are instinctively and naturally playing. Play
is the *language* of infancy, toddlerhood and the preschool years. So, if
you want to properly understand your under-five and help them to
know what any child of their age should *really* know, you'd better
learn the language of play. And this book is where to do just that.

The power of play

As a teacher and creative play specialist with over twenty years'
experience working with children and their families in a variety of
educational settings, I am evangelical about the power of play to
promote learning. I have seen little ones simply thrive physically
and mentally when their days, weeks and months are, above all
else, playful.

Over the years I've worked with thousands of children in a huge
variety of locations – from classrooms, gardens, woodland, parkland
and playgrounds to museums, art studios, venue foyers, libraries,
kitchens and even school dining halls. Whether I'm producing
materials and ideas for families to use together in a gallery or at

home, or I'm leading a session for a group in a herb garden, my raison d'etre is to provide young children with an enabling environment – somewhere Early Years Foundation Stage (EYFS) guidelines describe as a place where they feel safe, comfortable and 'at home'; where they can investigate, explore and learn in a way that is best for them. And that is always through play.

As an Early Years practitioner, these EYFS areas of learning and development guidelines inform all the sessions I plan, all the materials I produce – and because over many years I have experienced how young children learn best, I always deliver Learning and Development objectives with *playful* teaching methods and through *playful* activities.

For example, if I'm thinking about how to include the teaching of Communication and Language in my sessions, I'll plan for plenty of playful opportunities for families to talk and sing together, where a little one can talk with their grown up, learn new words, experience non-verbal communication and listen to rhymes, songs and stories. When considering Physical Development I try to include opportunities for the children to playfully practise their fine motor skills and gross motor skills doing practical activities. I teach Personal, Social and Emotional skills during my sessions too, and offer plenty of opportunities to develop skills like sharing, taking turns, listening to others and recognising others' feelings while playing. I also make sure I develop slightly more formal EYFS Specific Areas of Learning – things like Numeracy, Literacy, Expressive Arts and Design and Understanding the World – which can all be promoted through play.

Throughout my professional work, wherever I'm teaching, play is central to my planning and practice. This way, I know that the children in my care are happily and naturally learning, gaining all those essential skills that will make them really ready for school when the time comes.

By now, you might be thinking – *hang on a minute, all this play sounds well and good for a teacher doing their job, but how exactly does this fit in with parenting? Family life is just too busy for all that play-planning and all those 'Areas of Learning and Development'.* I know, I know. This was my thinking too. When I became a parent of two young children – only seventeen months apart – and then went back to work, albeit part-time, I also wondered how on earth I could integrate all this great and important play, in which I strongly believed and promoted professionally, into our everyday family life. I remember thinking that, sometimes, it would just be easiest to hand over my phone to my toddler when on a journey to the supermarket, for example. And what about the TV? How handy was that for keeping them still and quiet while I dashed off those vital emails, or loaded the washing machine?

It was then that I decided to *change the conversation* just as Don Draper from *Mad Men* would say. Instead of trying to fit all this play into our busy life, I decided to flip it on its head and instead try to see our busy life as a series of opportunities for play. Play was so important to me professionally, I just knew I could make it work personally. In fact, using this approach transformed my experience of parenting two young children into a more joyful, fulfilling and memorable experience than I ever could have imagined.

Using play didn't mean that I suddenly became the in-house entertainer, and it didn't mean I played with my children all day long. No, I just wanted to get my children involved and learning, thinking and growing, helping and cooperating as a matter of course throughout our normal busy day – and I realised that I could do this all under a kind of *banner* of play.

So, for example, loading the washing machine became a playful activity that my toddler just *loved*. Sometimes, he would help with a fun socks-sorting game and sometimes we'd sing a silly washing machine song as we worked. (There will be much more singing in this book, so be prepared.) And if I needed to make a phone call or try to get his baby sister to sleep, for example, instead of putting on the TV, I might surprise him with a little tote bag containing a few unexpected things – just some small toys he'd forgotten about. As I experimented with more and more ways to weave play into our everyday life I began to realise that some of these ideas actually freed me up a fair bit, because once I'd set them off with something irresistible to play with, my children would often find their flow and they became really rather good at playing independently. Some of the ideas actually saved my sanity – like when I arranged their clothes into silly positions on the floor in the mornings. When they were laid out like that, there was never again an argument about *what* to wear, and *when* to get dressed. I was so pleased because those arguments had been proper two-year-old ones, with rage and tears and stamping – you know the kind . . . Now they just laughed, said 'silly Mummy', and got dressed.

Parenting with play really paid off for me. I realised how much easier it was to motivate my children, and get good behaviour from them, when I applied playful positivity to the situation, rather than by trying to be all authoritative and go down the battle-of-wills route. My feisty and smart two-year-old got that I was being playful, of course, but because she, like all children, had this innate desire to play, she was more than happy to comply – to help tidy up, or clean her teeth or whatever – because it was all done in a fun and gentle, playful and mutually respectful way.

So this was me, beginning to find my feet as a parent, bringing my teaching experience to bear when I could, experimenting with different ways to make play shape our everyday. Some ways to play were time savers, some were sanity savers. Some were ideal for filling a bit of time, instead of putting on the TV, and some brought out top-notch creativity in my children or developed their independence. I discovered a sense of peace, purpose and fun in parenting despite hearing so many others with children of similar ages bemoaning the 'terrible twos', shouting at their kids, ignoring unwanted behaviour with a 'boys will be boys' comment or just going on and on about how *hard* it all was.

Yes, these are the messy years; yes, things get pretty hectic and, yes, sometimes there are tears and tantrums – but by identifying and implementing ways to parent with play I developed an approach to parenting that really worked for me. And it will work for you too.

Why 7 Ways to Play?

When I was asked to write about this approach to parenting I knew I had a fantastic opportunity to reveal the secret to a happier, calmer and more creative experience of parenting under-fives. And, of course, you've probably guessed that, put very simply, the secret is *play*; play in all its glorious forms.

When I started analysing how I integrated play and playfulness into my family's life I realised that there were, in fact, just *seven* different ways.

 Sometimes I would use play to enable me to complete the household chores.

 When I needed a minute to myself I would initiate play in super-quick time with a tempting toy or object.

 Whenever we had more spare time, I would invitingly set out a few toys or objects they hadn't played with for a while.

 If we had a free afternoon, I would encourage my children to get creative and play in a messy way.

 I always listened out for my children's *call-to-craft* moments, and on these occasions I would use playful tactics to help them make things.

 I would try to make time every now and again to actually stay and play a game or two with them.

I would use playful strategies to help keep my children's behaviour on the right track at potential flash-point times of the day or in particularly challenging situations.

The aim of this book is to explain and offer lots and lots of examples of these seven ways of parenting with play to help you adopt this peaceful and positive approach.

In summary, the 7 Ways to Play are as follows:

⭐ Chores: not bores
Household chores will always need to be done; it's about inviting your preschooler to 'help' you – or play alongside – while you tackle domestic tasks.

⭐ 10-second set-ups
This is perfect for when you need your children to play by themselves for a while; it's about offering them a super-quick, irresistible stimulus to encourage a period of happy independent play while you get on with something else.

⭐ Invitations to play
For this way to play you take just a few minutes to set up and demonstrate/model the activity before you step away and witness some wonderful open-ended play.

⭐ Invitations to create
The idea of this is not *what* they make; it's *that* they make – it's all about the process – giving them the materials and opportunity to explore different media and to get creative without necessarily finishing a piece of art or craft.

⭐ Make and take
Through this you can be with your child to make (or bake) something together, perhaps for a special occasion or particular time of year. For this activity, it is okay for the child to be aware that the aim is to create a finished product.

⭐ Stay and play
This is when you make time to simply play with your child. Often this way to play is special time with stories and books, games or song-based play.

⭐ Sanity savers
This is when you use quick-thinking tricks and play to keep children behaving as you would like, but with fun and games rather than stern discipline.

How to use this book

The Playful Parent is a guide to managing and enjoying your busy family life with play. It will help you identify, observe and initiate play, and enable you to integrate it into your everyday routine. It will help you feel more confident about encouraging a mix of activities from across the broad spectrum of play to fulfil your family's particular needs in most situations, from a spare five minutes to the times when something playful can absolutely save the day. It's a book to dip into again and again for details of practical and fun ideas to help you use play throughout your day, or to simply get some inspiration.

You'll be fluent in the language of play in no time, and you'll begin to really enjoy – not endure – those messy, marvellous and magical toddler and preschool years. It doesn't matter if you feel you have forgotten how to play; babies, toddlers and children instinctively know how to do it. It doesn't matter either if you think you haven't a creative bone in your body – children are the most creative people on the planet. And it doesn't matter if you feel you don't have the time or the inclination to be the family entertainer – children are naturally great at entertaining themselves. All you have to do is give *them* opportunities to play along the way, every day – and these can be found in the many tried-and-tested ideas in this book.

Use the 7 Ways to Play to plan your day

Planning play is like planning meals; just as you aim to provide your child with a balanced diet of food, you might aim to offer a balanced diet of play too. So, in the same way that you wouldn't want their diet to be all bread and cereal, say, their play shouldn't be all make and take. Some people like to create weekly plans for their meals, others like to take it one day at a time; the same principle can be applied to planning your play. When you're familiar with all the different ways to play you can begin to pick and mix the ideas to give your child variety; you can plan by selecting the right kind of play at the right time — to suit you, your situation and the needs of your child – and, of course, come up with your own ideas. If you wish, you could then make these into a daily or weekly play planner – just like a meal planner.

The key thing to consider when planning your play is how much *time* you have. If you really need your little one to be getting on with something by themselves or perhaps to be helping *you* get on with something, happily and cooperatively, then choose an idea from Chores: not Bores, 10-Second Set-ups or Sanity Savers. If you want to set up an activity that engages them while you merely supervise, choose an Invitation to Play. If you can be around to help them a bit, choose an Invitation to Create; if you have enough time to actually join in, then try a Stay and Play or a Make and Take activity.

Also, when choosing ways to play, think about the mood your little one is in. Are they full of beans? Can you stay and play? If they're bouncing around when you need to make a phone call, or you'd just like them to play by themselves for a while, choose an active 10-second set-up, like the balloon solution on page 62, or an active invitation to play as on page 102.

If your child is feeling poorly you could try a gentle stay and play – perhaps reading to them. Then, depending on how they're feeling, you might set them up with a gentle invitation to create – maybe with some play dough, or with an audio book – or a simple invitation to play – perhaps using small figurines and a little play scene on their duvet.

Whatever your situation – whether you want to mark high days and holidays with some kind of art or craft, have a cosy day at home because you're feeling unwell, fit play into a hectic morning of shopping and travelling, use it to cool down on a hot day or simply to get them outside for a while – there is a way to play in this book that will suit.

Family Favourites

You might like to make your own collection of playful-time favourites by trying out a few of the ways to play and making a note of any that worked particularly well in the Favourite Play chart at the back of this book. As your repertoire expands, and you add ideas of your own, you can check with this list and revisit those favourite activities when you're stuck for an idea. By continuing to add more winning ways to play to your list of tried-and-tested, go-to ideas, you will create a bespoke play-planner that's perfect for your family (see p.312).

A quick guide to baby and preschool play

How can we recognise play?

Young children have a natural drive to be playful and to find every opportunity to play; they have a talent to be totally and busily absorbed in whatever they're playing. It can be hard for us grown ups to recognise play sometimes – let alone define it – as we're often so busy ourselves, or feeding, changing and cleaning up around our little ones that we don't really see what's going on. But just take a moment, when you next get a chance, to observe your child at play – I still find it pretty captivating to watch my own children. Look at that tiny infant kicking her legs or watching the light bounce off the reflection in a window – she's playing. Look at that baby sitting up and crinkling some noisy fabric – he's playing. Look at that toddler digging a hole with a stick – she's playing. Look at those preschoolers with pillowcases round their shoulders, picking up leaves and taking them to a tree stump – they're playing. Look at that little girl tapping her water bottle along the park railings – she's playing. As I might watch a talented artist sculpting or a chef cooking, I'm often in bewildered awe at the sight of babies, toddlers and preschoolers playing. For me, their ingenuity, creativity, imagination and their ability to be fully immersed in their game is a wonder to behold.

What do they play?

What babies, toddlers and preschoolers actually play can be grouped into categories, which can help us begin to recognise play when we observe it, giving us a little window into their special, wonderful world. Children often exhibit more than one category of play at a time, and there are acknowledged to be around sixteen types, so it can get a little confusing, but to help you identify *what* your little one might actually be doing when they're, say, ripping up your newspaper or making those two pebbles talk to one another, here's a summary of some of the different *categories* of play in which your little one might be immersed.

Imaginative/fantasy play

In these games a large cardboard box will become a car, a tea towel a superhero cape, or the sofa a volcano with the carpet as the lava, or you might be made cup after cup of 'tea', or a toy hammer and screwdriver will be tucked into the top of shorts, a hard hat popped onto a head and your kitchen will be measured-up and 'mended'.

This category of play begins as imitation of what the grown ups do in a kind of role-play, but later it can take on a more filmic, adventurous quality. It's immersive and full of improvisation, and children are experts at this kind of play from as early as two years old.

Small world play

This is similar to the imaginative/fantasy play described above, but in small world play the child is the 'puppet master' – controlling the world and the action. Using play figures or toy cars, or even sticks and stones as characters, a child will act out their story or sequence of activities. Sets and scenes for the characters are useful (like dolls' houses, garages, farm sets, etc, and can even be made by older children) but they are not essential – a child's imagination is often enough.

Object play

This type of activity refers to the playful use of objects. These can be dolls, blocks, toy cars and puzzles as well as non-toys such as plastic bowls and empty cardboard tubes, wooden spoons and a silky scarf, or loose parts such as pine cones and giant buttons, as well as natural objects such as shells, leaves and pebbles or a few root vegetables. These objects are played with and explored, manipulated and lined up. Sometimes children over three years old will use objects imaginatively, as substitutes for something else – so a rectangular block might become a telephone, while a cardboard tube becomes a tunnel for a small car.

Books and stories

This is a well-loved form of play for babies, toddlers and young children who adore being told stories from books or in a grown up's own words, and this magical, special category of play is very important in developing listening, language and pre-literacy skills. Young children in particular find picture books irresistible, and they can very quickly learn the techniques of page turning and 'reading' the story (often out loud) to themselves.

Creative play

This is when children respond creatively, using a wide range of media, to different stimuli in order to make something: mark-making, music-making, art-making, sculpting, construction and model-making. Activities involve painting, sticking, cutting, tearing, rolling, print-ing, scraping, colouring, spraying, flicking, squeezing and moulding. Dancing and dramatic play are also examples of creative play.

Sensory play

This is a very important category of play for babies and toddlers as they do most of their learning about the world around them via their sense of touch and taste (that's why they go through that phase of 'mouthing' everything). Sensory play is about using all of the senses, so listening to music, and tapping and hitting things to create sound is included in this category. Sensory play is also playing with play dough, water, paper, plastic balls, leaves, mud, corrugated card-board, wooden shapes, fabrics and shaving foam. It's looking into mirrors, through coloured cellophane, at pictures, faces, the sky and watching the washing machine spin. Many examples of sensory play are multi-sensory.

Outdoor play

Considered by many to benefit the health and development of little ones more than any other form of play, outdoor play is not all about rough and tumble, running wild and getting up close to nature, although developing gross motor skills and experiencing flora and fauna first-hand is an important part of it. Most categories of play can be transferred to an outside arena and are more fulfilling and memorable for it.

How do they play?

How little ones play, and with whom, will change as their social and emotional skills develop. Babies and toddlers will mainly play alone, but sometimes they will do so *in parallel* with other children – they will play near to one another in a similar way but do not engage in play together. When they're a little older children enjoy social play – making up all kinds of collaborative games with other children. Babies, toddlers and preschoolers will enjoy playing with us grown ups too, of course; from the earliest games of Peekaboo, to sharing a 'cup of tea', to having a kick-about in the garden as they really find their feet and get moving. Young children love it if they can get an adult to join in the fun.

Why should we let the children play?

The crucial beginnings of the brain's building process occur between 0 and 3 years of age when there is a rapid production of connections between brain cells (synapses). By the time a child is three years old around 80 per cent of this development has already taken place; 90 per cent by the time they are five. Since *play* offers huge amounts of brain stimulation, it makes sense that it has a massive impact on the emerging cognitive, motor and social skills of young children. It's through a kind of *prism of play* that children, using their natural creativity and amazing imaginations, make important cerebral connections and basically learn *everything*; developing personal, social and emotional skills, communication, language and emerging literacy, problem-solving, reasoning and emerging numeracy, knowledge and understanding of the world and all their physical skills – a whole *spectrum* of thinking and knowing and learning. And to think they're just *playing*!

Ready steady play

Before we begin . . .

It's at about the time when a baby reaches toddlerhood that our homes might begin to fill up with numerous flashing, noisy, plastic, branded gadgets and toys. This is far from necessary, and actually can be a bit of a barrier to accessing the 7 Ways to Play. Rather than buying toys that do more and more of the thinking for them, now's the time to seek out those toys that really stimulate your children's brilliant imaginations and which will promote open-ended play. If this means having a toy audit and giving away, or at least putting into storage, a lot of their stuff – now's the time to do it. Honestly, those flashy plastic things won't be missed a jot. The 7 Ways to Play method will result in you actually needing fewer, not more, toys for your toddler and preschooler, which they will play with more and for longer periods of time.

Preparing for play

The 7 Ways to Play method supports the idea that toys are just *one* of the many things children need when playing. You will find that they will use more art supplies and general household stuff in their play. Non-toys – or *real objects* – are often fantastic playthings and, as long as they're clean, are not sharp or pinch hazards, or left out all the time, they can make for really interesting and useful tools and toys in play.

Here are a few things to look out for, and make room for, after all those bleepy, flashy plastic things have been *adios*-ed. It's all about *experiences* rather than specific *equipment*, though, so do adapt this list; make use of what *you* have – make it work for you, and your family, in *your* home.

☆ Toys that promote open-ended play – things that don't do all the thinking for them; like Lego and other construction toys, imaginative-play toys and books.

☆ Practical-life equipment – such as an extra washing-up bowl, cloth and sponge, a dust-cloth, clothes pegs.

☆ A child-sized soft-bristled broom and dustpan and brush.

☆ A sand-timer.

☆ Some child-friendly kitchen equipment: jug, grater (we invested in a kid-friendly grater, as seen on the CBeebies cooking show *I Can Cook*), juicer, pestle and mortar, wooden spoons, measuring spoons, bowls and children's scissors. (Really small children will need supervision with some of these sharper items.)

☆ Some child-sized basic gardening equipment: a small watering can, trowel or spade or fork, and an outside broom.

☆ Lots of clean, interesting, plastic, polystyrene and cardboard packaging that is otherwise destined for the recycling box.

☆ Clean and empty plastic food containers, tote bags and baskets.

☆ An acrylic (safety) mirror tile or two.

☆ A set of beanbags.

☆ Balloons.

☆ Play-silks and other large pieces of fabric, including a blanket or two.

☆ Natural objects – such as shells, driftwood, pebbles and leaves, sticks, dried grasses and seeds.

☆ Some child-friendly tools of investigation – tape-measure, plastic magnifying glasses, torches, plastic tweezers.

☆ Basic art and craft supplies, the smaller and messier of which should be stored out of reach of little ones, and used only under supervision: good-quality poster paints, watercolours, PVA glue, sticky tapes – double sided, masking (painters'), colourful tape – children's scissors, paintbrushes, paper – on a roll, A4, coloured and watercolour paper – thin card, paper plates, paper bags, stickers, pipe-cleaners, beads, buttons, feathers, sequins, googly eyes, glitter, Blu-tack, crayons, washable felt-tip pens, chalks and craft foam sheets.

☆ A scrap-paper collection: save sweet and chocolate wrappers, used wrapping paper, old greetings cards, ribbons, greaseproof paper, foil and magazines with lots of colourful child-appropriate images for cutting out.

☆ A selection of brushes – of various sizes, soft and hard, for all kinds of play.

☆ Loose parts: cotton reels, pine cones, tubes, big buttons, mini pom-poms, corks, small blocks, pieces of fabric.

☆ A collection of child-friendly musical instruments.

☆ A good-quality set of face-paints.

☆ A ball of string.

Make way for play

The 7 Ways to Play method supports the idea that your child's play shouldn't be restricted to just their bedroom, an area in the living room or a playroom. However, this doesn't mean that there'll be mountains of toys in *every* room, nor does it mean you have to convert your home into some kind of soft-play gym. Rather, it's about *making way for play* in your home by adapting the spaces you already have to accommodate play; play that's *appropriate* to that particular space. This adaptation of your home doesn't have to be permanent and it needn't be expensive. As IKEA interior designer Raphael Bartke says,

'Children aren't small forever . . . and your home will soon transform again.' And, of course, you don't need to reorganise your whole home at once – take it one way to play at a time and adapt as you play.

Ideas to get play started

Here's how you might make way for play in your home. Try just one or two ideas initially; you'll be amazed at the changes in how your little one interacts with the spaces in your home.

☆ Buy sink steps or step-stools for each sink in your home.

☆ Source a low bench or kids' table for your kitchen (or fix a fold-down table at your child's height if you're short of space).

☆ Put placemats, plastic plates, bowls, cups and cutlery somewhere low and within easy reach of your little one.

☆ Fix hooks for coats at child height, and place some accessible storage for shoes near your front door.

☆ Sort out your storage: a lot of art and craft supplies, toys and playthings can be stored out of sight and reach of your little one. Buy some cheap storage boxes, and buy twice the amount you think you'll need. Label them if they're not transparent – *you will* want to be able to access their contents quickly and easily. Display those that you do want left out on low shelves and in lots of small baskets and tubs.

☆ Make some, carefully considered, toys and playthings accessible in small storage stations all over your home – the bathroom, the hall, the master bedroom, the kitchen and garden – as well as in the living room and your child's bedroom.

☆ Find a space for construction play.

☆ Find a space for physical play, like target practice, inside.

☆ Look out for spaces for temporary dens and book-nooks.

☆ Have small baskets or boxes of picture books all over your home – don't just store them on one bookshelf.

☆ Create a dress-up area with a mirror.

☆ Make a creative/making station.

☆ Find a space for a listening station – with an easy to use CD player, cushions and a few audio books.

☆ Provide at least one designated doodle area.

☆ Make any outside space as safe and as interesting a place to play as inside – think accessible storage stations with kid-friendly tools and toys, a low work-bench, places for temporary dens – not just as a place for running around and other physical activity.

☆ Find space outside for those messy or wet-play activities – and, if possible, somewhere for digging.

You can prepare for play when you're out and about too. This doesn't mean you need to take a suitcase full of toys with you wherever you go, rather, it's about taking along a basic kit to encourage play. What you pack will depend on your outing, of course, but whether it's a small toy or two, a roll of Sellotape, some paper and crayons, a torch, a take-a-look book, or a little bucket for collecting things, you can initiate some wonderful play by handing over something other than your smartphone when you're out and about to get your child thinking, learning and playing in the real world and engaging appropriately with their environment.

So, now we're ready, we're set. Let's play!

Chores: not Bores

Chore *noun*. A small piece of domestic work (freq. in pl.); an odd job; a recurrent, routine or tedious task.

Whether we love or loathe chores, it's impossible to deny the fact that they are an ever-present aspect of domestic life. Anywhere along the sliding scale between *house-proud neat freak* and firmly in the *chores-are-for-bores* camp, our own relationship with, and attitude towards, chores becomes crystallised some time between the age of three and thirty-three. Once established, it's pretty hard to alter, until, that is, we have children. Most parents would agree that as soon as a baby arrives on the scene, chores not only multiply but they also swell and mutate, unearthing a brand-new set of domestic tasks just when our time to carry out such jobs has been totally eradicated by the newly arrived bundle of joy.

'Suddenly you have to do the washing up or the laundry, or whatever, as soon as you get a spare minute. There's no choice. There's no "I can't be bothered". There's no later. And if you don't do the basics when you can it can all quickly unravel – from a stinky, overflowing nappy bin and no clean bottles, to no clean mugs for that much-needed tea. It was a learning curve and a half.'

Dad of two, remembering the early days

During the baby years we, as loving, responsible parents, accept and maybe even relish the realisation that we must carry out chores for, and because of, our children; there is usually a tacit acceptance of our fate. But at some point, perhaps as our children turn from tots to preschoolers, or from preschoolers to school-age children, or even from school-age children to teenagers (it hits every parent at a different time), there comes a day, or a moment in a day, when we suddenly feel like the maid. This is neither a positive nor pleasant feeling to experience and it can soon lead to feelings of resentment towards those chores caused directly by children, which, let's face it, feels like all of them, doesn't it?

However, it seems that in the UK and the US, parents are more reluctant than their predecessors to ask children to carry out household tasks. Recent studies have shown that children are increasingly not expected to contribute in any real way to the domestic chores of everyday family life, and older children often receive bribes or payment for completing their chores. At what age and exactly how children might become involved in domestic chores is, of course, a parental prerogative, but according to this poll many parents believe that they should involve their children in chores, even if they don't.

Apart from avoiding that feeling-like-the-maid moment, there are many other good reasons for introducing age-appropriate chores to children at some point in their childhood. For example, by carrying out chores children can:

☆ learn to be confident and responsible
☆ feel an important part of the family
☆ learn to care for themselves
☆ learn to care for others
☆ increase their self-esteem (for a job well done)
☆ develop specific skills like hand–eye coordination and problem-solving

It seems children are perhaps even predisposed to wanting to help with chores; they certainly develop a natural inclination to be kind, even selfless, at a younger age than we might suppose. German psychology researcher Felix Warneken, PhD, showed that at 18 months old toddlers are capable of exhibiting altruistic behaviour. In one experiment, Dr Warneken had an adult, laden with books to put away, pretend to be unable to open the doors to a cupboard. More often than not – without being asked or offered a reward – the toddlers helped.

But here's the rub: how do you get children to continue to develop those altruistic flashes of behaviour and carry out chores happily as they grow into preschoolers and beyond? How do we avoid the nagging (ours) and the rolling eyes (theirs)?

Certainly our own personal relationship with chores has a bearing on how we present them to our children; if we consider them to be boring and tedious, it's hard not to transfer this message. I'll never forget coming in from school – I must have been about twelve years of age – to my little sister, then three years old, playing with her toy iron and board next to my mother who was doing the real thing – the family's ironing. My sister caught my eye as she wielded her toy iron menacingly and muttered, frowning, 'Bloody ironing.' Fortunately, my mum saw the funny side!

However, the same point is relevant to personal chores too. As Steve Biddulph points out in his recent book, *Raising Girls*, our children definitely take in and will eventually make our attitudes their own – whether we sing while we shower or enjoy putting on our clothes, or whether we frown, stress, grump and hurry our way through life.

Many parents find that older children can be encouraged to complete chores through rewards, praise and recognising the feeling of satisfaction of knowing they've completed a task well. My husband, to this day, will be first to offer to put clean covers on the duvets.

He puts this enthusiasm down to the fact that when he was about ten years old his mum told him how good and quick he was at it; we are still reaping the rewards of this great, and possibly honest, note of encouragement.

Younger children have different motivational drives though. If we can tap into their intrinsic desire to be kind, busy, productive and playful we really can make chores more than bearable, and actually – wait for it – fun. This is how chores have become my first way to play for toddlers and preschoolers.

Chores aren't bores; they're a way to play

By changing the way we present household tasks – not as mundane, boring jobs that need to be done, but as opportunities for playful activity – they can instead be seen as a way to spend quality time with our children. This is especially useful for busy working parents for whom chores and playtime with their children have to exist in the same concentrated period of time.

The key to integrating chores into playtime is to stop thinking that household tasks have to be isolated, parental tasks.

Ways to play and chores for preschoolers

Here are some points to keep in mind when trying to get preschoolers involved in chores:

☆ Make the chore irresistible and fun with a game, a song or a challenge.

☆ Keep it playful.

☆ Change the nature of the chore-play regularly to keep it fresh.

☆ Don't feel you have to involve your child in every chore.

☆ Don't expect perfection.

☆ Always supervise.

☆ Use green (and safe) cleaning products around children.

☆ Be encouraging.

☆ Show how pleased you are every time a chore is completed (even if it is not done perfectly).

☆ Always say thank you for helping.

The most common question that parents ask is what exactly is the appropriate age to a) introduce chores, and b) what kinds of chores should children actually be able to complete at specific ages.

If you think of chores as a way to play then you can introduce them from as early an age as you like. As for the actual complexity of the chore, well, of course that will depend on the age of your child, their specific abilities, their dexterity, their maturity and the set up of your home. But by making a job a game, in fact *all* areas of chore-work can be happily accessed by children as young as two. In some cases they will, of course, simply be playing alongside you while you complete the task, but on occasion they may be able to contribute to the actual outcome in some way. The point is, by making chores fun the domestic tasks get done, your child is happily involved, they don't learn that chores are tedious and something to avoid at all costs, they practise important life skills and numerous other skills with you through playful activity and you get some quality time together.

Below, I've listed the main household chores. I've grouped them according to how frequently they might need to be carried out, but, of course, this varies in every home.

Everyday – or most frequent – chores:
Laundry ☆ Dusting ☆ Vacuuming ☆ Sweeping ☆ Washing up ☆ Dishwasher loading/unloading ☆ Setting and clearing the table ☆ Making beds ☆ Changing sheets ☆ Cleaning the bathroom ☆ Tidying up ☆ Putting rubbish in the bin ☆ Picking up after oneself ☆ Putting groceries away ☆ Cooking

Less-frequent chores:
Cleaning the car ☆ Defrosting the freezer ☆ Washing windows ☆ Garden upkeep ☆ Sorting out clothes – outgrown and worn-out

The Mary Poppins Approach

What better way to explain chores as a way to play than to refer to the wonderful cleaning queen and playful governess, Mary Poppins. Her take on how to get the chores done is brilliantly illustrated in the song 'A Spoonful of Sugar' in which she tells us, 'In every job that must be done, there's an element of fun. You find the fun and – SNAP – the job's a game. And every task you undertake becomes a piece of cake, a lark and a spree.'

So here are some adult-led spoonfuls of sugar – or rather, playful ideas – to help any household chore become a way to play for you and your little one. Remember to change the nature of the game or challenge every so often to keep it fresh for you and irresistible to your child. Of course, this is not a finite list – I hope these ideas will inspire you to think up your own playful ways to make chores less of a bore.

Laundry

☆ Complete the laundry chores, with your child helping as best they can alongside, in the manner of robots or fairies, magicians or spies.

☆ Make a game of dividing the laundry into piles of different types – colourful, whites and pales – ready for the machine.

☆ Play the colour game – as you sort the laundry, give your child one particular colour to search for and collect.

☆ Set playful challenges for you and your child – how fast can we sort the washing or load the machine? Can we do it faster than last time?

☆ Play 'What am I?' – a great describing game as you sort, hang out or fold the clean laundry. 'I am blue. I have buttons. I have long sleeves. I have cuffs. I belong to Daddy. What am I?'

☆ Try the match the socks game. You could add to the challenge by seeing how quickly your child can complete the task, or by playing a song from a favourite CD or listening to a song on the radio to see how many clean and dry socks they can match before it finishes.

☆ Sing a laundry-themed song to 'move the job along' like Mary Poppins does. You could sing 'A Spoonful of Sugar', but here are a couple of other suggestions to get you started and add some variety!

On a cold and frosty morning ♪

(To the tune of Here we go round the Mulberry Bush)
This is the way we sort the clothes, sort the clothes, sort the clothes*
This is the way we sort the clothes
On a cold and frosty morning.

See them go round in the washing machine, the washing machine, the washing machine
See them go round in the washing machine
On a cold and frosty morning.

*change the action to sing about different types of laundry jobs like 'hang out the clothes', or 'fold the clothes'.

To be washed ♪

Mummy's found some blue trousers, blue trousers, blue trousers
Mummy's found some blue trousers – to be washed.
Daisy's found a white towel, white towel, white towel
Daisy's found a white towel – to be washed

☆ Set up a mini laundrette in the kitchen while the washing machine does its thing. Most small children will love to handwash dolls' clothes in a bowl of warm soapy water. Put an old towel down underneath to prevent slips.

☆ Let them have fun folding things – small towels, pillowcases and tea towels are great items with which to practise. Just don't expect precision corners.

☆ Secure a length of string at each end, to two chairs perhaps, at your child's shoulder height and let them peg out the socks.

☆ Get to know some laundry-themed stories to recount to each other while doing the laundry. Or your little one could 'read' you the story from the book itself.

Laundry-themed picture books

Here are a few of our favourites:

Mrs Mopple's Washing Line – Anita Hewett
Bare Bear – Miriam Moss and Mary McQuillan
Pants – Giles Andreae and Nick Sharratt
The Queen's Knickers – Nicholas Allan
The Smartest Giant in Town – Julia Donaldson
Paddington: Trouble at the Laundrette – Michael Bond
Mrs Lather's Laundry – Allan Ahlberg

Dusting

☆ Children, armed with their own cloth or feather duster, will love following you around, copying you while you dust. Best not to put any cleaning product on their cloth though.

☆ Pop on a motivational tune and see if you can finish the room by the end of the song. Here are a few of our favourites:
'Heroes' – *David Bowie*
'Take on Me' – *a-ha*
'Jump Around' – *House of Pain*
'Give it Up' – *KC and the Sunshine Band*
'Don't Stop Me Now' – *Queen*

☆ Try singing this song while dusting a room; it's adapted from the Disney film *Peter Pan:*

We're following the leader ♪

We're following the leader, the leader, the leader
We're following the leader wherever (s)he may be

We're gonna dust the table, the table, the table*
We're gonna dust the table wherever it may be

*Change to other areas or pieces of furniture such as the banister, the bookshelf, the TV, the windowsill or the picture frame

Vacuuming

☆ When they were very young, my own children were scared of our vacuum cleaner – so much so that one of us used to vacuum while the other took them out for a walk! But some children like the noise and some babies are even soothed by it so much that they fall asleep to it, apparently.

☆ To make the vacuum cleaner more appealing, why not turn it into a hungry, crumb-eating creature by giving it a face. Just add some googly eyes, paper or craft foam brows, ears and nose with some double-sided sticky tape (or Blu-tack for less permanence) just where your little one thinks they should go.

☆ Every time the vacuum cleaner needs to come out, say it's time for another 'Adventure with the Crumb-Eating Creature'. The children will love helping with the story (shouting it out above the noise) about where it needs to go to today, what it will eat, and how it has to go to bed when the cleaning is finished.

☆ You can buy a range of toy vacuum cleaners (these are very popular with most preschoolers), but if you don't want that expense you could simply raid the recycling box for tubes and boxes and, sticking them together with some heavy duty gaffer tape, help your child make their own mini vacuum cleaner. Your children will love copying you with their own scaled-down, lightweight model. I have also seen some children as young as four using a hand-held dust-buster most effectively. If you feel your child is up to this, let them have a go (closely supervising them, of course) and enjoy the fact that they will actually be effectively contributing to getting the carpet clean. (For other details of junk modelling using recycled materials, see pages 143–147.)

Sweeping the floor

Sweeping is actually quite a complex task that requires a great deal of dexterity and coordination. It's unlikely that a child under five will be able to achieve what we might call *effective* sweeping but this doesn't mean it can't be a way to play. Usually, soon after the sweeping action is explored, young children drift to playing with the broom in an altogether different way; I am of course talking about using it like a horse, or a balance beam, or if they've had any exposure to witches in stories such as Julia Donaldson's brilliant *Room on the Broom* – they'll be flying round the room on it. Or maybe they've just seen you being particularly playful with your broom at some point, and are just copying what they've seen.

☆ Invest in a miniature (but effective) broom and dustpan set – otherwise you'll end up tussling over ownership far more than sweeping or playing. Recently I read that just a few years ago, Montessori teachers in the US – who promote sweeping as an important developmental play opportunity for young children – had great difficulty in finding miniature, non-gendered brooms in natural materials – in fact they worked with a manufacturer to enable the making of such 'specialist' brooms to be continued. It's amazing how many good-quality miniature sets are available now, and it means that if your child insists on using the grown-up version, you can still carry out the task effectively while your child is copying you, albeit with equipment on a scale that makes you feel like a giant.

☆ You can have fun mixing up the order of the three parts of the sweeping process by using a song to help you do it right while you and your little one sweep:

Sweep the dirt *(sung to the tune of* 🎵
'Head, shoulders, knees and toes')

> *Sweep the dirt into a pile, to a pile (repeat)*
> *Sweep and sweep and sweep and sweep*
> *Sweep the dirt into a pile, into a pile.*
>
> *Push the pile into the pan, into the pan (repeat)*
> *Push and push and push and push*
> *Push the pile into the pan, into the pan.*
>
> *Tip the dirt into the bin, into the bin (repeat)*
> *Tip and tip and tip and tip*
> *Tip the dirt into the bin, into the bin.*

Remember to give praise and tell your child what a good helper they are – even though you may well have to re-do the sweeping they attempted after they've scooted off to do something else. They'll definitely be back for more, and gradually their sweeping (and broom-flying) skills will improve.

Washing up

Washing up is often seen as one of the more tedious chores for grown ups. Despite this, young children seem to find it a real treat. When I asked via social media which chores are children's favourites, washing up came out on top. Of course we can't get our under-fives to scour pans, safely wash cutlery or clean the best china, but they will easily and enthusiastically manage plastic plates, bowls, cups and wooden utensils.

☆ Invest in an extra washing-up bowl, washing-up brush and a sponge or cloth so that they can sometimes wash up as you do. Just set it all up nearby – either on the floor (with an old towel underneath to prevent slips) or on a low table that they can stand at. You won't be able to rely on their skill at cleaning, but you can rely on their skill at playing. To them, washing up means a sensory play opportunity; they'll splish-and-splash in the warm, bubbly water for ages – pouring and swirling, scooping and wiping. And if some of the lunch things get clean in the process – that's a bonus! They'll still think they're washing up whether the items are spotless or not. Young children are more likely to stay interested in washing up if you keep it as an occasional activity that's different to other water-based play. Offering it as a grown-up job, to help you, is all part of its irresistible charm, it seems.

Dishwasher

☆ If your household has a dishwasher, you can still get your little one to help with the dishes; they'll happily help load it with the dirty stuff or empty it of its sparkly clean contents as long as you make the process fun.
☆ Set yourselves a challenge – can the dishwasher be emptied before a certain song on the radio finishes? Your toddler could help by collecting the non-breakables.
☆ Play a spotting game where *all* of the dirty or clean cups, then forks, then bowls and so on are identified by the children and put away by the grown up. Do this against the clock and you'll have a really fun game on your hands.

Setting and clearing the table

Setting the table can be a fun activity for young children. When my daughter turned four, she went through a phase of turning our dining table into a restaurant every time I asked if anyone would like to do the job. She would make a central flower arrangement, menus, place cards – the lot! This became quite time-consuming in the end, so I had to make sure I asked at least twenty minutes before the meal was actually ready, but it did mean that she happily, and creatively, took on the task.

Make a 'let's pretend' cafe:

☆ Make some personalised placemats; trace around the shapes of where the plate, cup and cutlery should go if your children find it hard to remember. Decorate large paper doilies or A4 paper for temporary mats (or if you have access to a laminator, cover them and they will last longer and be wipeable) with drawings, stickers or pictures cut from magazines.

☆ It's fun and useful for young children to remember where everybody sits and to think about what the family needs to use during the meal. If they're feeling particularly creative, let them make place cards, or a menu, or whatever they wish, to create the desired ambiance.

Mealtime rituals and routines differ vastly from family to family, but quite commonly the end of the meal is often the time when children seem to magically disappear and the grown ups are left with the devastation that is the post-dinner dining table. You can occasionally involve the little ones in clearing up the mess with some fun and games, however. For example:

☆ Clear the table with your children helping as best they can alongside, in the manner of robots or fairies, magicians or monsters.

☆ Make some attractive and tactile 'job stones' to pick out of a cloth bag to allocate tasks. These are easy to make by painting, drawing or sticking pictures from magazines onto smallish pebbles with PVA glue. Each stone's picture should represent one of the jobs required to clear the table, for example: collect cups, cutlery, plates and bowls, wipe the table and sweep the floor. The aim is to empty the bag of stones – and complete the jobs – before going off to play something else.

☆ Offer an incentive of a game or some other playful activity at the table once it has been cleared. This can be a real motivator for children of all ages; it's an example of the When/Then technique (see p.20).

Making beds

☆ Making the beds is a daily chore that usually takes us grown ups mere seconds in the modern world of duvets, however, small children can find bedding incredibly cumbersome and heavy to manoeuvre. You can still include them, though, by allocating them aspects of the job that they can manage.

☆ Start by making it a job you do together – you could shake and straighten the duvet while your little one plumps and places the pillow.

☆ Young children love to arrange bedtime soft toys. This can be made even more fun with a song:

There was one in the bed 🎵

There was one in the bed
And the little one said, 'Roll over, roll over.'
So he rolled over and another popped in,
Cuddled up tight, and gave a grin
'Please remember to tie a knot in your pyjamas,
Single beds are only made for one, two. . .'

Continue with 'three . . . four . . . in the bed' until all the toys are in position.

Changing the sheets

This is not usually a daily chore, but it still fills some parents with dread – especially if their children have reached the bunk-bed or cabin-bed phase; I know how difficult it is to get the sheets into those bed corners. However, try these playful activities and include your children when you can, and you may even look forward to sheet-changing day.

☆ Have a game of 'pile-up'. See how quickly you can strip the beds – your child does the pillowcases, you do everything else. The person who finishes their job first gets to 'flomp' into the big pile of discarded linen.

☆ 'Monkeys on the bed.' We have a rule in our house that this game is only allowed when there are no sheets on the beds and when the grown up is close at hand, putting the covers on duvets and pillows; it definitely requires supervision. It's a fun game that gets them burning off lots of energy. Your little monkeys simply jump up and down on the bed singing the following song (other actions optional):

Monkeys on the bed ♫

Three little monkeys jumping on the bed
One fell off and bumped his head.
Mummy called the doctor, and the doctor said,
'No more monkeys jumping on the bed.'

Two little monkeys jumping on the bed,
One fell off and bumped his head.
Mummy called the doctor and the doctor said,
'No more monkeys jumping on the bed.'

One little monkey jumping on the bed,
He fell off and bumped his head.
Mummy called the doctor and the doctor said,
'No more monkeys jumping on the bed.'

☆ 'Wonderful wafting.' When my two children were very small, they
loved nothing better than to lie on the floor while we wafted the clean,
fresh-smelling sheets and covers over them again and again – and
occasionally we covered them up, pretending they'd disappeared. It
made them giggle and wriggle so much. If you try this, but need a way
out of the game (it is rather open-ended), you might try starting to
waft a pillowcase at a doll or teddy. Your child may well take the bait
and join in, then take over, that game instead – leaving you free to
complete the job in hand.

Cleaning the bathroom

This job often requires the use of cleaning products, so it's not ideal
for young children to get too involved, even if you are using green
products. Instead:

☆ Try cleaning the bathroom during bath-time when your child is playing
in the tub. You can get a lot done then, whilst being able to supervise
the children; you'll just need to clean the bath at another time. You do,
of course, need to keep a close eye on your little one in the bath, so this
activity is only suitable for your nearly-five-year-old or an older child.
☆ Make it dolls' bath-time by setting up a washing-up bowl or a baby bath
of warm bubbly water on the floor in the bathroom (with an old towel
underneath to prevent slips) to occupy your little one while you clean
around them.

Tidy-up time, putting rubbish in the bin and picking up after themselves

I've put these chores together because they are all about learning how to live tidily – it's a journey we all have to make and, let's face it, often we never get far. When children are babies and toddlers, most parents accept that their little wonders are going to make a mess; they're going to play with things, sort things, unpack things, throw things, leave things, forget things. They leave a kind of trail-of-play in their wake, or in other words – they make a big ol' mess. It's up to us to reset the rooms and put things away after bedtime so it's ready for the next day of mess-making (otherwise known as playful exploration and discovery). Do bear in mind that it's definitely worthwhile doing this daily reset; children's interest soon wanes in anything left out for too long, and it's amazing how old toys and playthings suddenly become the bee's knees again after a day or two of absence.

Toddlers can begin their learning to live tidily journey by helping with this end-of-day tidy-up. It really helps if you have lots of tubs, boxes and baskets for their toys and playthings – and shelves at a suitable height. However, don't expect them to clear away with any great efficiency to begin with. It's merely the idea and concept of a 'time to tidy up' that we're trying to introduce here.

☆ Have some sort of signal to indicate the start of tidy-up time – perhaps a little bell, shaker or tambourine. Give your child the opportunity to announce it every once in a while, as they'll love the feeling of power it gives them. The sound signal can be used during tidy-up time too, should anyone forget and start playing again – and that includes the grown ups.

☆ Give your child a choice as to what they'd like to tidy away; for example, cars or books.

☆ 'Gimme five.' This game works well for preschoolers as they only have to put away five things – but they all have to be different things, so not five Lego bricks, for example.

☆ 'Colour code.' This is a fun and challenging game for preschoolers who are confident with their colours. Everyone chooses a colour and only puts things away that have that colour somewhere on it. The challenge for slightly older children is that at the end of the game they must guess what colour code the others chose.

☆ Race against each other, the clock, or the length of a song. Most children cannot resist a challenge like this – just decide the race conditions and they'll be off in a tidying frenzy. Remember that small items scattered all over the floor, such as toy cars and Duplo blocks, can be swept into one place with a broom or dustpan brush before being put away. This can make a job much less daunting, and cut down on the back-and-forth-with-one-item scenario.

☆ Keep spirits high with a favourite song. We've enjoyed a hearty rendition of 'Whistle While You Work' many a tidy-up time.

☆ Tidy up in the manner of various animals or book characters. Say 'freeze' every minute or so and choose a new style of tidying. Ask your children for suggestions – you'll be amazed at what they'll come up with and how well they'll embody the spirit of the craziest things. We've tidied up like cupcakes before now. Yes . . . cupcakes.

☆ You've probably seen the basketball-hoop bin that is loved by teenagers the world over. Who can resist the challenge of a slam-dunk, even if it is only rubbish being thrown away? Young children won't have the skills for this kind of precision challenge, of course, but preschoolers love a race against the clock – to the bin and back – to dispose of a handful of rubbish.

For children, picking up after themselves is perhaps the hardest of the tidying-up lessons to learn. It's the one from which parents often feel their children are deliberately shirking as they approach or reach school age. It's the moment when the trail of discarded coats, shoes, bags, tissues, jumpers on return from nursery or a day out, or the mess of a day's worth of play suddenly smacks of our children having no respect for us, their things or their home – although it is important to remember that children are not deliberately trying to make us feel this way. Pave the way for their future independence with playful tidying techniques when they're little; it'll definitely help them learn to look after their things themselves as they grow up.

We can get a lot of tips from Montessori educational practice here – which promotes independence and responsibility for one's self – by ensuring our learning and living spaces reflect this philosophy. We can easily replicate some of their practical ideas in our homes without too much fuss, or expense:

☆ Have hooks for coats and shoe storage close to the entrance of your home – and at an accessible height. As your children master the art of de-coating, make it an automatic next step for them to try to remember to hang it up. Putting up special pegs at their height could be a reward for being so big and grown up. Offer an incentive, a playful activity, once the arriving home jobs have been done. This can be a real motivator for children of all ages; it's a playful example of the *When/Then* technique: *when* they've put away their shoes, *then* they can play with some play dough.

☆ As your child approaches school age, or when you feel they are ready, introduce a few more tidy-up times throughout the day; for example, just before lunch and teatime perhaps, as well as a big one at the end of the day. During these the children can tell you what they've finished playing with so just a few things can be put away.

☆ 'Points make prizes.' This is a game to kick-start, or reinvigorate, interest in picking up after yourself. Make a score chart, however you like, to record every time you or your children notice that they or someone else has picked up after themselves. When you've reached a certain score there should be a family treat, like watching a movie or something similar.

Putting groceries away

Grocery shopping with young children in tow is, in my book, a great achievement in itself. It seems most unfair that when we get back home there's a whole new challenge to undertake. Where is that fairy godmother when you need her? Putting away the groceries is a time-consuming chore which, if left unchecked, can last all day and lead to the unscheduled and unofficial distribution of edible treats to one and all.

The following ideas might help to distract your little one from the 'I spot, I want' nightmare as you unpack and get them counting, sorting, stacking and playing alongside you as those treats and special things-for-another-time can be discreetly secreted onto high shelves and into cupboards.

☆ Put your child in charge of the more robust fruit and vegetables – hand them over with the storage utensil of your choice and get them to put them away. Of course, they'll be playing with them more than actually carrying out the official task, but they'll love doing it and there'll be lots of opportunity to find out how many apples or potatoes you bought, or which is the biggest potato or the longest leek.

☆ Give your child a fun, manageable mission and get them to take some non-kitchen items – perhaps things for the bathroom – to the right place. If you time them there and back I bet they'll not be able to resist trying to carry out the task as quickly as they can, again and again.

☆ 'Pass the packets.' This game is a fun spotting-and-sorting challenge. Choose one type of grocery item to put away at a time, i.e. packets, tins, boxes or bottles. Work together to spot them all and put them away before moving on to the next category.

Cooking

I'm not talking about baking biscuits and cupcakes here, I mean the daily task of making breakfast, lunch and dinner for the masses. Some people love to cook, they find it relaxing and creatively reward-ing, but having to prepare toddler-friendly morsels – every day – whilst simultaneously being in charge of small children, can break even the most dedicated foodie. There are lots of clever things people do to avoid this repetitive chore, such as cook in bulk and freeze in portions, or have weekly menus, but here I'm hoping to break the relentless monotony by making cooking a way to play for you and your little one.

☆ Involve your child in one or more of the cooking tasks once in a while, perhaps even making it their speciality. For example, they could wash the vegetables, break the eggs, grate the cheese, snip the ham, squish the tomatoes, slice the mushrooms or banana with a blunt knife, juice the lemon, choose the herbs by smell – that kind of thing.

☆ Toddlers will also be very happy to occasionally play along with cooking in the kitchen. Hand over a selection of safe kitchen utensils and equipment, for example a real saucepan with a wooden spoon – which is often more tempting than a toy version – and some dried pasta (you can re-use this for play cooking over and over again) and they'll be 'cooking' up a storm in no time.

☆ 'Play along with play dough.' This activity has got me out of a tight spot many a time when my two children were toddlers. At the kitchen table or equivalent, give your child a ball of herb-infused play dough (recipe on page 205), a few toy kitchen utensils, a couple of plastic plates and an empty shoe box (which makes a great oven) and they'll be happily occupied while you get on with the real deal. Play dough is so versatile; your little one will be able to make anything from peas and pasta, to potatoes and pizza.

Less-frequent chores

Cleaning the car

I only ever contemplate cleaning the car if there are children involved. I've yet to meet a child who doesn't love it, and this makes the whole thing seem much more of an attractive proposition in my book. The car may not get a thorough clean by child alone, but there'll be fun and laughter in bucket loads to accompany what might otherwise be a rather arduous task. Make sure everyone is in appropriate clothing and footwear so that getting wet isn't a problem – because they will definitely get wet.

☆ Set up your carwash together before you start: assemble buckets and bowls full of warm soapy water, sponges, brushes and cloths and drinking-water bottles for rinsing. Chamois-leathers and soft cloths need to be kept out of reach until step 4.

☆ Use a sand-timer or equivalent to help move smoothly from one stage of the job to the next. There are five steps:

1 *A first rinse:* everyone can help rinse the whole car with clean water to remove the scratchy surface dust and dirt. Flinging water from drinking-water bottles is great fun, and easy for little ones to master.

2 *Soaping and scrubbing:* the grown up should clean the wheels (using a heavy-duty scrubbing brush if possible) as these are likely to be the dirtiest part of the car. The children can soap-up wherever they can reach.

3   *Rinsing off the soap:* as step 1, but the aim of the game is to rid
    the car of bubbles rather than to just wet it. Start from as high
    as possible and work down the car, for efficient de-soaping.

4   *Drying:* use a chamois to dry the bodywork – wring it out
    frequently while your little one uses a piece of newspaper to get
    the windows smear-free. They may need to stand on their sink-step
    to do this.

5   *Cleaning inside the car:* you could vacuum while your child cleans
    the dust off the dashboard and so on. Soft paintbrushes can often
    get into the hard-to-reach dusty and crumby nooks and crannies.
    I swear by baby wipes for a thorough de-stickying of door handles,
    gear stick and steering wheel. Young children will find being allowed
    to sit in the front of the car very exciting – do allow time for their
    imaginative play, as they will undoubtedly 'drive' you to the beach
    or the zoo.

Defrosting the freezer

This is a relatively infrequent job, but sometimes it's imperative. You
know that moment? It's when it becomes impossible to open or close
the freezer drawers without using the force of ten men, and there's
only the freezer's own ice in there anyway. Sometimes, you have no
choice but to carry out this chore while in charge of little ones – so
here are a few ways to manage that eventuality:

☆ While you're emptying the frozen stuff into cool bags to preserve what
   you can, empty your ice-cube tray onto a large flat metal or plastic tray
   for your little ones to play with. Ice cubes glide, skid and crash brilliantly
   – a bit like bumper-cars. Add a little silver glitter, plastic toy animals
   and figures and you'll have a brilliant small-world Polar landscape for
   your little one to enjoy. (See pages 92 and 112 for more ideas for small
   world play.)

☆ If you have one of those no-mess Aquamats, let your child draw with the melting ice cubes instead of the water-filled pens it comes with; it's a very satisfying experience.

☆ If the ice cream is simply not going to stay frozen enough to make it back into the freezer, why not treat yourselves to a home-made sundae while your freezer is defrosting? Let your little one help with scooping the ice cream, adding any sprinkles, fruit and sauce that you have to hand. These extras could be presented to the children in your empty ice-cube tray (if there's a few of you) so there's just enough of everything displayed and ready for self-service.

Cleaning windows

Some people recommend cleaning the windows twice a year, but I know that we wash some of our windows more often than that – and others (those we can't easily reach) about . . . never. If you use your windows in play (which I really hope you might consider, if you don't already) – you will need to wash them more frequently, of course, but at least it'll be because they've been dirtied through use and not just accumulated grub. I don't know why that makes me feel better, but it does. My mum said she loved it when her grandchildren came to visit her because she would see their little hand marks on the glass doors out to the garden and note them getting just a little higher up the pane each time. Apparently, she sometimes didn't wipe them off, just to remind her of our last visit. I suspect that's a grandmother-love-thing, but remembering this means I'm never miffed at finger marks on our windows.

☆ Allocate an accessible windowpane for your child to clean while you clean others nearby. Of course you will have to go back and properly wash their window later, but this chore is much more fun if you have a little help-mate close by.

☆ Hand over some neoprene (craft) foam shapes or those foam shapes or letters for use in the bath, plus a little water in a plastic pot or cup and small paintbrush. Your child could then decorate one of the windows.

Sorting out outgrown and worn-out clothes

There's nothing like the simultaneous change of season and a growth spurt to suddenly render 70 per cent of a child's wardrobe useless. If your children's clothes need a bit of a sort out, try this three-pile sorting game. My children loved playing this when they were under five, and although it would often lead to some sudden sentimentality about clothes that had been fiercely refused before, it worked as a fun way to get the job done, with the children conveniently there to check what fitted and what didn't. Tumble the contents of their wardrobes and drawers onto their bedroom floor and let the Goldilocks Three-pile Sort begin. The three piles could be:

 Clothes that are *too small* (or too worn out) to keep – to give or throw away

 Clothes that are *too big* (perhaps inherited from older siblings or cousins, and the like) – to store away

 Clothes that are *just right* and fit your child now

The third pile will inevitably, and annoyingly, always be the smallest pile, but at least you'll have had fun finding out, and got a handy reminder about some of your children's clothes that may have got lost in the mix.

Gardening

Whether you have a huge garden or just a windowbox and front porch, the general maintenance and upkeep of your outside space can be a way to play for young children. Of course, for many, gardening is an activity that is not a chore, but rather is a hobby – a passion even – and green-fingered parents happily and naturally want to pass on to their children their love of gardening.

The benefits of gardening with little ones are numerous and well documented; learning through outside play, growing things, looking after plants, finding mini-beasts and getting muddy, allowing children to connect with nature and develop an understanding about the world around them. There are numerous concerns for safety when gardening, though, so children should always be supervised when outdoors, and hands should always be washed after any gardening activity. We will discover more ways to play in the garden later in this book, but starting with the basics, here are a few ways in which you can begin to include young children in some very gentle, general gardening jobs:

☆ Get them to collect up litter or debris like fallen branches and twigs. This can be made fun by putting a time limit on it – challenge yourselves to see how fast you can clear the garden together. The best twigs and sticks can be kept for playing with at a later date, and this promise could be used as a motivational carrot, to find for example, the best stick to become their new wand. We've painted sticks and twigs with poster paint before; they look marvellous. If you gather enough you could also make a tepee for toys. Just tie the tops of the twigs with twine and splay out the other ends.

☆ Sweep or rake up stray leaves on lawns, walkways and paths. You can buy miniature versions of good-quality garden brooms and rakes for your little one to try to help; this will need careful supervision, though, as rakes can be a bit pointy and pokey if not used correctly. Or you could sweep up the leaves yourself, making it playful by piling them up into artful shapes or maze-like pathways for your little ones to enjoy. Hand over to your children the most beautiful of the leaves as if they're treasure – they'll soon be collecting their own. These can be played with there and then, or saved to use in an art activity later. Or set them a challenge to find the biggest/smallest/brightest/pointiest leaf.

☆ Clear moss from stone or brick walkways which could become slippery. How satisfying for little ones to be allowed to prise away the green stuff. Let them use a small trowel or teaspoon for this. Save the moss for making a miniature garden later.

☆ Children love helping with watering. This job is best done in the early morning or late evening, when you will lose the least amount of water to evaporation. There are some great lightweight mini watering cans available for little gardeners. This is a good time to teach children about where water comes from, and how we use it. Make your own rain collectors by using large, empty water or soft-drink bottles. Simply cut off their tops (where the neck of the bottle begins) and rest the offcuts on top, upturned, to prevent large bits of unwanted debris (or animals) getting stuck inside.

☆ Weeding is a job that requires supervision; although many weeds can be easily pulled up, roots and all, by small children, you need to make sure they check with you before pulling anything up, in case it's a plant! Rather than composting the weeds, many smallish weeds make fabulous shrubs and trees for miniature gardens. If the roots are intact as you pull them up, pass the best-looking weeds to your little one to plant up in a flowerpot, planter or small wooden container.

☆ Give the children a mucky job that won't cause damage to your plants! Discovering mini-beasts and worms is all part of the gardening experience, and collecting such creatures for investigation will keep them busy while you work. You need a suitable container (with air-holes) as a temporary base for the mini-beasts, some damp soil and a few stones. Add magnifying glasses and torches for the budding biologist. If your children find snails, slugs or caterpillars (or their eggs) on the underside of the leaves, make sure they tell you, so you can decide how to deal with them. My daughter adores snails and insists on making little habitats for them, but none of us are that keen on slugs (a huge pest in our garden), so I always get a call to come and remove the wee beastie if she discovers one. Above all, lead by example: show the children how to hold the creepy crawlies without hurting them, and that you respect them by always putting the little creatures back when you have finished with them.

☆ Pruning and trimming is a job for the grown up, but depending on their length and number, the offcuts are great for play. Smallish, tender offcuts can be handed over for some imaginative garden 'cooking' – to be ripped up and stirred into old pots and pans along with grass cuttings, mud and water. Larger and more numerous branches and trimmings can make outside dens, or as the scenery of a small world setting for vehicles, animals or fairies.

☆ Planting may well be a seasonal or infrequent job, depending on the size and type of your outside space, as well as your interest in gardening. You may have no flowerbeds whatsoever, so any planting will be constricted to containers. If you have a large mature garden with well-established plants, shrubs and trees you may wish to allocate a small flowerbed for easy-to-grow plants to be cultivated by yourself and your little one.

Quick and easy plants to grow with the kids

Here are some of the easiest plants to grow and look after:

☆ Sweet peas: You don't need a big garden to grow these beautifully scented flowers, they are ideal for a large pot or a windowbox.

☆ Sunflowers: One of the best plants to get children started on. They are easy to grow and the seeds are cheap to buy. Children of all ages love them, and because they are quick-growing they keep them interested over several months.

☆ Lamb's ears: Children love stroking this plant's soft velvety leaves, and the spikes of purplish-pink small flowers are attractive to bees, so ideal for a bug watch.

☆ Snapdragons: These flowers are pretty and easy to grow. If you gently pinch their blooms they look like roaring dragons.

☆ Marigolds: The blooms are vibrant yellows and oranges, and the plants are pretty forgiving if you forget to water them. The kids can plant them in pots or, if they are prone to forgetting to water them, they will find their own way in a sunny flowerbed.

☆ Nasturtiums: Sow the seeds in pots in spring and the foliage then large orange and yellow blooms will quickly appear. Great for playing food games with, as the flowers are edible.

☆ Tomatoes: Every gardening beginner's favourite. You can grow them from seedlings planted straight into a compost bag or large pot. They need a sunny spot and a fair bit of watering, but there's nothing like growing your own to encourage young children to try eating tomatoes.

☆ Herbs: These plants are a wonderful source of scent. Lavender and rosemary are pretty tough, and both have purple-ish small flowers that attract bees. Rosemary can be used in cooking, and the petals of lavender can be dried and then used to make sweet-scented pocket-pillows or pot pourri.

☆ Get your children interested in nature while they are out in the garden with you, and make their job the one of feeding the birds. You can very simply make a birdbath by using a terracotta flowerpot saucer or an old ceramic plate placed on top of an upturned flowerpot. Make sure it is kept clean and is filled with fresh water often – young children love to help with this. Providing birds with food, especially in the winter when the ground is frozen, is very important. Most garden centres sell seasonally-appropriate food to scatter on the ground, or on a bird table. You can also make bird-feeders with your children to hang from trees. Our favourite are apple- and seed-feeders which seem to attract most birds to our garden. (See page 207 for how to make this garden bird-feeder with your children.) The Royal Society for the Prevention of Cruelty to Animals has further tips for looking out for garden birds. Visit: www.rspca.org.uk/allaboutanimals/wildlife/inthewild/ feedinggardenbirds/birdfeedingguide

Brilliant books for budding gardeners

There are some funny and beautifully illustrated picture books about gardens and gardening to pique interest and entertain you and your little ones. Here are a few of our favourites:

The Enormous Turnip – a classic folk tale retold by many and available
   worldwide in various editions
The Carrot Seed by Ruth Krauss
Monkey and Robot in the Garden by Felix Hayes and Hannah Broadway
Ben's Butterfly Garden by Kate Petty and Axel Scheffler
Flora's Flowers by Debi Gliori
Eddie's Garden: and How to Make Things Grow by Sarah Garland

How about singing while you do your garden chores? Here are a few of our favourites:

D'you know the parts of a plant? ♬
(Sing to the tune of Head, Shoulders, Knees and Toes)

> *D'you know the parts of a plant, of a plant?*
> *D'you know the parts of a plant, of a plant?*
> *Flower and leaf*
> *And stem and root*
> *D'you know the parts of a plant, of a plant?*

Lavender's blue and Roses are red medley ♬

> *Lavender's blue, dilly dilly*
> *Lavender's green*
> *When I am king, dilly dilly*
> *You shall be queen.*
>
> *Roses are red, dilly dilly*
> *Violets are blue*
> *Sugar is sweet, dilly dilly*
> *And so are you.*

For more information and seasonal suggestions for gardening with children, visit the Royal Horticultural Society website at www.rhs.org.uk/Children/For-families

10-Second Set-ups

'The quickest way for a parent to get a child's attention is to sit down and look comfortable.'

Lane Olinhouse

As a parent, you know how the concept of time radically changes as soon as there's a baby around. Minutes can seem like hours when your little one won't stop crying or refuses to sleep, and hours can pass like minutes when it seems you've surely only just finished feeding your baby and yet somehow it's time to do it all again. Babies just don't follow the conventions of time as we know it. As Catharine Kedjidjian of the website *BabyZone* writes, 'Babies start life with a distorted concept of time: night can be day and everything is now.'

We are at the behest of our babies. We find ourselves asking questions like, 'Is there time for me to get dressed before the baby needs feeding again?' or even, 'Do I have time to go to the toilet before the baby needs me?' And the truth is, there really is no way of telling if there is actually time or not; when our children are babies there are countless days when we never quite have enough time to get fully dressed, or to brush our hair, or even to drink a cup of tea while it's still warm. As parenthood begins, time is no longer our own, and either gladly or reluctantly, we hand it over to our babies and join the ranks of selfless providers and carers as per the tacit new-parent contract: any time, any place, anywhere.

'While I feed my baby I can eat my lunch with one hand or pick things up off the floor with my feet. I have my hair tied back in a pony-tail – well, that stays put for days without any attention. You learn to just get by when you have a baby.'

Mum of two – master of multi-tasking

Carla Poole, Susan A. Miller EdD, and Ellen Booth Church explain on Scholastic.com how this early parenting is important in forming the beginnings of a baby's understanding of time:

'A multitude of nurturing moments helps babies' natural body rhythms and schedules take shape. Loving relationships are formed and life becomes a more predictable pattern of people, things, and events.'

As our babies move towards toddlerhood, time begins to take on a more recognisable and predictable structure again. But there is no concept of hours or minutes in a toddler's mind; instead there's nap time, milk time, nappy-changing time, lunch time, snack time, story time, play time, bath time and bed time. They're grasping the abstract nature of time through the routines and patterns of their daily activity. They're certainly not sticking to any clock, and woe betide any parent who tries to keep their toddler 'on time.' I'll never forget my own battles at the sandpit when my son, then two, would clearly demonstrate that his time to play had not finished – despite whatever I might think. He just would not have it that it was time to leave, that the park was closing. He would lie down on his back, stiff as a board, refusing to budge. Ah, happy memories.

As Carla, Ellen and Susan point out, two-year-olds have all the time in the world; it's us adults who never have enough. When your child is a toddler it's clear that they are still in charge of time – and they can be incredibly forceful in deciding how it will be spent, and often frustratingly unrealistic.

The good news is that as toddlers move towards preschool age, they begin to understand the concept of 'before' and 'after'. This can be very useful in moving the day along smoothly; we, the grown ups, can then start to be more in charge of time, with simple authoritative statements that include these concepts: we'll play outside *after* nap time, or, *before* we have our snack we must wash our hands.

Preschoolers also start to get the idea of *when* and *then*, which is lovely for either reviewing the day, reporting it to granny, say, or using it to talk about the future: *when* you've taken off your shoes and coat, *then* you can go and play. There are lots of positive and playful methods of establishing rules and routines in the chapter Sanity Savers.

But what about the times *in between* the transitional moments in the day, when we're not needed to direct, help or move things along to the next, or more suitable, activity?

When children play

These *in-between* times – when your little one is oblivious to time passing and is happily occupied, independently busy, involved in an activity – are like manna from heaven when we first encounter them. And it's in these moments we discover that, while they still need subtle supervision, our children really don't need us to entertain them, or to be involved. This begins very early on, even when our children are babies, as parenting expert Janet Lansbury discovered with her three-month-old baby.

'I placed her on her back on a blanket near me and watched. My needy, vocal baby, the one I'd been entertaining and engaging almost every moment she was awake, spent nearly two hours in this position, peaceful and content. She knew I was there, shot an occasional glance my direction, but didn't seem to need a thing from me except, perhaps, my appreciative presence. And, oh, I was *beyond* appreciative.'

On her website (www.janetlansbury.com) Janet has beautiful video footage of babies happily playing on their own, playing with their toes, just looking around them or at something close-up, or happily reaching out and making efforts to get toys and objects, for much longer than we might think possible.

As a child grows into a toddler and preschooler he or she becomes increasingly capable of entering this zone, and for longer, where they find their *flow*; they are busy, they are concentrating on something with an impressively long attention span; they are playing independently. When we see this 'magic' happening we are often tempted to watch and marvel at their brilliance, and for some parents it's very tricky not to interrupt them – albeit unintentionally. But also, it may occur to us that we might be able to take advantage of this little bit of freedom. If we simply let the children carry on playing, maybe we could make that quick phone call? Or read the newspaper for a minute? But as writer Lane Olinhouse points out, it seems the moment we sit down and look comfortable (or equivalent) we suddenly have the undivided attention of our child.

Sometimes, young children can't help but to tune in to us and what we're doing, the moment we think they're immersed enough for us to tackle that chore or dash off that email. For every time we successfully step away and achieve something while they're playing, there are many times when our little one is suddenly round our feet, needing us *right now*, when we were quite invisible to them just seconds before. And flag up to a toddler that you need them to 'just wait a minute' while you finish fixing the TV remote, or applying for a new car tax disc and you're usually on a hiding to nothing. They need *help* to find their flow again, and it is on these occasions when 10-second set-ups can save the day.

Can young children really wait?

It seems not *all* young children challenge their parents in this way. Pamela Druckerman, author of *French Children Don't Throw Food* has discovered that Parisian children definitely know how to 'wait'. They are simply told to do so by their parents and teachers from very early on in their lives, and they apparently learn this skill rather success-fully, developing the self-control and resourcefulness to self-distract until the waiting is done. By doing this, French children have earned themselves a reputation for being a tantrum-free, non-clingy and independent lot. This strict, no-nonsense tactic of simply being abso-lutely authoritative in stating when children need to wait clearly works for French parents, but to me it seems rather unnecessarily brutal. It also encourages unwanted behaviour, known in France as '*betises*', which are basically the times when children are 'getting up to no good'. According to Druckerman, in France this is apparently a common and almost expected side-effect of getting children to wait.

Fortunately, it is possible to help young children learn not just to wait, but how to wait – how to find their flow again – by tapping into their intrinsic desire to be busy, productive and playful. We can guide them back to independent play by using gentle, simple and playful methods. Being able to find something *to do* – something that is constructive, calm and absorbing – is a highly useful skill that can stay with toddlers right through childhood and into adulthood. Knowing our children have this skill means we parents can get the space we need should we wish to do something for ourselves (without wondering if our child is 'getting up to no good') even if it's just sitting down and collecting our thoughts for a minute or two.

So, my second way to play is about helping toddlers and pre-schoolers find their flow of independent play again; when we need them to amuse themselves constructively while we get on with something else.

TV or not TV? That is the question . . .

Of course, a very tempting way to get young children to wait – to be quickly absorbed, quiet and captivated – is to plonk them down in front of the TV, or, if we're out and about, by handing over our smartphone or iPad. And the truth is this tactic will usually work like a dream; our children become quiet, still and occupied, giving us that much-needed downtime or the opportunity to complete a task that needs adult-only attention. But problems will arise if we rely too much on the screen as a babysitter.

When the TV is constantly on, often it becomes just something in the background to our little ones, even if it is set to a channel showing programmes aimed at them. They either end up ignoring the screen in the corner all together – and so it loses its power as an attention-grabber or babysitter – or they become totally addicted to it. It is a drug, after all.

Where a generation ago nearly all preschool programming was limited to certain times of the day (and was advert-free), now there's TV for tots around the clock. Turning it off can be a real battle because there are no longer any natural breaks, not least because we are always shown what will be on next to keep our little ones tuned in. Apps and computer games are the same – there's no sense of them ever ending, you can simply 'play' the games again and again.

In a recent Yale Family Television Research study teachers described children who watched excessive amounts of TV as less imaginative, less cooperative, less enthusiastic about learning and less happy as those children who watched little or no TV. The reason being that by watching too much TV or playing with computer games too often, children may eventually find it difficult to keep themselves busy at play in the real world, and might lose their natural creativity. Sue Palmer, author of *Toxic Childhood*, explains that in the first few years of childhood, genuine interactive first-hand experiences are much more important than technological toys. She quotes Dr David Walsh of the National Institute on Media and the Family, 'If we orientate our kids to screens so early in their lives, we risk making media their automatic default activity.' Whatever your App says it can do for your child's learning, it cannot provide the real-life, hands-on activities that are so important for young children's healthy development – it's how they learn about the world around them. A hands-on approach to toddler learning beats high-tech hands down.

From a physical perspective, too much TV watching and playing computer games can drain a little one's naturally high energy levels, making them far too sedentary. Physical play is very important to toddler growth; it builds strong muscles and helps children discover what their bodies can do. Small children naturally want to run, jump and climb, but as Sue Palmer suggests, too much screen time may result in them becoming sluggish, frustrated or fractious. She also cites some research in Scotland showing that three-year-olds weigh more than their counterparts of twenty-five years ago because physical activity levels have dropped off so dramatically.

I'm not saying that a little TV watching or a short time on screen-based activities can't be useful (in fact, it features in the chapter Stay and Play), it's just that now there is so much on offer 24/7 that we have to be really on top of just how much our little ones are exposed to.

But here's the good news: by having other, more playful, options up our sleeve, we can nurture independent play habits for our children as they approach school age; play that is creative, often physical, involves learning and is in the real world, in real time. As the National Literacy Trust tells us, encouraging independent play is much more beneficial to toddler and preschool learning than anything our children will see on screen.

Setting the rules for screen time

If you do occasionally want to use screen time, here are some tips that may help to keep you in control:

☆ Set limits in advance and be disciplined about keeping them.

☆ Consider showing full-length feature films in a series of instalments.

☆ Choose what your tot watches and uses wisely and always supervise them as they watch. Even better, stay and play with them while they are involved in any screen-based activity.

☆ Think of TV and App use like sweets; you'd never hand over a whole bag of assorted treats to your tot – too many would make them sick, and you never know if there's a hard toffee or a choking hazard of a boiled sweet in there. Select, share and limit the treat.

10-second set-ups are a way to play

By offering simple, self-explanatory and open-ended play prompts that either surprise or are somehow linked to what the adult is trying to do at the time, we can provide an initial spark of interest. The activity should then captivate, involve and absorb a young child for many independent minutes at a time, so freeing us up to feed the baby, make that call or open the mail. In time, they will start to come up with their own ideas – self-initiating positive play when they find themselves at a loose end.

There are numerous benefits to 10-second set-ups, both for you and your toddler or preschooler:

☆ you get some downtime.

☆ you have the opportunity to complete that task that needs adult-only attention, enjoy that cup of coffee, or have that conversation with another grown up.

☆ your child goes back to being happily occupied, playing.

☆ your child masters how to play independently and how to keep their *flow* of concentration.

☆ their attention spans are given a good workout and will become more robust and lengthy.

☆ your child becomes used to parents or carers being present but not required.

☆ he or she develops numerous skills through playful activity.

☆ you both get some quality time alone, but together.

☆ a child's temptation for sneaky 'mischief-making' behaviour is vastly reduced.

Which 10-second set-up?

The aim of any 10-second set-up is to promote independent play without you getting too involved – ten seconds should be long enough for you to offer the bait, and then your little one can take the play where they like. The actual complexity of the play will of course depend on the age of your child, their specific abilities, their dexterity, their maturity level, the set-up of your home and where you are.

Below are some tips to bear in mind when offering a 10-second set-up for your little one:

☆ Don't stop them if they are already immersed in independent play; just keep an idea up your sleeve in case they tune in to what you're doing and can't get back their flow, even when encouraged to.

☆ A 10-second set-up should be about discovery and experience, not end product.

☆ Keep it very simple, using just an idea, perhaps something you have prepared earlier, or something you have to hand wherever you are.

☆ Make sure that you involve objects that are not always accessible to your little one, so they become more interesting and alluring.

☆ Be low-key in your offering of the object or activity; if you make too much of it, your child might well be put off. Even better if they discover its presence by themselves.

☆ Check the activity is open-ended, will naturally lead your child on to playing something else independently, or has the potential to be a long enough challenge or game that will keep them engaged for as long as you need.

☆ Make sure the activity is pretty much self-explanatory and self-exploratory.

☆ Don't intervene if they're playing with the stuff in a wholly different way to how you'd envisaged. Leave them be and let them play.

☆ Try different set-ups often to keep them fresh and irresistible.

☆ Think about the set-up's element of surprise; it needs to be something that immediately grabs their attention.

☆ Do listen out for genuine needs and always be subtly supervising.

☆ Don't expect every set-up to work every time.

☆ Always be close at hand to keep an eye on your child, but try not to become involved in the activity – let them play independently.

☆ Always check that the objects used for the set-ups are not choking hazards. This is especially important for the under-threes.

☆ Older children might respond well to a timed activity, e.g. 'when the timer goes off, Daddy will be finished and we can play something together'.

☆ Be aware of your little one's go-to type of play; if they're mad on construction or imaginative play, for example, you can rely more on 10-second set-ups that spark playful activity in that direction.

☆ Acknowledge to your child that they've allowed you to get your job done, if you made them aware that this was the purpose of this independent play time.

When I asked parents on Facebook what things their little ones seemed to resent them doing or just plain didn't allow them to do without them wrapped around their legs, or equivalent, making phone calls or going to the toilet seemed to be most problematic. But there were numerous other everyday activities mentioned too, and some of these are listed below:

Grown-up activities, when children might need to 'wait':
Drying hair ☆ Eating ☆ Taking a shower ☆ Shaving ☆ Cleaning teeth ☆ Daily stretches, exercises or yoga practice ☆ Making a phone call ☆ Going to the toilet ☆ Getting dressed ☆ Sitting down ☆ Making a cup of tea ☆ Making a sandwich/cooking ☆ Fixing something ☆ Changing a light bulb ☆ Taking out the rubbish ☆ Opening the mail ☆ Clearing up after a meal ☆ Paying bills ☆ Making appointments ☆ Listening to the weather or traffic news on the radio ☆ Helping other children ☆ Feeding a baby ☆ Having a conversation with another adult

Out and about:
Waiting in a queue ☆ Interaction at the counter in a shop, at the bank or post office ☆ Having a (brief) business meeting ☆ A doctor's appointment ☆ A dentist appointment

So, here are lots of examples of 10-second set-ups for those instances when you need your child to be calmly, happily and busily playing independently. This way to play is a quick-fix solution that will take 10 seconds or less to explain to your child. Some 10-second set-ups *do* need to be prepped in advance, but this extra work will pay dividends when you're feeling the pressure and can't think of anything to tempt your little one to play on their own.

Each suggestion given here will help to promote independent play, encouraging toddlers and preschoolers not only *to* wait, but to learn that waiting can be fun. This is in no way a finite list, of course – I'm sure you'll discover different set-ups that work a treat for your little one as you start to introduce them into your daily play.

Personal care

In the bathroom

When my two were very small, I remember taking their baby-bouncer chair into the bathroom while I took a shower. If I timed it right, the whole experience was wonderfully sensorial and they would happily sit and bounce and look around, just enjoying the warmth, sights and sounds of my shower-time.

However, such simple distractions will not be enough to capture your child's attention as they become toddlers and preschoolers. If your child finds it difficult to wait while you have a shower, i.e. they are unable to choose something – and stay with something – to do that doesn't need you, try one or two of these 10-second set-ups to help them get into their flow:

☆ **Shaving foam art:** Here's one that is especially good for dads. One blob of shaving foam put onto a lid of an ice-cream tub or similar goes a long way and will provide a wonderful, sensory substance for your little one to enjoy while you shave. If they need more help with how to play with it, challenge them to make as many different patterns on the lid as they can, using their fingers to move the foam around.

☆ **Aquamat doodle-time:** If they need encouragement to play with the Aquamat, challenge them to cover the whole thing with patterns and pictures for you to see when you step out of the shower.

☆ **Bathroom busy bags:** This needs some prep in advance. Fill a couple of small tote bags, make-up bags or inexpensive pencil cases with different things. Produce them only when you need to and change their contents every now and again. The surprise of a new bag is usually a big hit. In these bags you could put:

☆ Foam bath-time letters or shapes. A wet sponge in a small bowl will provide enough moisture to make the letters cling to any tiled or porcelain bathroom surface.

☆ Hair styling stuff. Bag up a few big clips, a soft brush, some soft hair scrunchies and a safety-mirror tile.

☆ Empty bottles and big lids to match up and twist on. Check the lids are not so small that they pose a choking hazard.

☆ Plastic stickle bricks/Duplo or Octons. If your child needs a little help to find their flow with these, challenge them to make something tall or funny or beautiful by the time you're out of the shower.

☆ Small figurines' bath time. Make up a simple kit with, say, a small plastic bowl plus soap plus a small sponge and a flannel, for a mini let's-pretend bath time. If you put a little water in the bowl, place a towel underneath to prevent slips.

☆ Sponge construction shapes. Cut up some colourful new sponges into shapes and bricks for some brilliant, and quiet, bathroom-themed building.

☆ Waterproof craft foam cut into sections of road (you can also buy these pre-made) and a selection of small toy vehicles for some road building, and zooming and racing car action.

☆ A selection of waterproof bath books.

☆ Lots of mini-pom-poms or the foam 'peanuts' you get as box packaging and a small, empty, dry water bottle. Challenge your little one to fill the bottle with pom-poms by the time you have finished in the shower. You can use the pom-poms or packing peanuts again and again, of course.

☆ A message-in-a-bottle kit – you need a small, empty, dry water bottle, strips of paper and a pencil. Challenge your little one to 'write' you messages on the strips of paper and post them in the water bottle. See how many different messages they can make before you step out of the shower or finish brushing your teeth.

☆ Let's pretend wash bag – *What you'll need to do beforehand:* Make up a special wash bag for them to investigate. It's great if it has lots of pockets. It should look like a grown-up's version, but with kid-friendly contents; a hand mirror, brush, comb, small wash cloth, mini water sprayer, some empty cream bottles, a nail buffer and emery board, cotton wool pads, a shower cap, a hair roller, a hair scrunchie, and the like.

Drying your hair

Offer your child a harmonica or other noisy musical toy to play on while you use the hair dryer. Let them know they can play as loudly as they like, in the same room as you, only while you are drying your hair. The noise – sorry – music, will get totally drowned out by your hair dryer and is the best way to really appreciate it, I think.

Getting dressed

Getting ready for the day when you have babies and very young children can often be a rather snatch-and-grab affair. But if you have your little one with you in the room you could try to take the time pressure off yourself by letting them discover a game while they wait for you to get dressed. Try one or two of these 10-second set-ups, if they aren't able to find something to do themselves, to help them find their flow through calm play:

☆ **Dressing teddy:** Offer some play silks or scarves plus a teddy they can dress up while you are doing your thing.

☆ **Dressing skills bags:** These are good opportunities for young children to practise their own dressing skills without feeling under pressure to get ready quickly because of time constraints.
What you'll need to do beforehand: cut out hand-sized shapes in thin card or craft foam and punch holes round the edge. Fill a bag with these lacing cards plus a few shoelaces or yarn – sticky-tape the end to prevent

fraying. Fill another with short and long strips of Velcro or zips, and another with big buttons to post into a plastic tub with a slit cut to size in the lid.

☆ **Button-up:** I remember a wonderful book made by my sister, for my little sister, of felt – each page had some kind of 'getting-dressed' skill to try – like a picture of a shoe with real laces, and a picture of Humpty Dumpty with a real belt with a buckle. The idea below is a little less ambitious, but should capture the attention of your child just as well.

What you'll need to do beforehand: sew about ten colourful large buttons onto a piece of felt or non-fraying fabric just as you like. Then cut out shapes from felt – hearts, triangles, circles for example, and cut a slit through each to make a button hole. The shapes can be attached and removed again and again by your little one – great buttoning practice.

☆ **Junk-jewellery box discovery:** Have a special-looking jewellery box for your little one to explore. Make sure they know that it's a real treat to be allowed to look at your special things. Do keep all expensive and delicate stuff out of reach obviously – we're talking plastic bangles and chunky beaded necklaces here.

☆ **Make-a-necklace kit:** *What you'll need to do beforehand:* into a shoebox or basket put a couple of handfuls of coloured pasta tubes, big chunky beads or cut-up pieces of drinking straws along with a shoe lace or yarn. Wrap a little sticky tape around one end to stop it fraying and tie a big knot at the other end. This kit will keep your little one independently busy, threading and necklace-making while you dress. Do check any beads used are not so small as to pose a choking hazard.

☆ **A special bag of books about getting dressed and clothes:** Little ones feel very special lying on a grown-up's bed, and will really enjoying looking at a few picture books in such a luxurious setting.

Some of our favourite books about getting dressed are:

Thomas Goes Out – Gunilla Wolde

Bare Bear – Miriam Moss and Mary McQuillan

The Emperor's New Clothes – Hans Christian Andersen

The Tale of Peter Rabbit – Beatrix Potter

The Smartest Giant in Town – Julia Donaldson

☆ **Magnetic dress-up:** Dig out those magnetic shapes plus a board – or a metal baking sheet works well. If the magnets have a clothing theme, all the better.

☆ **Puppet costumes:** *What you'll need to do beforehand:* gather a few finger puppets and some small fabric squares. Fold the fabric squares in half and make a small slit in the middle of each, big enough for the puppet's head to be pushed through. This should start a spot of dramatic puppet play with the chance to change the characters' costumes.

Exercising with a toddler-in-tow

Whether you are a fitness fanatic, an occasional runner, play competitive sport in a team, love dancing, cycling or swimming, there is no doubt that having small children will have had an impact on the amount of time available to exercise, and your attitude towards it. Whether you're desperate to continue, get back to it, or start a new regime, you of course have to take into consideration what happens to your little one while you exercise. For some, it's a matter of dropping them off at the gym's crèche, or getting childcare while your team plays a match or you go for a run; for others it's about waiting till the little one is napping, or in bed at night.

For many parents and carers, incorporating exercise into playing with their child is a good way to go. You can read more about ideas for this way to play in the chapter Stay and Play, but if you want to try to get your daily or weekly fix of exercise when you have your child with you, but not necessarily joining in with you, your little one needs to learn to wait while you exercise. With a 10-second set-up or two, you should find they get used to playing independently while you do your thing.

Exercising at home

If you exercise at home – say, doing yoga, Pilates, or dance, for example – and your children are swirling round your legs like puppies but are adamant they don't want to join in, here are a few 10-second set-ups to distract and happily occupy them until you've finished your practice:

☆ **Plastic bubble-wrap popping challenge:** Few young children can resist the lure of bubble-wrap. Small pieces can be set out like puddles – for leaping and jumping practice; make sure your little one has bare feet and the bubble-wrap is on a non-slip surface or secured to the floor with a little masking tape to keep the fun safe. Larger lengths can be used for marching, crawling, running and rolling practice. The challenge, if required, could be to see if they can pop every single air pocket before you're finished with your exercise.

☆ **Target practice:** Challenge your child to scrunch pieces of scrap or newspaper into balls – they'll need to make at least ten – and then throw them, aiming into an empty waste-paper basket. Of course, the challenge can be made harder by standing further from the target.

☆ **Skittles:** Sealed plastic bottles, with a little water in them for a bit of weight, make great skittles. Raid your recycling for at least three, and challenge your little one to see how many times they can knock them over and set them up before you're finished. A small soft sponge ball or beanbag can be the projectile.

☆ **Walk the line:** Make a couple of masking (painters') tape lines – one straight, one zigzag, say – on the floor, away from where you're exercising. That should start up some tight-rope walking, and who knows what else; toys and cars may also become involved. Just let them go with their flow – and you'll have the space to finish those stretches.

☆ **Tracks and runs:** If you have a toy train track or a marble run that your little one can make independently, now's a good time to challenge them to see what they can make by the time you've finished your exercise; they'll love showing you their design when you're done.

☆ **Soft-toy Olympics:** While you exercise, challenge your child to find out which of their soft toys is best at running, jumping, rolling, skating and the like, with an athletic competition. Medals could be given at the end – maybe you'll get one too, for being so good at your particular exercise.

☆ **Books about sport or physical activity:** Your child may relish a quiet few minutes near you, looking at stories about sport and exertion, while you finish yours. A couple of our favourite picture books with a sporting theme are:
Ambrose goes for Gold – Tor Freeman
The Tortoise and the Hare – an Aesop fable

☆ **Tunnel-time:** These cheerfully coloured pop-up tunnels are a good investment – crawling babies love them and toddlers and preschoolers are still drawn to their enclosed, colourful space. They'll slither and crawl through it again and again, but might also use it as a camp, or involve other toys. Its sudden appearance could intrigue your little one for at least the time you need to exercise, and probably longer.

☆ **Toys play Twister:** If you have the game Twister (which I highly recommend getting) you can set it out for your little one with a few soft toys as the contestants. Your child can be in charge of the spinner and move the toys to the correct colour spots on the play-mat. They'll make up the rest of the rules as they go along.

Sustenance

Whether we want to make a cup of tea or have a quick sandwich, finding time for our own sustenance is often a huge challenge for parents of the under-fives. One of my friends told me how she would surreptitiously eat most of her meals and snacks standing in her kitchen, facing away from her kids while they were in their high chairs. She had to hide what she was eating because they would always abandon whatever they were doing, even if it was having something identical, in favour of her food. Another friend's two-year-old had a serious obsession with kettles for a while; he desperately wanted to open and close the lid and put the kettle on its stand over and over again if he ever got the faintest whiff of anyone wanting a cuppa. It was often easier to just not ever think about having a cup of tea. Some young children are very intrigued for a while with the process of food preparation and, as another mum told me, 'sometimes, just sometimes, I'd rather they just let me get on with it.'

'. . . very little ones grabbing at/climbing up your legs, or trying to get in the oven when you open it, or wanting to be carried so you have to do everything with one hand. Bigger little ones demanding food instantly when you are trying to cook it, "but Mum, I want something to eat NOW"! If you give in and do snacks then the cooked food doesn't get eaten.'

A mum of two, trying to make lunch

Maybe the dream scenario, while food and drink is being prepared and partaken, is for your little one to be – as the French would have it – *sage*; a word I rather like. By this they mean that children, and very young children at that, are calm and self-controlled around food and at mealtimes – they certainly do not clamber to take your food, or food that's destined for them but that is not ready yet, nor do they ask for different food. The way in which French parents achieve these dream eating habits and table manners in *les enfants* is, as you may have guessed, by setting strict rules; there is certainly no pandering to the potential fussy eaters out there. But I can totally see how the *sage* child, the calm and well-mannered child that waits patiently while food is being prepared, eats when and what they're given, and allows their parents to do the same, might be something that makes this particular aspect of parenting easier. It's how to achieve this, though, and that's the tricky bit. Unless you're French, of course.

If your child is finding it difficult at mealtimes – is not *sage* – and is exhibiting unwanted behaviour, then take a look at the chapter Sanity Savers, which might help. If, however, your child can't find their flow of independent play while you *prepare* food or drink for yourself or them, try one or two of these 10-second set-ups to help them wait:

☆ **Play dough:** This is a kitchen basic in my house. It's such a wonderful way to get young children busy and concentrating at the kitchen table or on a plastic mat on the floor while the grown up cooks. There's a recipe for homemade play dough on page 205 – and a batch will last for ages if you keep it in an airtight container. One of the best things about using play dough as a 10-second set-up is that it is so versatile – you can ring the changes in a flash, refreshing children's interest by offering different things to use with it; from favourite figurines, shells and sticks and rubber stamps, to toy kitchen equipment like plastic cookie-cutters and rolling pins, cupcake cases, buttons and pipe cleaners. The only thing they mustn't do is eat it.

☆ **Empty muffin tins and ice cube trays:** These compartmentalised containers are irresistible to young children. Just add pom-poms, favourite mini figurines, toys or play dough and see how the play develops.

☆ **Egg boxes and cardboard tubes:** These recyclables are brilliant for little ones. Grab what's to hand from your recycling stash and add some things to hide in the boxes or slide down the tubes, such as small figurines or toy vehicles. Or make a sensory tub for your little one to explore, right before their eyes, by placing the tubes and egg boxes in a large, wide-based box along with some uncooked rice (the rice can be used again and again), some plastic scoops, bowls and a funnel or two.

☆ **Pestle and mortar and herbs:** We have a wooden pestle and mortar which my two children have loved since they were tiny; it makes them feel very chef-like or scientist-like. Just put out some handfuls of things for them to crush – like herbs from the garden, eggshells, a cracker or a few cornflakes.

☆ **Pincer practice:** If you have a set of small tongs in your kitchen, or a set of kids' chopsticks or tweezers, you can entice your child with a challenge to sort pom-poms, uncooked pasta shapes (which you can use again and again), fresh apple skin or carrot peelings – these are great materials for scissor practice too.

☆ **What's in the drawer?:** My mum had a drawer in her kitchen which could be easily reached and opened by my two children when they were tots. She realised this, and so always had some wonderful kitchen-y things in there for them to haul out and investigate. If you have a drawer that your little one always delves into, why not make it a 'magic' drawer and occasionally change or add to its contents? It could have a range of things inside from wooden spoons, a colander, sieve, and tubs and bowls, to more surprising contents from time to time like:

 ☆ a few tote bags, cardboard boxes or socks with interesting things inside to investigate

 ☆ a book or two

 ☆ a soft toy

 ☆ stuff for a tea party – a toy tea set, tablecloth and a toy guest or two

 ☆ a clean metal baking tray, which will be magnetic, plus any magnetic dinosaurs, letters, vehicles or whatever you have to hand

 ☆ plastic cups, bowls, containers and wooden spoons

☆ **Colander and pipe cleaners:** This has become a bit of a classic 'as seen on' the Pinterest boards of the world – and with good reason. Young children really love posting and weaving pipe cleaners in and out the holes of a colander.

☆ **Salt-trays:** A little fine table salt goes a long way. Thinly cover a tray with salt, and let your little one make their mark – just as they like (though do keep an eye on them to make sure they don't eat it!). You can add paintbrushes and forks to let them create different marks. A little side-to side shake allows them to start over again. Set them up somewhere where they're comfortable and can really see into the tray easily – a low table, or the floor (with a wipe-clean tablecloth or play-mat underneath).

☆ **Busy bags:** *What you'll need to do beforehand:* Take a couple of small tote bags or simple drawstring bags and fill them with different things from time to time. The surprise of a new bag appearing is usually a big hit. In the busy bags you could put:

   ☆ Build-a-meal activity. *What you'll need to do beforehand:* Cut various shapes out of felt to make some *let's pretend* foodstuff – carrots, sausages, cheese, tomatoes, pizza base, ham, bread, broccoli and the like – for some wonderful open-ended dinner-designing. Just provide a plastic plate for the assembling of the meal.

   ☆ Create a food feast poster. Our local Post Office always stocks loads of stickers, often with food and drink themes, but you can buy them very cheaply online; postage is never much because they're so light. Invite your little one to create a poster of a feast on some colourful paper using some food and drink stickers. Once made, the poster can be displayed in the kitchen, say, and used for a game where everyone chooses what they would eat at the feast.

   ☆ Wooden spoon art. Adding colour to a wooden spoon is very satisfying. Provide watercolours, crayons or felt-tips (for older kids) – whatever you think your little one might like best – and a new wooden spoon or two; you can buy them very cheaply at pound shops or online.

☆ Paper plate art. A bag with a paper plate and some crayons, watercolours or pencils inside should inspire your little one to decorate the plate just as they like – there's no right way of doing it. Dry markers work well on shiny plastic-coated paper plates and are great if you would like to use the same plate a few times. Test which colouring instrument works best on the surface of the paper plates you have first.

☆ Foodie magazine collage. *What you'll need to do beforehand:* Scan freebie supermarket magazines, veggie-box delivery catalogues or food supplements in the weekend press for pictures of food. Cut out and collect these over a few weeks before making up a busy bag with lots of these images, a glue stick and a thin piece of card or a paper plate. Let your little one rip, snip (if they're confident with scissors), arrange and stick the pictures on the card just as they like.

☆ Jigsaws and puzzles. If your child loves a puzzle, surprise them with a forgotten (or new) puzzle in a busy bag. *What you'll need to do beforehand:* For a foodie theme, try making your own puzzle by finding a cool picture of a 'showstopper' cake or any other *wow* picture of food. Stick it onto some thin card, and then, on the back with a pencil, mark it up into however many pieces you'd like the puzzle to have – these can be regular or irregular in size and shape; it's up to you. Cut along the lines and pop the pieces into a busy bag.

☆ **Books:** Have a special kitchen book basket which occasionally appears to surprise and catch the attention of your little one. You can change the selection of books often to keep it fresh, but here are a few of our food-themed favourites:

Ketchup on your Cornflakes? – Nick Sharratt
The Very Hungry Caterpillar – Eric Carle
Smelly Peter the Great Pea Eater – Steve Smallman
The Tiger who Came to Tea – Judith Kerr
I Will Not Ever Never eat a Tomato – Lauren Child
You Choose – Pippa Goodhart and Nick Sharratt
Cake Girl – David Lucas

Sitting down for two seconds together

Sometimes, if a toddler or preschooler is in the zone – playing independently and with flow – we think to ourselves, I'll have a little sit down for two minutes myself; I'll read a chapter of my book, or skip through the newspaper, or I'll just drink my tea and maybe make a list. Or if we have another, younger child, we'll think, now's a good time to settle down for a few moments and feed my little one. And sometimes, especially if the older children are well practised at independent play, they will ignore our presence and we might indeed get a few precious minutes to ourselves. But if you sitting down near them is a rare sight for your child, then the moment you settle they could well take it as a sign that you want to interact with them.

Often a gentle check-in and then an encouragement for them to carry on with what they were doing will be enough to get them back their flow – especially if you don't do anything too interesting-looking for a bit. However, if not, with subtle sleight-of-hand you can orchestrate their discovery of something new, interesting and intriguing, buying yourself some quality down-time, or time to feed the baby. Here are some of my go-to 10-second set-ups for such occasions:

☆ **Books with a CD:** There are some wonderful picture books that come with an audio CD. These are especially useful if your child is not in the habit of 'reading' to themselves; having the audio version on can break the 'mummy or daddy must always read to me' cycle. Some of our favourites are:
Biscuit Bear – Mini Grey
The Little Red Train – Benedict Blathwayt
The Enormous Crocodile – Roald Dahl

☆ **Time to build:** The sudden appearance of a box of Lego (or Duplo) bricks, train track, wooden blocks, Octons, marble-run pieces – or whatever construction toy you know your little one can build happily and independently – will remind them of its brilliance. Chop and change, and don't have any of them out all the time, otherwise they'll soon lose their play-lustre.

☆ **Make a quick book nook:** To get across that looking at books is sometimes an independent activity, it can be useful to define a special temporary space for it. Create a quick cosy corner with a chiffon scarf or table cloth pegged up to make a little roof – or use an old-fashioned clothes horse with a cover draped over it. Add a few cushions underneath, along with a basket of freshly selected books. How could they resist?

☆ **Play scenes and figurines:** Even when he was a toddler, my son would play for the longest time with two figurines (or toy vehicles), one in each hand, using the whole room as their world. They'd slide down chairs, skid along the walls and jump from shelf to shelf with dialogue, sound effects and often a slow-motion replay of the action. My daughter, on the other hand, would be more likely to stay with this kind of play if the figurines were more grounded in an environment. We do have a doll's house and a garage – classic and expensive – but often the most popular play scenes for their 'small world play' were, and still are, the most simple and non-specific. Anything from a large plant or a few stones, to a blanket or some polystyrene packaging, for example, can be a fantastic world for figurines – and often the more improvised and specific the play scene, the more open-ended and imaginative the play.

The surprise arrival of a few figurines and a potential landscape should kick-start some wonderful, independent, imaginative play and buy you some precious time to have a sit down. Here are some of our favourite combinations:

☆ Dinosaurs and some big stones.

☆ Fairies and a robust plant.

☆ *Star Wars* characters and some polystyrene packaging.

☆ Action figures and a piece of cardboard.

☆ Soft toys and a white blanket.

☆ Mermaid figurines, a blue piece of chiffon and a small cardboard box.

☆ Small plastic figurines – ready for a swim – and a small plastic box of water (with a towel underneath to prevent slips).

☆ The dolls' house family and some furniture.

☆ Spiderman and some netting – from fruit packaging, say.

☆ Box of small toy cars and a long cardboard tube.

☆ Small wild animal figurines and some natural-looking fabric – brown or green hessian, for example, and some large stones.

☆ **Doctor, Doctor:** We have had so much play out of our toy doctor's kit, which is now full of child-made extra equipment like tissue bandages, x-ray pictures and the like, and I think this is partly due to my keeping it as just an occasional toy. If you need to buy some time to have a sit down, it's the most brilliant and quick thing to produce to engage and help your child find their flow. Remember, though, if you don't want to be the patient, make sure there's already one there waiting, requiring urgent attention – any doll or soft toy will be up for this.

☆ **Make a place to play with a puzzle:** Some children are mad-keen on puzzles, and if your little one enjoys them you can definitely use this as a 10-second set-up. However, some children see puzzle-making as something that only happens with a grown up helping, rather like reading. Of course, like reading, it should *sometimes* be this kind of activity – but it doesn't have to be. If you want it to be an independent play activity, make sure the puzzle you offer is of a suitable level for your child to enjoy and is good-quality, so they have the best chance of knowing when the pieces fit properly. Encourage your child to complete it themselves by making them a clear and comfortable place in which to settle.

☆ **A big cardboard box:** How simple is this? It's well known how fascinated young children are when it comes to cardboard boxes, and they can be used for all manner of open-ended play. As a 10-second set-up you're on to a winner with a cardboard box, especially if it's big enough for your child to climb into by themselves. Just sit back and let the magic happen.

☆ **A sound button:** I first used sound buttons with young children in a museum setting – pre-recording short sounds and songs for them to activate themselves. It wasn't until I was asked to prepare some at home that my two children got their hands on them. Once they were shown how to set the machine to Record mode and switch it to Playback to hear their recording, they were occupied for ages; collecting noises, leaving messages, singing songs and the like. Audio play – a vastly underused 10-second set-up!

☆ **A piece of string and an action figure:** One of the play staples in our house is a ball of string. While one does need to be supervising, of course, the ways to play with string are infinite. Before my son could tie knots, he would sticky-tape one end to a car of a mini-figurine – usually Spiderman – and there would follow all kinds of crazy imaginative dramatic action.

☆ **Bag of large fabric pieces:** Play-silks and other floaty fabrics lend themselves to all kinds of open-ended and imaginative play. From dressing up, dancing with them, wrapping things up in them, using them as blankets for toys or hiding under them – I've seen it all.

☆ **Dress-up box:** The magical, sudden appearance of the dress-up box or a bag of grown-up clothes destined for the charity shop usually does the trick of capturing the attention of little ones. Few can resist trying on Daddy's old jumper, or Mummy's unwanted summer t-shirt or that hat-that-was-a-mistake.

☆ **A blown-up balloon:** If a brightly coloured, freshly blown-up balloon makes an unexpected appearance it usually delights and captivates little ones for longer than you'd expect. Keepy-uppy, fancy-football skills and simple throwing-and-catching games are sure to ensue.

☆ **Sports section of the newspaper:** Make yourself a paper hat out of one sheet and see how long it takes for your little one to notice. Hand over the rest of the section (just check there's no disturbing or inappropriate images on any of the pages you offer) and tell them you've finished reading it, so now it's theirs to play with, just as they like. They may well rip it up, screw it up, or hide under it – just let them explore it, and let them play.

☆ **Clean plastic and cardboard stuff from the recycling box:** I've brought in the recycling box before now, with the excuse that I need to check for something in there. Its presence is often enough to spark interest, and if your children are anything like my two were, they'll be asking if they can have that box, or that bottle or whatever. They'll have an idea of what they want to do with it, and you can bet it'll be playful.

☆ **A blanket:** It might sound a bit strange to suggest offering a blanket as a 10-second set-up, but rather like the cardboard box, it can be a wonderfully open-ended play object. Just you unfolding it will probably be enough to interest your little one and, however they take over the play, it should buy you some sitting-down time.

☆ **Pop-up tent:** Our pop-up tent got so much use – I used to love surprising my two children with it. It takes seconds to assemble (hence its name) –

and if you put a toy or a book inside, you should certainly set your little one off on a new and independent play journey should they need a little help to regain their flow.

Home-maintenance and DIY

If the thought of fixing something, a bit of DIY or simply changing a light bulb, fills you with dread then I would suggest waiting till your child is napping or in bed before tackling any house-maintenance. If, however, you're not daunted by such adult-only tasks, then you might want to consider one or two of these 10-second set-ups as a way to keep your little one close, but occupied, with their own house-mainte-nance-themed activity should they find it difficult to let you carry out the task unhindered.

☆ **A tape-measure:** Many young children love measuring things. Hand over a tape-measure and a small notebook and pencil and ask them to measure the height and length of stuff in the room you're in. I find those automatic-shut tape-measures a bit frightening, but many young children get the idea of them incredibly quickly and are not fazed by their snappy closing-action – there are even some gorgeous kids' versions out there, with a gentler quick-release mechanism. The soft dressmaking tape-measures look just as professional, though, should you be worried about the safety of the snappy-types.

☆ **Kid-friendly tool kit:** If you're a keen DIYer then I would recommend purchasing a toy tool kit to occupy your tot at a safe distance away from your real tools, but engaged in a similar activity. There are some great ones on offer – with chunky nuts and bolts, working screwdrivers with things to join together and boards with 'nails' to hammer down.

☆ **Big nuts and bolts:** Some little ones love the idea of filling the length of a bolt with nuts – or making sure every bolt has a nut (and a washer, maybe). These are available at most hardware stores, or there are toy versions too. This is definitely one for the over-threes and those past the mouthing stage. . .

☆ **A spirit level:** The bubble of a spirit level is quite mesmerising to young children, and they'll love the challenge of finding out what's level and what's not.

What you'll need to do beforehand: You can even make your own spirit level by simply filling a small, smooth-sided, plastic bottle with water, nearly to the top, and securing the lid. With a permanent marker, make a bold line on the surface of the bottle, tracing the water's level bubble when it's lying down flat, or standing up, on something you know to be level – like a table, say. If you give them a little notebook and pencil, they might like to draw or make a mark or two in their notebook to show their findings. What's level in your house?

☆ **Can they fix it?:** Some children love nothing more than being given a hard hat and a toy-spanner and being asked to fix the door handle or the chair. This will often be enough to spark some wonderful imaginative play.

☆ **Screw-box sort:** This one is definitely for the over-threes; if you have collected screws from here, there and everywhere over the years, why not get your little one to sort them out? If you give them some containers they will love sorting them into big and little, or positive and negative-headed groups. They'll feel like they're helping too – all the better for giving them a sense of importance to their play.

☆ **Hammer and tack:** If you're using your hammer for some DIY, why not offer your child a similar opportunity should they become interested in your activity? There are some great hammer and tack toy sets available with reusable cork bases which are suitable for three-year-olds and over. Polystyrene packing can be used in lieu of cork or wood, and golf tees instead of nails.

☆ **Magnetic magic:** Magna tile sets are great for children who are intrigued by magnetism, and who like construction play. They can be a little expensive, though; cheaper are those kid-friendly horseshoe magnets. Why not give them a bunch of smallish magnetic objects to test? They could be DIY-based like allen-keys, nuts and bolts, washers, rawl plugs and the like. If you can get hold of a magnetic base (remember those old office toys of the 80s?) your little one might like to sculpt with magnetism. Large nuts, paperclips and washers can be fashioned into cool shapes – very arty.

Home-keeping

Keeping on top of the everyday jobs of a household is hard enough without children, but add a baby or toddler or two into the equation and it stands to reason that only the bare minimum gets done; and that's totally normal. Embracing chores and including my little ones in them is the only way I could face them in the early years (see the chapter Chores: not Bores); making them playful and positive parts of the day certainly worked for me. However, sometimes you just want to put a wash on, take out the rubbish, or clean up after a meal quickly and without necessarily involving your child. If this is the case, here are a few 10-second set-ups that should occupy your little one if they can't find something playful to do themselves while you finish that quick chore:

☆ **Laundry basket play:** Add a bit of glamour to your laundry basket by handing it over to your little one, with some ribbons and scarves, for some weaving practice. You'll almost enjoy using it when it's been transformed.

☆ **Painting the garden fence:** If you're dotting in and out – taking out the garbage or hanging out the washing, for example – you could easily keep your little one in one place and happily occupied by giving them a chunky paintbrush and a pot or bucket of water to 'paint' the fence (or garden furniture).

☆ **Prepare for play:** The promise of some together-time after you've finished your job can work really well for young children, especially if you give them the task of preparing for the play themselves. For example, ask them to find a few books they'd like to share with you and set them out ready with cushions, etc., or to set out a tea party for you to attend, or to select cars and get them ready for a race. Make sure you do actually make good on your promise, though, and *stay and play* with them as soon as you can.

☆ **Send them off on a colour hunt or treasure hunt:** If you are immersed in a domestic chore or two and you just need your little one to wait while you finish, but they can't find something to do, this is an easy-peasy trick: hand over an empty egg box, basket or bowl and send them on a mission to find five – or ten, if they're quick – yellow things that fit in their container. If you revisit this one, ring the changes with the colour or the kind of object you want them to collect; we've had plastic, shiny or things-with-corners as our collecting rule before. Great fun – and so easy to set up.

☆ **Timed challenge:** If your little one likes puzzles or colouring with crayons, for example, you could set out the activity attractively and ask if they think they could complete the jigsaw or picture while you finish your jobs. Older children might like to set the kitchen timer or a 5-minute sand-timer to see how long it takes them to complete the challenge and you to finish your chores.

Household admin and working from home

Even if you are a full-time stay-at-home parent, there are still plenty of admin activities that need attention during traditional working hours. Paying bills or making appointments online, making phone calls, filling out forms and opening the mail are just some of the table- or desk-based tasks often made challenging by our little ones. And if you've ever tried working from home, or you are trying to help older children with homework (maybe you are homeschooling) with toddlers twirling round your legs, then these 10-second set-ups might well be for you. These are for the moments when you've snuck to the computer to check your messages or write that email, or when you want to help another child with their spelling practice because your little one is playing independently and happily. Suddenly what you're doing is far too interesting, and they're there, tugging at your trousers, wanting to join in, or have your attention at least. These activities will keep your little one happily busy whilst sitting next to you.

Sit-by-me activities

☆ **A calculator and paper and pencil:** Both my children loved to be given a calculator – a very grown-up piece of office equipment – and make up crazy long numbers. 'Doing sums' on the paper just means they'll be scribbling away then probably proudly telling you their totals – but it can be a surprisingly absorbing activity for many preschoolers.

☆ **Wipe-clean mark-making:** This is a great sit-by-me activity. We have a set of lovely wipe-clean animal-themed cards that get used again and again. The pictures are incomplete and the aim of the game is to add detail like expressions, tails, or the other half of the animal. But you can make your own wipe-clean paper and it will look a lot more grown up and office-y, and thus very appealing to the young business person; just pop a piece of A4 paper or card into a sheet protector, *et voilà!* Kid-friendly dry-erase markers are widely available in lots of lovely colours, and usually come with a little cloth included. You can ring the changes by marking the paper in some way before it goes into the protective sheet – maybe with dots or squares or part of a car or an eye – to start them off on their mark-making.

☆ **Stamps and inks:** This is a great sit-by-me activity, especially if you keep the inks and stamps as just an occasional, special treat for when you're working at the table or desk. We've collected loads of stamps over the years with various themes; pictures and stories will grow on the paper very quickly.

☆ **Play 'office':** Some children love the idea of working in an office environment – well, all those grown-up gadgets and office supplies are tempting. Cardboard boxes make great computers and if you add an old diary, some Post-it notes, a date stamp, some office stickers and an old phone into the mix, they'll be off; mimicking you on the phone and being very busy and business-like.

☆ **Letter-writing play box:** *What you'll need to do beforehand:* collect a few used envelopes of varying sizes and colours, add some scrap paper suitable for mark-making – maybe some lined, some plain, some coloured, a strip of office labels – with family members' and friends' names written on them, some snazzy pens and pencils, some old postage stamps, a glue stick, some cool pictures or interesting puzzles or photographs cut out from magazines that might interest individual potential recipients, and a few stickers. Just let them have fun with the stuff and explore the process of letter-writing.

☆ **Folders of fun:** *What you'll need to do beforehand:* like busy bags, these take a couple of minutes to put together but you can make up a couple and have them ready for when you need them. Inside each is a special surprise sit-by-me activity – here are some of our favourites:

  ☆ A page of new stickers and a plain paper bag to decorate.

  ☆ A gold or silver crayon, a simple picture of an outline of a crown or a robot, and some play gems for embellishing their picture.

☆ An undecorated paper plane, boat, bird, hat or fortune teller plus crayons and/or stickers.

☆ A couple of pieces of paper with masking-tape strips spelling their name (or the first letter of their name) or a pattern or shape, plus some crayons. If they colour over the whole sheets of paper and tape just as they like then peel away the tape, the shape or letter(s) are revealed, like magic.

☆ Some black paper plus sticky stars and a metallic crayon or pen to create a night-time picture.

☆ A picture of something missing its spots – a leopard, a Dalmatian dog, a jumper or dress, a sprinkle-less cupcake – plus some office-supply coloured circle stickers to rectify the situation.

☆ Make-a-watch kit: pre-cut a kitchen-roll tube to make wrist straps and circles and/or squares of pale thin card or paper with a bit of double-sided sticky tape on the back for the watch faces – if you like you could add the numbers, or cut out those large luxury watch-face pictures from adverts in magazines – plus pencils, crayons and stickers. Challenge your little one to make a watch for each member of your household.

☆ Make-a-picture kit: collect a few bits and bobs for your child to make a collage – scraps of patterned paper, foil, net, sequins, fabric squares, neoprene foam and the like, cut into various shapes and sizes. Add a piece of thin card and glue stick and see what they make.

☆ Sticker books. My children didn't really get into these before they were about five years old, but I've seen some three-year-olds totally absorbed by sticker books. I love that when they're really young, children have no idea of where the book's creators expected them to put the stickers so there's a wonderful freedom to where those stickers get stuck – and often unstuck again, of course. Just let them do what they will – and enjoy the space it gives you to do what you need to do.

Adult-to-adult interaction, out and about

If we have to take our young child or children with us when we have an appointment, then the setting of that appointment will have a huge impact in how comfortable we feel about our children being there. The environments of, say, hospitals, dentists, banks or hairdressers all have pros and cons when it comes to how welcoming they are to young children. And there is often a *waiting* aspect to these kinds of outings; 10-second set-ups work really well for waiting-room time. Just make sure you eke out the goodies, as it were, so that you've always got something new and exciting to produce from your bag, just when they need it. There are lots of things you can do *with* your child whilst waiting too – see the chapter Stay and Play for ideas for waiting-room fun and games.

The ideas below are especially good for during your actual appointment, too, when you need to interact with the doctor or bank manager and you really need your little one to be busy and occupied until you're finished.

Pull it out of the bag

☆ **Busy purse or wallet:** This will take a bit of preparation, but young children will love the idea of having a proper purse or wallet full of things – just like Mummy or Daddy.
  What you'll need to do beforehand: fill the notes section with play money or blank note-sized sheets of paper – for them to make their own – and the credit-card section with sample cards and the like. Out-of-date library cards and so on look authentic and will help to fill the sections. Add a few large coins (or play money) if your child is definitely past the mouthing stage or, if you are worried about coins being a choking hazard, make paper coins by rubbing pencil over paper-covered coins and cutting them out. Fill out the wallet with a pencil and a bit of notepaper, a photo or two, unwanted tickets, receipts – whatever you

have to hand. If the purse has poppers and flaps and zips and is full of wallet-treasure this will definitely interest and occupy your little one until you're done with your meeting.

☆ **Forgotten treasures:** Grab a handful of small toys without teeny tiny parts that could get lost and produce them at intervals throughout your appointment, as needed. Things like Duplo, pocket ponies, an insect eye lens, a mini-torch, a mini-magnetic drawing board, pocket puzzles or those freebie toys you get on the front of kids' magazines or in party bags. Things that might have lost their appeal are usually greeted with renewed enthusiasm when offered unexpectedly.

☆ **Cars and an empty kitchen roll tube, or similar:** If your little one is a vehicle fan then bring along a couple of cool matchbox-size cars. I often take an empty cardboard tube with me too – this simple addition really adds to the adventures of the cars.

☆ **Clicker-counting:** When we were small my sisters and I were obsessed with a gadget that my father had – I think it might have been an unused car mileage counter. It had a very satisfying little handle that when turned would click the numbers up and up. We felt so privileged to be given a turn with it, and oh my goodness, I remember the excitement of a *9999 number clicking on one more digit – it was so satisfying. You can buy quite cheap clickers online; if you get a grown-up-looking one and produce it as a gadget to try, rather than a toy, then your little one will not be able to resist its allure, clicking up the numbers higher and higher, and resetting it, of course.

☆ **Wallet calculator:** One purse of mine came with a little solar-powered, credit-card-sized calculator. You can imagine my children got a real kick out of being allowed to borrow it while I was otherwise engaged during an appointment. The key thing here is to only allow them to have it on occasion, to keep it special.

☆ **Mini-books and comics:** My two children are massive bookworms, and always have been. Before heading out on any outing we will grab a smallish book or two and a comic each. Do choose kids' magazines carefully though, as some of them have loads of cut-out-and-keep pages or tricky make-y activities and so are not particularly useful for keeping your little one *independently* entertained.

☆ **Bed-in-a-box**: Once, we decorated an empty kitchen matchbox and transformed it into a mini-bed for two small figurines, with little fabric and felt blanket and pillows. This would sometimes magically appear from my bag to squeals of delight, but I got the same response if the bed was just a small plastic box with a tissue napkin blanket in which a favourite figurine could sleep. Then the box and lid could become other things with which the figurine could interact; a simple and open-ended play object to fire your child's imagination for some great independent play.

☆ **A box of delights**: Any smallish box with something unusual, or a few forgotten toys, inside is usually very desirable, and a great way to hook your little one and keep them happy and interested for a while.

☆ **Notebook and pencils**: A rather grown-up-looking notebook and pen or pencil produced from mummy or daddy's bag is often seen as a very tempting offer. They'll probably tell you what needs to be made note of or drawn.

☆ **Colouring sheets and crayons**: I'm not a great fan of the colouring-in book, probably because my children would, when they were very young at least, do one little mark on each page and then that was it and then they would never go back to it. My secret of success in using these is to not give the whole book to your child. Spend a few minutes when not with your children tearing or cutting out the pages, and then take just a few out with you at a time. Less is definitely more; the pictures have more status and seem more special if they are one of four rather than forty. A little plastic-lidded box of crayons, especially for this kind of situation, also makes the prospect of 'colouring-in' more attractive to a small child, and they could well be absorbed in the activity for the duration of your meeting or appointment.

Invitations to Play

'. . . A poor life this if, full of care,
We have no time to stand and stare.'

From *Leisure* by William Henry Davies

The pleasure of leisure

As adults we know what we like; the things we do for leisure are usually very personal – sometimes even a little idiosyncratic. Show me a copy of the magazine *Elle Decoration*, for example, and I'll be eyeing up the nearest cosy corner to immerse myself in a bit of glossy interior-design escapism before you can put the kettle on. Show my husband a Frisbee, or a pack of cards and a cribbage board, and he'll be as exuberant as a puppy at the prospect of a game.

Some *places* are naturally inviting to adults, too – maybe a set of rolling hills or a clear, still swimming pool is your cup of tea. Such environments can tempt us to engage with them. Things or places that have the common characteristic of being *inviting* can invoke many different activities. They might encourage us to stay, sleep, rest, look, daydream, be, think, talk, climb, dance, run around, eat or drink, imagine, investigate, design, explore, make, watch, swim, read or write. Whatever the activity, the power of that place is in initiating the desire in us to stop and stay, and participate somehow in something we believe to be pleasurable.

Some people are rather clever at *creating* inviting environments; think of a cafe or pub you know that has that warm glow at dusk, tempting you inside out of the cold, or a fantastic shop window display that never fails to catch your eye and lure you in. Places not necessarily always associated with the pursuit of leisure, like libraries, museums, offices, laboratories and classrooms, can have this inviting appeal too. Some achieve this more successfully than others; it takes talent and a great deal of thought to make such environments inviting to a wide range of people. Knowing the potential audiences and what they might find attractive and welcoming – making them happily stop and stay and participate for a while – is the key to success here.

Open to invitation?

Seeking out things that are linked to leisure is often seen as a 'guilty pleasure' as we reach adulthood, and we rarely allow ourselves the time to indulge in such frivolities. How many times have we hurried past that wonderfully scented rose bush without stopping to smell its perfume, or not taken a moment to sketch that building or finish the crossword puzzle even though such invitations might be staring us in the face? It often seems we really do not have *time to stand and stare.* Children, however, do. They don't even have to make a conscious decision to accept an inviting opportunity, let alone deal with any guilt an adult might associate with it. If something makes them want to stop and stay for a while, then that's it – it's simply time to play – perchance to climb, dance, run around, jump up and down, imagine, investigate, touch, design, build, explore, make or observe – whatever activity is called for. As poet Kathy Williams so aptly put it,

'*Childhood is that state, which ends the moment a puddle is first viewed as an obstacle instead of an opportunity.*'

One can often clearly see adult sensibilities at odds with a little one's innate ability to find the playful opportunity in so many things; when a toddler is compelled to continually press the buttons and turn the dials on the washing machine, for example, or when a pre-schooler absolutely has to walk along that little wall holding your hand on the way up to nursery however late you are. Yes, sometimes their desire to engage in playful activity needs to be re-directed, or stopped for safety reasons or because of time constraints. But there is something in their amazing aptitude for the detection of possible play opportunities that can be incredibly useful to us as carers and parents. By tapping into their talent of finding the playful in the mundane, the opportunity to playfully engage with the most surprising of things and their ready acceptance of an invitation to play, we can, in fact, use this to our advantage, encouraging learning, family happiness and harmony. If we recognise, seek out or indeed deliberately set up playful opportunities for our toddlers and preschoolers, we can make invitations to play a way to play.

Invitations to play are a way to play

Recognising ready-made invitations to play – they're out there

Young children are absolutely brilliant at seeing the playful invitation in almost everything, so if we are out and about, it is up to us grown ups to recognise when our children have found ready-made opportunities to play. If it's safe, and if there's time, letting them accept these invitations to play will be one of the greatest gifts you can give them. Green Hearts, the Institution for Nature in Childhood, write and consult on the power of nature and play and believe that if the time young children have for unstructured outdoor play – that is, play that they make up themselves – is frequent and in diverse natural settings, then their social and emotional, creative, intellectual development, physical fitness and overall health, and the creation of lasting personal bonds to the natural world will be vastly enhanced.

The benefits of outside play for the minds and bodies of our children are well documented, and there have been many studies which have shown that it can increase physical activity and levels of vitamin D; it can have a positive impact on a child's sense of wellbeing; it can help avoid near-sightedness; it can promote the imagination and creativity; it encourages the use of their senses; it offers opportunities for doing things in different ways and on different scales to indoors; it offers first-hand contact with weather, the seasons and the natural world. It's no wonder the Early Years Foundation Stage (EYFS) curriculum guidance documents in the UK have described it as an enabling environment. It goes on to say that outdoor play should *not* be an optional extra, so a recent UK study finding that almost half of preschool children do not venture outside to play each day is a sad statistic at odds with the well-documented benefits.

Often, because we aren't necessarily on the lookout for them, we hurry on our children without stopping to let them notice these invitations to play. If it's inclement weather, we hurry them inside, unenthusiastic to be out in the rain or wind or cold ourselves. How does that Scandinavian saying go? 'There's no such thing as the wrong sort of weather, only the wrong sort of clothes.' If little ones are in the right gear for the weather conditions they will happily stay outside, and play in the wind, rain or sun for as long as we allow.

But even if the weather isn't an issue, we're still often all too keen to stop them playing in the dirt and come along, ushering our children into the official, recognised, widely-accepted and relatively clean place to play – the playground. However, there are so many fantastic ready-made invitations to play on the way there. Yes, your little one may get a little dirtier, or a lot dirtier, than if they spent the entire playtime in the playground, but that's half the fun of childhood, surely? Children are, as they say, 100 per cent washable. Play-clothes are likely to get grubbier, waterproofs are likely to get wetter, but isn't that why we have them?

Recently I read that someone had overheard a dad saying to their child, 'Stop playing in the dirt and go and ask Grandma for her phone to play with.' How depressing is that?

Here are a few fantastic ready-made invitations to play that you are likely to encounter when you're out and about with your little one. They are incredibly valuable play opportunities, so take a moment to see them as invitations, and then let your child play:

a tree that's a good climber ☆ a grassy bank that's great for rolling down ☆ a lawn full of daisies ☆ a pile of fallen leaves ☆ a wooded area full of good sticks to collect ☆ a pavement full of puddles ☆ a shallow pool of water ☆ a sand pit ☆ a set of tree stumps ☆ a low wall ☆ some crazy paving ☆ shadows on a sunny path ☆ a log-slice path ☆ clumps of mown grass ☆ a wide expanse of long grass ☆ a cove with treasure of sea ceramics or beautiful pebbles or sand ☆ a bunch of boulders ☆ a 'secret' niche under some trees or bushes ☆ a plank of wood or log ☆ an earth pit ideal for digging with a stick ☆ pebbles and a stream ☆ fallen flower petals on a path ☆ a shrub den or shelter

Seeking out invitations to play at home

There are plenty of invitations to play to be had at home too; after all, it's a busy place full of interesting things and opportunities. But because we don't necessarily want our little ones to be playing with those washing-machine buttons, or emptying out that cupboard again and again all day long, we tend to seek out those areas where our little ones can safely play, such as a playroom, if you have the room, and we seek out those things we deem safe and appropriate for them to play with.

In truth, we often absolutely fill our homes to bursting with these safe and appropriate playthings – otherwise known as toys. We might, in fact, bombard our children with an overload of them. Sometimes so numerous and always-available are their toys that our children ignore most of them, or play with them for a matter of seconds before moving onto something new; they simply can't see the wood for the trees. Various discussion threads on Mumsnet share many a parent's common concerns; do our toddlers and preschoolers have too many toys? Do some toys do too much, leaving little to the imagination? And why are so many of them only played with for only a few minutes at a time?

One mum wrote about her three-year-old:

'We went to stay with my parents a couple of weeks ago and took very few toys with us. My parents have a bag of cars they've had for donkey's years plus a doll's house with plenty of the original bits and pieces for it. My three-year-old played for three days straight with these things, didn't once ask for TV or the iPad or his other toys. It was so lovely to watch him concentrating and playing properly instead of spending a minute with one thing, a minute with another, then looking for the iPad! It was a real eye-opener.'

Children, naturally great at seeking out an invitation to play, will head for a place or thing that's most inviting; frustratingly this may not be their toys, especially if these are the same things they see every day. Instead, they move on to something that is more appealing – like a recently emptied cardboard box, the not-allowed remote control, or your wallet, for example. 'What about your toys?!' we may cry, but you can't force a child to want something. Their drive to be busy, productive and playful will always guide them to the best and most enticing opportunity.

But we do not have to be powerless. As babies, toddlers and preschoolers are so good at seeking out the playful opportunity, we can help them to do this by making those things that already exist in our homes more obvious, accessible and inviting. This may mean we have to put a lot of stuff away and possibly consider a bit of toy rotation – more on this later. That old adage 'less is more' is really true: *less* stuff to play with will definitely mean the things that are there will be *more* inviting to your children, and they will stay with those toys for longer. If you can, have a toy stock-check and try having less out. As Ashley Phillips of *Parents* magazine writes, we should try to be our child's toy editor:

'Having a large number of toys can actually make a child more distracted; like adults, toddlers can become overwhelmed when they're presented with too many choices. In fact, stashing items in the toy box for a few weeks can end up giving them a certain appeal.'

Deliberately setting up invitations to play

I first witnessed deliberate invitations to play for teeny-tinies as a mum, when I began taking my children to a local Sure Start play scheme – known as the One O'clock Club. Every time we popped in, I noticed how they had different things put out attractively in different areas of the space for the children. These invitations to play were truly appreciated by my toddler, and being occupied with my youngest, then a babe-in-arms, I happily observed my son trotting off and immersing himself in the various play opportunities while I settled my baby girl in the babies-only zone. I noticed he would always go first to a particular permanent play feature – almost to check-in with it – and then he would happily try out most activities; some construction, some messy, some dramatic, some imaginative, some outside activities, with a calm and immersive playfulness. As a teacher I could see how all these playful opportunities were designed to fit in with the EYFS curriculum and offered meaningful and open-ended resources for exploration and play. And with experience as an Early Years educator I also knew that this way of setting up an environment in which children can direct their own play and learning has much in common with some aspects of Reggio and Montessori educational philosophy too, where environments are cleverly and thoughtfully designed to maximise meaningful and calm self-directed and free play. There was low shelving, accessible selected playthings, natural materials, open-ended playthings and areas for different activities. There were unusual combinations of toys and playthings and different items set out every day. The whole environment was, in fact, an invitation to play.

It got me thinking, with my mum hat on, about our environment at home, and how we might increase the enjoyment of our time there – which for us, despite going to various classes and play dates, still meant hours and hours at home most days – by thinking about how inviting it was as a place to play. And I realised that deliberately setting up invitations and places to play at home might be possible.

I began to organise our tiny flat a little differently; not as a nursery or classroom, but definitely as a place where there could be lots of open-ended, self-directed play opportunities for my two young children. By making this simple shift, even just in my head, a world of possibilities opened up; from simplifying our play spaces by storing away – out of sight anyway – just some of their toys and play things with a view to rotating them every couple of weeks, to finding more playful uses for different areas of our home and offering my children new ways of using their toys.

By deliberately setting up invitations to play in our homes – using what's already there in a smart way – we can harness our little ones' powerful urge to play, making the most of their intrinsic desire to be busy and productive. We can give them what they seek; clear opportunities to play.

In case you need any more convincing to set up invitations to play and places in which to play in your own home, here are some of the benefits of doing so:

☆ fosters immersive, independent play for long periods of time.
☆ encourages children to try different types of play.
☆ satisfies a young child's urge to find the most inviting play opportunity available.
☆ ensures that all toys and play things, no matter how old, get their moment in the sun.
☆ there's actually less mess to clear up at the end of the day without all of the toys out, all of the time.
☆ refreshes old toys by giving them new ways to be played with.
☆ taps into your child's intrinsic desire to be busy, productive and playful.
☆ gets them playing all over your home without them playing with things you'd rather they didn't.
☆ mixes toys with non-toy play objects, giving those imaginations a good workout.
☆ develops numerous skills through playful activity.
☆ encourages social and emotional development through meaningful playful activity.
☆ your child's creative and intellectual development will be enhanced by different play experiences.

Static and semi-permanent inviting places to play

Different areas of our homes can be set up invitingly, inside and out, for different types of play in a semi-permanent way, with static and large focal opportunities for play. If you fancy doing this, here are some things to bear in mind:

☆ Look around your home for areas that could become inviting places for play – where a low table might go, for example, or a full-length mirror and a box of dress-ups, a wall suitable for low shelving to house toys for easy access. Is there a place you could put cushions and a basket of books, or a place outside to dig and investigate the ground, or an area that could be great for climbing, building stuff, gardening or hiding?

☆ Small, open containers or baskets of favourite toys and playthings are more inviting than huge tubs that hide them.

☆ Open, low, accessible shelves with baskets, bowls or boxes of themed or categorised longstanding and basic playthings will be inviting and have longevity of play allure.

☆ A few larger items displayed attractively will be much more inviting to your child than a kind of stockroom scenario with a jumble or stacked-up pile of too many toys.

☆ Put lots of their things away and then chop and change what you bring out every week or two. This is called toy rotation, and though it might seem harsh it really does make toys seem SO much more interesting when they make a sudden appearance, and you will get to use all the toys much more in the end.

☆ Tidy the shelves each night. Children are much more likely to find something inviting if they can see what's there.

☆ A few books in a basket on the floor are much more accessible and appealing to a toddler and preschooler than rows of spine-out shelved reading material. Swap and change them, and have these baskets all over your home.

☆ Favour open-ended toys and natural materials when possible. Bright, flashing, all-singing, all-dancing and 'branded' plastic toys might be engrossing for a few minutes but they won't lead play on to new and fabulous immersive places as simpler objects can.

Temporary invitations to play

These are set-ups which can be changed every day, if you like. These invitations to play might be a range of selected toys set out invitingly, or a deliberately chosen selection of varied toys and playthings to be experienced in combination. These can be put out on the floor, a low table, on a waterproof tarp or old shower curtain (if messy), a rug or mat, or just about anywhere you like for your child to discover. The complexity and choice of the invitations will of course depend on the age of your child, their specific abilities, interests, their dexterity, their maturity level and the set-up of your home, but here are some things to bear in mind if you are thinking of setting up some temporary invitations to play:

☆ You don't have to set these up every day; having inviting places with favourite toys on shelves and in smallish containers will be enough for happy and busy free-play some days.

☆ You can set them up when your little ones are napping, after they've gone to bed, or are otherwise occupied in independent play.

☆ Use toy rotation techniques for temporary invitations to play: choose from their toys that you've got in accessible storage, giving the forgotten ones a revival.

☆ Combining toys with non-toy playthings and materials is a quick and easy way to make an invitation to play.

☆ You can be suggestive with the set-up, but invitations to play always work best if they are open-ended.

☆ They can tap into every type of play, and can combine more than one play type.

☆ Many invitations to play will be accepted straightaway and it's a delight to behold, but sometimes they'll be denied until later, sometimes altogether. You win some, you lose some!

☆ Some invitations to play will be suited to being left out for a couple of days, and will be revisited, while others are suited to being played with once, and then cleaned up and put away.

☆ A few invitations might need a minute of you modelling an aspect of the play, just to lead your little one into the play. Do step away as soon as you can, though; invitations to play really shouldn't need much grown-up involvement, and are about prompting independent play.

☆ If you have more than one tot playing at a time – then that's all the better for learning those valuable social skills. Invitations to play are a great place to try out those sharing, negotiation, or waiting or coming-back-later skills. Sand-timers are quite useful if there's a 'waiting list' for something in particular.

Gate-keepers of the play party

Like 10-second set-ups, invitations to play are practical ways to foster flow in your children, but unlike the quick-fix 'you need to wait' scenarios, these activities can be planned a little more in advance and are designed for a settled period of discovery play time in your home or out and about. Parents should be available to dip into their little one's play, offering general encouragement and bits of guidance should they so wish, but it's not about taking over or leading the play here or giving direct demonstration or entertaining them, this is about discovery-based learning. Here, we are just the facilitators of great free-play times – we are merely the gate-keepers of the play party.

So, here are lots of examples which will maximise the chances of toddlers and preschoolers finding meaningful busy, calm, self-directed, independent and free-play at home, or out and about. Of course this is not a finite list, and I hope you'll use these ideas to inspire many more of your own.

Outside spaces at home

Static and semi-permanent inviting places to play at home: When my children were very small we lived in a fourth-floor flat with no outside space, and it was a complete hassle to get outside, but I made sure they did so at least once every day; we'd have been climbing the walls with cabin fever if we hadn't. It was wonderful when we moved to a place with an outside space. It's tiny – just a little yard really – but maybe because I'd had three years without easy access to any outside space at all, the door to our backyard was always open, or easily opened in the winter months, for most of the day. The increase in quality of play when my tots could move inside and outside, outside and inside whenever they liked, has made me an enthusiastic advocate for outside play – whatever the weather.

Let them move

Some people's experience of outside play is mainly about letting off steam, racing around and playing large, physically active games. Certainly many outside spaces (not ours, because it is really very small) lend themselves to this kind of play. If you have a largish outside space at home then you will already have one or some of these invitations available. Think about playtime outside as an opportunity for a set of experiences rather than a set of equipment, then you'll soon identify the great ready-made invitations and occasionally set up others to get your little ones *moving*.

Let them jump and reach and stretch up high

Get them jumping and reaching by attaching a few bunches of old and unused keys, toy bells or tin cans with a penny inside to pieces of string and onto various branches. If they jump high enough they should be able to make the keys jangle, the bells ring or the tin pennies jingle.

Let them run, roll and crawl

A grassy bank is great for running or rolling down, crawling up or stretching out on.

Let them hide and swoosh

A wild area with long grass, however small, will provide a fabulous and exciting place for them to hide in and move through.

Let them kick and toss the leaves around

A pile of fallen leaves can be simply kicked around by your little one, or make them into shapes for them to jump between, or rake them into little maze paths for them to zoom around.

Let them jump and splash and get wet

Children love jumping and splashing around in puddles, so make sure you are ready for them to get wet; wellies are a must or, if it's warm, bare feet are waterproof, of course.

Let them leap, tippy-toe and climb

A few low tree stumps provide a wonderful place for this. A quick internet search should throw up a local source of tree stumps if you don't have any, and often they're free. They do need a bit of setting up, because they have to be made stable to be safe. Bury them in the earth slightly, at different heights for variety, and watch them be jumped off, climbed on, run round and stepped across. Other climbing opportunities can be provided if you are lucky enough to have large stones or a boulder or two in your garden.

Let them balance

A low wall is a common feature of many back gardens, and they make wonderful balance beams for little ones. Check the structure is sound before you invite them to walk along it, and if you're worried about the unforgiving nature of the ground next to it, you can always cover it with lots of bark chippings for a softer landing. A plank of wood or a stable log are also irresistible to children.

Let them hop, skip and jump

A path of crazy paving or log slices (sometimes known as log cookies) will provide a great opportunity for honing their hopping and leaping and skipping skills.

Let them ride

A flat surface for bikes, trikes and other things that go is great for encouraging them to pedal, push or scoot around.

Let them throw and kick and catch

Bring out a bag of balls for your children to roll, bounce or kick, make a few paper planes for them to throw, find a Frisbee for them to launch (polystyrene pizza packaging also makes fun temporary throwing discs), or you could invest in a bubble-making machine – it will fill the air with bubbles for your little ones to catch and pop.

Time outdoors can help *all* areas of child development, not just the physical aspects. The EYFS states that outside learning has equal value to inside learning. If you can make the outside play space accessible for little ones, this will mean their flow of play can go from one to the other without breaking stride; they shouldn't always feel compelled to rush outside like caged puppies set free. You could think about it as just doubling your play space. If you think about outside play as a set of experiences rather than a set of equipment, then with even just a couple of the following semi-permanent and static invitations to play you'll definitely observe all types of immersive and calm play outside. Of course, the number and type of these you arrange will depend on the age of your child, their interests, the season and the size of your outside space, but they will enable you to:

Let them dig

Find an area – it doesn't have to be very big – for a mud-pit or sand-box, or both if your little one particularly loves to dig. Set up a low shelf or crate with spades, buckets, sticks, moulds, stiff brushes and maybe a mini-rake so your child can choose their tools themselves.

Let them imagine

Dens and shelters in the shrubs make great settings for all kinds of fantasy and dramatic play; container plants and mini-gardens make magical small world scenes for a few resident mini-figures – dinosaurs or fairies perhaps; large blocks and/or lightweight crates made available to move around just as they like will enable them to make their own fantasy location. A low table or bench can be made into a mud kitchen with the addition of circular cork mats or the like as hob-burners, with a few old pots and pans, wooden spoons, perhaps a muffin tin on low shelving or in a crate; just add some mud, grass clippings and weeds for some let's-pretend cooking.

Let them observe and interact with nature

A small pond can be created by sinking a washing-up bowl into the ground; this can be integrated into the landscape by adding some large pebbles and planting around its edge. A shelf or box of exploration tools in the garden – magnifiers, tweezers, insect boxes and the like – will definitely encourage curiosity and investigation of mini-beasts or botanical specimens. Add a low bench, table or surface to encourage the displaying of the nature treasure that's sure to be discovered.

Let them talk

Tree stumps or cookies, and other natural seats like a log, an arrangement of large stones, or an inviting space demarcated by planting are wonderful places to encourage young children to be still, to sit with others and to talk.

Let them listen

The natural and numerous noises of an outside environment will definitely be noticed by your little one. From birds singing, planes flying over, to the wind rustling through the trees, there's plenty for your child to listen to in the garden. There are ways to enhance your garden's sound-scape and encourage your child to listen. For example, you could place a couple of 'sound-spots' around your outside space; a few painted or labelled pebbles indicating that here is a good place to listen will be enough to get your little one pausing and listening. Wind chimes are a great addition to an outside space – you can even make your own.

Let them collect

Young children often go through a stage where there is nothing that rocks their world more than loading up a bag or cart or barrow with stuff, and carrying it around with them. Even if they're not obsessed with this at present, having a few tote bags, baskets or containers available on shelves or pegs in the garden or a mini-wheelbarrow on hand will undoubtedly spark the idea of collecting all manner of small toys and natural stuff from around the garden.

Let them invent, construct and tinker

A low work-bench with shelves or a few crates nearby with things to use for construction like small pipes and blocks of wood, sticks, stones, masking tape and maybe some fine sandpaper, a wooden hammer and the like will get your little ones thinking, building and inventing.

Let them grow things

If you have enough space, why not allocate a small area as a grow-your-own garden especially for your preschooler. Children could have their own container gardens if you don't have flowerbeds. See page 30 for the easiest plants to grow with children. Have child-friendly but functional gardening equipment at the ready – perhaps stored in a crate or on a low shelf nearby, so your little one can water the flowers and weed when they like.

Let them look and be captivated

Hang a few old CDs to the branches of a tree. When they turn and twist in the breeze they'll catch the light and the eye of your child. On sunny days you may even spot the rainbows they create, which is quite mesmerising for young children.

Temporary invitations to play outside

When deliberately setting up temporary invitations to play, remember you are just setting up something for them to discover themselves; to initially entice them and get them started. They'll surprise you with where they take the play and all the different ways in which they'll participate. You can set these up when your little one is napping or otherwise engaged in independent play.

Let them play inside outside

Invite them to play with some of their inside toys outside, should the weather suit:

☆ Arrange their favourite construction toy invitingly on a rug or play mat – blocks, Lego, stickle bricks and the like. These have a different feel and appeal if played with in the garden, and different things may well be constructed.
☆ Set up one of their small-world toys outside – somewhere not too muddy. A dolls' house, toy garage, train track or a homemade play scene along with figures and accoutrements will have a different feel and appeal when in an unexpected location.

☆ Small toy animals or figures will have a whale of a time outside. Add some natural materials like straw, rocks, grass or water in a small container on a tray, or a container plant, as an exciting and different environment for the adventure.

☆ Bring out the dress-up box and, if possible, a mirror, for some warm-weather costume changes. Your little one may want to put on a show, or just immerse themselves in some imaginary play in costume.

☆ Set out some of their toy instruments and a few soft toys who might want to get involved in an outdoor concert.

Let them play somewhere new

☆ Make a sun canopy or cloth den and add some books to create a temporary inviting quiet place, or some boxes, further cloth pieces and a few plastic containers and bottles to help transform it into something altogether different – a car, a spaceship or a submarine may well appear.

☆ Set out the picnic blanket, some favourite soft toys or dolls, a toy tea set or some plastic cups and plates from the kitchen, with some leaves and grass and so on for 'food'.

☆ Let them create their own new place to play. For example, fill a beach bag with everything you can find around your home that might contribute to creating a let's-pretend visit to the beach. It could contain a beach towel, some shells, a nearly empty suncream bottle, a sun hat, some sunglasses, some toy sea creatures, a net, some pebbles, an umbrella, a bucket and spade, an inflatable water-ring and their swimming costume (if it's summer). If you have a paddling pool out or you have a sandbox, then either or both of these might feature in the creation of their beach. Then again, they might make something else altogether.

Let them play at being someone new

☆ Bury a few plastic dinosaurs or pieces of plastic tea set in the sandbox, or transfer some sand or soil to a washing-up-bowl-sized container so your little one can become an archaeologist or a pirate digging for buried treasure. Provide brushes and a small spade to help with their investigation.

☆ Fill a washing-up bowl or bucket with warm soapy water, lay out some soft cloths, sponges and brushes and get out the kids' vehicles; you'll probably have a trike-and-scooter washer ready to work in no time.

☆ Bring out the baby dolls, their clothes and blankets, toy medical kit, and any other equipment you might have for them – from buggy to cot to dolls' bath – for an opportunity to play baby-carer.

☆ In the summer months, gather whatever you have to hand to make a let's-pretend ice-cream or soft drinks/shakes stall. We've used cotton wool balls, large beads, glitter, pipe cleaners, coloured water, crushed melting ice, cardboard cones, pastel-coloured play dough, lolly sticks, wooden fruit and cupcakes before. Plastic cups and spoons, plastic bottles with lids – for shakin' up those smoothies – can be put out ready to be discovered. Be prepared for things to get a bit messy and wet, and to buy lots of ice cream or shakes. Soft toys can also queue up very sensibly for a treat.

☆ Let them be a potion-maker. Making potions was one of my children's most favourite activities when they were very small, and they still absolutely love it now. It's definitely one to set up outside if you're worried about mess. The ingredients of the potions can be changed every time you set up this invitation to play – you could gather things for, say, a science experiment, a magic potion laboratory or a perfumery. We use empty plastic food containers destined for the recycling bin to hold our ingredients. You could offer:

　☆ blobs of poster paint, little piles of glitter, sequins, water (fizzy or still)

　☆ little piles of out-of-date spices and sauces – like ketchup and mustard – water (fizzy or still) and a little olive oil

　☆ vinegar, bicarbonate of soda, water, blobs of paint (this one should fizz!)

☆ herbs from the garden, fallen petals, a pestle and mortar, water or orange-blossom water

You'll also need some equipment for your child to mix and make the concoctions; like plastic funnels, spoons, stirrers, plastic pipettes, bowls, a sieve and plastic bottles or tubs with lids to store the finished potions. The best place to set up this invitation is anywhere you have a low table or bench, or you can put down a plastic play-mat – it definitely has to be a flat surface, though, to give those containers and bottles a fighting chance of staying upright.

Let them play with water

A water table is definitely a worthwhile purchase for your garden, however small, but any large and shallow plastic container will do the job, and is often a lot cheaper. We always use a large plastic under-bed storage box, sometimes set on a low table, sometimes just on the ground. Make sure you are happy for your children to get a bit wet while playing; aprons, waterproofs or swimming costumes (if it's the summer time) are of course an option. Change the water every time you set up a new invitation to play, and vary what your child discovers by adding:

☆ different things in with the water, like toy boats, or action figures and plastic animals for racing, swimming and scuba-diving adventures

☆ plastic bottles, containers, scoops, nets, sieves, a colander and funnels for exploring the characteristics of water

☆ a bit of sparkle with some glitter, or some colour with a few drops of food colouring

☆ a few natural objects, like pine cones, flowers, leaves and twigs, shells and pebbles for all kinds of sensory play and investigation of floating and sinking

☆ bubble bath or soap flakes, bubble wands, whisks and the like for a lot of foamy fun

☆ toy cars and plastic track for the ultimate in splash-racing-with-water-chutes

Let them play with things that go!

Matchbox-sized cars set out on a paved area, along with some chalks, will tempt your little one to design a brand new town for the cars to zoom around, or perhaps a new Formula 1 track. Draw a couple of little roads yourself, just to start them off.

Put out a flat piece of cardboard as a track area and gather together a few wind-up toys for some races. Snails will also participate in this kind of thing, should you have a lot of these in your garden and, like me, a little one who *loves* them.

Let them play out after dark

Even if it gets dark pretty early in the afternoon in the winter where you live, it's still possible to set up invitations to play in your back garden. Young children find it rather thrilling to get out after the sun's gone down – and as long as there's a bit of light from street lights, or spilling from your home or what have you, playing out in the night is super exciting.

☆ Put bike lights on trikes and scooters for an after-dark ride around the garden.

☆ Glow-sticks are cheap as chips, and as long as your little one knows they're not to be mouthed or snapped, they are pretty safe. Just place them round and about outside for your child to discover, or hang them from tree branches. They often come with connectors so they might want to construct a glowing structure, or simply wave them around as they run around.

☆ There are some great torches for kids on the market, but even if you haven't got a lightweight, wind-up child's version, any torch will be a tempting offer for a toddler or preschooler. If the beam is too bright (young children will look into them, however much you tell them not to, cover the light with a couple of layers of masking tape (painters' tape), or put small torches or bike lights into empty, dry, plastic milk bottles which are translucent – they'll glow not blaze. Offering your child a torch/light, and a chance to 'take a turn' in the dark garden might well start some wonderful independent play in the garden.

☆ We were given some wonderful bouncy balls a couple of years ago. They were full of glittery liquid and when they hit the ground they lit up. So magical. They don't work anymore, but my goodness, my children loved to take them out to our night-time garden and get them to light up whilst playing all kinds of imaginative games with them.

Let them play out in the rain

Get that wet-weather gear on and let your little one play out in the rain – they'll jump in puddles and play with whatever is available to them out there, regardless of the conditions. To make it just that extra bit special you could occasionally set up some of these invitations to play for your child to discover:

☆ Put up a few of your umbrellas as little shelters or bases in the garden. You could put something surprising sheltering underneath each one, like a ball, or a plastic bottle, or some waterproof figures.

☆ Get out some chalks and mark an area on your paving to invite your child to experiment with colour and rainwater.

Let them out in the snow

Snowy weather shouldn't put you off letting your child play outside. Of course, appropriate snowsuits, hats, mittens, boots and the like are a must, and playing out in the snow can't be an all-day event. Short and sweet playtimes are the key to keeping snowy days fun, to ensure young children don't get too cold.

☆ The novel and beautiful white environment will be invitation enough for most children – just get them out there and they'll be running, jumping, rolling on it and throwing it about in no time.

☆ Offer the accoutrements of the sandbox – buckets and spades, sticks and stones, rakes and moulds – for your child to play creatively with the lying snow.

☆ Natural objects like pine cones, leaves, pebbles and sticks can be buried in a bucket of snow and left ready for your child to discover.

☆ Plastic action figures will really enjoy a snowy environment, and if your water table has iced over, the small figures (or toy cars) can skate and skid across it most satisfyingly.

Let them make a marvellous mess

A garden is the perfect place to set up sensory invitations to play. These are often the messier activities which will provide your child with unforgettable and important experiences of play. Before setting up these fabulous provocations, do consider the aftermath. Is there somewhere nearby your little one can clean up? An outside tap or a washing-up bowl with some soapy water and a wash-cloth and towel nearby will be essential. Demarcate the area in which the messy play will take place with a waterproof play mat, tarp or old shower curtain if you are working in a small area close to anything you don't want to get messed up. Although you can let your child play freely with these invitations, careful supervision is absolutely required for safety reasons.

☆ **Sensory tubs:** These are intriguing for toddlers only if they're past the mouthing stage. We use a plastic storage box but a washing-up bowl would work well too. Add some uncooked rice or dried lentils (which you can use again and again), polystyrene peanuts, shredded paper, dried leaves, mown grass cuttings or even some thick mud if you are feeling particularly brave. Add whatever you have to hand to these tubs to encourage your child to play with the stuff in different ways, such as scoops, cardboard tubes and boxes, tongs or giant tweezers and small containers, or perhaps hide a few action figures or animals in the tub.

☆ **Sensory tables:** These are similar to the tubs except the sensory substances are best explored and played with by hands (or feet) on a shallow surface. Things like play dough (see p.205), gloop (made from mixing cornflour with water and food colouring), shaving foam (mix in a little paint or glitter occasionally), or kids' hair conditioner and flour are also great things to put on the table. You don't need too much – a little will go a long way.

☆ **Panning for gems:** My children were a little obsessed with this for a while after experiencing it at their nursery's summer fair at '10p a go'. We've recreated this activity in the garden many times and it never fails to please. You'll need a plastic container or washing-up bowl and about a 5cm depth of play sand in the bottom. Hide gems of your choice in the sand – attractive stones and pebbles, pennies, or metal buttons or beads (that don't float) – then add about 5cm of water to the sand. The only other things you'll need are a scoop for your little one to pick up a good quantity of sand, and a sieve for them to sift the sand for the gems.

Invitations to play inside

Semi-permanent inviting places to play

Anywhere in your home can be made into a play zone – from the living room and their bedroom, to a hallway or kitchen. Set up a few permanent places for them to stay and play, and:

Let them imagine

With a place to dress-up. Put the dress-up box or hooks full of intriguing costumes and lengths of fabric and so on in a little corner or nook along with a wall-mounted mirror. Or create a place that's somewhere else sometimes – maybe set up an area as a cafe, or a shop, or a kitchen, or a puppet-theatre or a space-station for a while. Or just keep it as a blank canvas for them to make it into whatever they want to imagine.

Let them be still

With a reading nook. These are very easy to set up and are often irresistible to young children. Just find a corner or alcove to create a comfortable, quiet reading zone by adding cushions or a beanbag and rug plus a basket or two of books (change these every now and again). You can convert this to a listening zone too by keeping a CD player and a few story CDs or music CDs nearby (but out of reach until your little one is confident in how to look after discs, and use the technology). You could also create a quiet area, either with cushions and floor space, or a low table, for the quiet exploration of busy bags, cuddling of soft toys or calm puzzle-completing and the like. This area will be used more if it is kept uncluttered, and they will see it as a refuge or a relaxation zone first, and a place to play second.

Let them build

With a clear and defined floor space for construction toys. Lego, Duplo blocks, track, Octons, books to make roads and tunnels, marble runs and the like are more likely to be played with if there's a suitable space to build adjacent to where these toys are stored. A short-pile rug is great for this kind of play (too shaggy and pieces get lost in the pile, and if there's just a hard surface then the noise can be too intense for us grown ups to tolerate). Don't leave all construction toys and loose parts out all the time, though, or they will definitely lose their appeal.

Let them look and be captivated

With a sun-catcher or a rainbow-maker fixed to one of your windows. When the sun comes out they'll catch the light and will be mesmerising for young children. If you are feeling crafty, you could make your own sun-catcher (see p.179). Mobiles can also be wonderfully captivating for young children as they gaze at them gently moving and turning. One or two pictures or posters displayed at their sight-height will also capture the attention of young children. We've put up double-spread scenic photographs from newspapers if they were particularly stunning or interesting, but anything you come across from magazines, maps, or prints of famous paintings will encourage your children to look carefully and talk about what they see. Change these regularly to surprise them and keep them interested.

Temporary invitations to play inside

Temporary invitations to play can be set up on a rug, or a low table, on the floor, in the kitchen, in the bath even; wherever play can take place safely. Use different places in your home to surprise them – with train-track making in the hallway, to a hospital for soft toys in the cubby-under-the-stairs, for example. You don't have to set these up every day – having inviting places with favourite toys on shelves and in smallish, accessible containers will be enough for happy and busy free-play some days. And remember you can set them up when your little one is napping, or otherwise engaged in independent play.

Let them move

Most grown-ups' ideas of *inside* play is not about children racing around and playing physically active games. This is probably because most inside spaces do not lend themselves to this kind of play. However, many puppy-like two-year-olds will not share this opinion, and often have to be repeatedly reminded that it's not appropriate – or safe – to zoom around and climb the walls indoors. If you have a very active toddler or preschooler, then I imagine the back door to your space outside is open most of the time to avoid those bull-in-a-china-shop situations. However, sometimes it's just not possible to get our little ones outside to run around and so it becomes necessary to allow for physically active play inside our home. There won't be many, or any, great ready-made invitations, of course, but you can set up temporary invitations to play. Of course, careful supervision will be needed, but at least your little ones will *get moving* safely and be able to let off some steam.

Let them jump and leap

Take off the cases and covers from a few pillows and cushions and scatter them on a carpeted (non-skiddy) surface. Add a few Arctic soft toys (I bet you've got some) and invite your children to leap from iceberg to iceberg rescuing/transferring/saving the animals along the way. A pack of anti-slip rubber 'spots', as used by toddler gyms across the land, are a great investment for wooden or tiled floors. Lay them out like lily pads on your floor for your little one to leap and jump from spot to spot. They'll make different arrangements and try different jump-patterns. If you can't get hold of those, try cutting out some dinner-plate-sized circles from some colourful craft foam or thick fabric instead. Remember these won't be anti-slip, so only use these on a carpeted area for less-skid, more-jump fun. Alternatively, you could use masking tape to make outlines of floor islands. Three or four of these strategically placed around your biggest space will invite your little leaper to jump between the 'landmasses'.

Mini-trampolines can be used inside, and are often fitted with soft grips on the base or feet so floors aren't damaged. I've seen versions suitable for children under two years of age, with handles for them to steady themselves while they bounce. Of course supervision is required, as well as plenty of soft space around the trampoline itself. If you have taken delivery of something fragile recently and you have some bubble wrap to hand, why not stick it to your floor with a bit of masking tape at its edges, then let your little one jump on it until all the air-pockets have popped? Grown-ups can rarely resist this invitation to jump up and down either . . .

Let them ride

There are lots of inexpensive ride-ons available; from ladybirds to motorbikes and everything in between. Toddlers especially will find scooting or bouncing around the living space most satisfying and highly energetic.

Let them dance and do actions

Clear the floor, put on some tunes and turn up the volume. This will be invitation enough for most little ones to hear the Call to Dance. Try different genres from rock, pop and dance tunes, to film-tracks and classical pieces. Add play silks or floaty scarves and ribbons and watch them express themselves with the music. Try a sing-along kids' album for classic action-songs to play along with.

Dance party 🎵

Why not theme your playlist for your invitation to dance? Here's one we used one winter afternoon:

☆ *Waltz of the Snowflakes* from Tchaikovsky's 'The Nutcracker'
☆ *Frosty the Snowman* by Walter 'Jack' Rollins and Steve Nelson
☆ *Sleigh Ride* – a light orchestral piece by Leroy Anderson
☆ *Troika* – the fourth movement of 'Lieutenant Kijé' by Prokofiev
☆ *The Skaters' Waltz* by Émile Waldteufel
☆ *Ice, Ice, Baby* by Vanilla Ice
☆ *Wake Me Up Before you Go-Go* by Wham!
☆ *Frosti* by Björk
☆ *Frozen* by Madonna
☆ *Ski Chase* from the soundtrack of *On Her Majesty's Secret Service* by John Barry

Let them roll, crawl and bend

Take a yoga mat or a big beach towel and lay it out on the floor along with a poster or print-out of some kids' yoga positions. My children especially love the *Star Wars* Yoda Yoga pictures. Seeing a little set-up like this might well encourage them to copy a few of the moves.

Rolling themselves up in the yoga mats or towels is another tempting manoeuvre, and as long as you supervise them they'll expend a lot of energy rolling and unrolling in it again and again – enchilada-style.

Pop-up tunnels are such a great plaything for inside and out. Not only can you surprise a little one with them, but you can easily put them away when the fun has finished. They'll love crawling and slithering through its colourful space. Offer a soft ball as well and they might try getting that through the tunnel too.

Let them 'ice-skate'

This works well on a wood, tiled or lino floor. Ask your little one to keep their socks on, roll back the rug and get them skating. You could make an Ice Warden's announcement like *'Skaters, please take to the ice'* to start things off. You could add to the atmosphere by playing some music ideal for skating, e.g. *The Skaters' Waltz* by Waldteufel.

Let them throw and catch and kick

While you may have already had to reinforce the necessary rule of 'no playing with the football' in the house, it is worth considering the variations of ball-skills which *are* suitable for inside play. Try offering newspaper scrunched up balls (or home-made 'snowballs' – see p.184), or beanbags, and a basket either placed on the floor or an armchair or sofa for a high-octane game of throw and target practice. Balloons also make great inside alternatives to footballs and provide safe, slow-motion versions of soccer-favourites like keepy-uppy or penalty-practice. Balloon-tennis is an easy provocation to set up. Simply produce an inflated balloon and suggest they play a game with it. They can use their hand as a racquet and the wall to get returns if there's no partner available. This can lead to much squealing and expending of energy.

Let them catch butterflies

Those battery-operated air-blowers that send out little fabric butterflies are well worth investing in. Toddlers and preschoolers love catching the airborne critters with their hands or the little nets that come with the game. They'll probably make up their own rules as they go along. What's important here is that they will be stretching and leaping and catching to their heart's content – so getting lots of aerobic exercise.

Let them do target-practice

We've made a tin-can alley from empty, clean baked bean tins. If you're at all worried about any sharp edges, cover the rims with some gaffer tape before piling them up into irresistible target-towers. Use beanbags or newspaper balls for projectiles then cover your ears; this game can get a bit *clattery*, shall we say.

You can buy very lovely skittle sets, but we've always made ours from those two-litre water or soft-drink bottles destined for the recycling box. You can theme them if you're feeling creative; see p.190 for ideas. Set them up just as you like, or in the traditional bowling alley 1-2-3-5 formation, and mark a point with masking tape, say, to show the best position for the bowler. Your little one will love to roll a soft ball or throw a beanbag at these targets. Put about an inch of water in each one for added difficulty and a bit more wobble-when-hit hilarity.

Let them be someone else

It doesn't take much for little ones to imagine, and I mean really imagine, they are someone else. I'll never forget giving a plastic spanner to a two-year-old during a free-play session and telling her that my chair was broken. This was all she needed to become a veritable Bob the Builder for about twenty minutes. Everything in the classroom was fixed with her trusty spanner; she even tucked it into her waistband between jobs.

We needn't buy fancy, expensive dress-ups for our little ones to immerse themselves in a role. Often pieces of fabric, hats, and homemade or found objects can approximate convincingly as the signifying accoutrements of a character or role. Our old grown-ups' clothes, and roughly-made tunics and cloaks have got much more use than those shop-bought princess or movie-character costumes – and they sort of grow with them. Look out in thrift or charity shops for scarves, hats and other potential dress-up items. Their alter-egos can be pure fantasy or based in the real world.

Invitations to play at being someone else are pretty easy to set up and happened to be my children's favourite way to play for a long while. They could never resist the lure of a bit of costume, some interesting equipment and the opportunity to play 'let's pretend'. You might think it's a bit of an effort to source things from various places around your home, but honestly it's so worth it. We've often kept the 'stuff' together in a cloth bag for a bit afterwards anyway, because they wanted to use it again and again. Here are a few provocations I've set up for my children to start their imaginative play. Of course you can include whatever you have to hand in your home, and you only need set out one or two things from these lists; your little one will think of other things they might need in their play and get them themselves as they take the game off in their own direction. These are just examples of the kinds of things you could put out to let them discover.

Hairdresser:

Hairbrushes and combs, a few scrunchies and clips, some soft curlers, a water-spray, a safe mirror, a few colourful ribbons, a low chair or cushion, a towel, a magazine and a cup from the toy tea set (but no scissors, obviously). We've also had a reception desk with cash till brought into the play on occasion. You might find a sign gets made too.

Pet parlour:

Lots of cuddly toy animals, plastic animals, insects and aquatic life, a toy doctor's kit, plastic bowls for pet food, ribbons for dog-leads, a selection of squeaky pet toys, various boxes and cushions to make pet beds and containers.

Shoe shop:

Shelves or largish cardboard boxes for displaying shoes, shoes (the children's own plus a few grown-up ones will help to get the shoe-shop look). Ribbons and small fabric bits and bobs to jazz-up shoes. A ruler and/or a tape-measure for measuring feet (we've occasionally made a kind of shoe-measuring machine, but of course that's not necessary). Spare laces and tissue boxes (big enough for shoes) with holes punched round the hole for custom-made special footwear, and bag or two to use whilst shopping. They've sometimes had a cash till or calculator to price up the shoes, and sometimes we make a shop sign.

Doctor or vet:

White shirt, play glasses, a toy doctor's kit plus some scraps of white sheet (for bandages), plastic bottles and boxes from the recycling as medicines for the animals, an assortment of soft toys in need of medical attention, cushions and magazines for the waiting room, an examination table, an x-ray machine (this has been a box and a chair in the past), blankets for the animals, bowls and the like for feeding the animals and a clipboard with paper and a pencil – for important medical note-taking and information.

Shopkeeper:

My children have played 'shop' countless times. Their favourite type of shop was always the toy shop. This is where our box of plastic toys came into its own. These toys – I call them the *plastique* – were often free with magazines, or were stocking-fillers, or little gifts from birthday parties. Set out some cardboard boxes or upturned containers, chairs and a low table or two for the toys to be displayed attractively by the shopkeeper. This should lead to some wonderful 'selling' patter, explaining to the other person playing how to use a particular toy; it might start a discussion about who it's for, and so on. They might want a cash till (a cardboard box with drawn-on buttons will definitely do the job), a little shopping basket for the customer and some tote bags in which to put the purchases.

Cook, chef or baker:

Play dough is great as the main medium. Play dough easily lends itself to being made into cakes, biscuits, pizzas, burgers and many other savoury dishes. You can also scent play dough with various smells by using cinnamon, orange or lemon oil, or with herbs, to theme the type of cuisine being imagined (see my recipe for play dough on page 205). Just add whatever toy cooking equipment you have, along with any safe kitchen equipment like wooden spoons, plastic bowls and cookie cutters, kids' forks and so on, and some plastic or foil platters, some paper-cases or a cardboard cake-stand for presenting the finished food. An oven can be made from a shoebox and a hob can be quickly approximated with black or red card circles placed on their little table or bench, or a chair. You do not need to have an expensive toy kitchen range to play cooking. Raid your craft stashes for feathers, pipe cleaners, large beads and buttons and or sequins to be added to the recipes. If you're worried about mess with this one, either put a tarp or old wipe-clean tablecloth on the floor, or work in the kitchen. Play dough trodden into carpet is not a happy occurrence.

Office worker:
A toy computer (or a plastic container from the recycling box), or an old keyboard plus hard-backed book as a screen, or an old typewriter if you have one, an old landline or mobile phone, pot of pens and pencils, an old diary, some deely-boppers (my daughter will always wear some if she's playing offices), a calculator, paper and envelopes, a small table as a desk. Offer something as an in-tray – a shallow cardboard box perhaps – and a corkboard or magnetic board for Important Things to be displayed on.

A treasure-seeking pirate:
Piratical clothes; headscarves, raggedy trousers or skirts, waistcoats, eye patches, stripy t-shirts. A pirate's ship; the sofa with a broom-handle sail, or a big cardboard box, or a pile of cushions and a collection of chairs. A pirate's things; a telescope, a map, some ship's biscuits, a bucket and cloth to mop the deck, a spade, some soft-toy shipmates, a bottle of 'rum', some treasure to hide, some treasure to find.

Astronaut/space explorer:
Space clothes; thermo-foil blankets work a treat but anything shiny will do, even if it's just a foil utility belt or shiny scarf, foil-covered bicycle helmet, moon-boots (wellies). Walkie-talkies (cardboard boxes

or plastic packing will do), containers to collect space dust, soft toy aliens to meet, a rocket or spacecraft (the sofa, a little den made with a thermo-foil blanket perhaps), computer/control gadgets (plastic packaging or calculators and the like), rocket packs, special space-viewer – cardboard tube (with holes punched in the side for a bit of galaxy view-finding and planet-spotting).

Super-hero:
A cape made from lengths of fabric, long-sleeved grown-up t-shirts or newspaper, a simple eye masquerade mask. Gadgets; torches, special wrist cuffs with 'buttons', utility belt, special sunglasses with powers, some soft toys to rescue.

Schoolteacher (for toy wizards and witches, toy fairies and pixies, toy animals):
Magnetic letters and board, paper and pencils, soft toys or favourite figures as extra students', wands, the chalk board, register on a clipboard.

Polar explorers:
A snow-cave or igloo (white sheet or blanket den). Some equipment; walking sticks, slippery magazines as skis, balaclavas, sunglasses, scarves and gloves, a map. White pillowcases and the like for ice-floes, pale soft toy animals, binoculars, 'rations', sleeping bag and torches.

Let them be somewhere else
In the countryside, camping:
A pop-up tent, a pretend campfire with sticks and red and yellow tis-sue-paper flames, sticks with polystyrene 'food' like sausages stuck

on the end to cook on the fire, torches, sleeping bags, a toy kettle and beakers, maps, binoculars.

At a posh tea party:
A toy tea set, with water in the teapot, cereal on plates, or some wooden toy cakes and so on, some guests (soft toys), a little table or box with something to approximate a tablecloth, a little table decoration.

Getting ready for Christmas:
A few ready-wrapped prop presents, a couple of knitted socks as stockings, reindeer antlers headdress, a Santa hat, wig and glasses, a few plastic baubles, some salt dough decorations (made by the children), tinsel, few (very cheap) crackers, a small artificial Christmas tree.

We've also had weddings, birthday parties, expeditions to rainforests and setting up an art gallery, to name a few. Often all these adventures started with just one or two items as inspiration.

Let them imagine with small world play
Many young children get absolutely absorbed in small world play. With different combinations of toy figures and non-toys, these invitations to play are very easy to set up and will entice children to take up the story and go on from there to who knows where. Try setting out one of the following combinations for your little one to discover in a place where you don't mind them playing:

☆ Superhero play figures, a few cardboard boxes and a few pieces of string
☆ Small figures and a homemade play scene (see p.191)
☆ Small dolls or figures and hard polystyrene packaging
☆ Small toy cars, cardboard tubes and a big cardboard box
☆ Clear plastic containers and small toy animals

☆ Natural objects like pebbles, shells, driftwood and some plastic dinosaurs, or other figures or animals

☆ Small soft toys and a picnic box

☆ Roll of masking tape (painters' tape) and some small toy cars

☆ Track and toy trains

☆ Toy car garage (or a cardboard version will work a treat) and some toy cars

☆ A large snow-white blanket, sheet or tablecloth tied up high in one corner and draped just how you like, a selection of soft toys, favourite toy characters or action figures to visit the scene, Lego – for skidoos, sledges and toboggans and the like – and small cardboard-box mountain lodges

☆ Small plastic animals and some straw, some cut grass and some pebbles

☆ A selection of wind-up toys and a plank of wood

☆ When it's cold outside, bring in some snow, pop it in a large plastic bowl and add some plastic figures with a taste for adventure (pop an old towel underneath the bowl to prevent any slips as the snow begins to melt)

☆ A shoebox with blue cellophane in, plus a tube slide into it alongside some dolls or figures ready for a 'swim'

Let them construct

Many preschoolers love to build. Putting out just one construction toy at a time and presenting it invitingly on a flat surface with plenty of space will encourage most little ones to sit for a while and build. From stickle bricks, colourful wooden or fabric blocks, to jenga bricks, Octons or shop-bought marble mazes, you'll see some wonderful constructions being erected, and of course demolished with a crash.

Let them carry, combine and redesign with loose parts

Loose parts are anything from cotton reels to pine cones, to tubes, big buttons, mini pom-poms, corks, small blocks, pieces of fabric, natural materials like pebbles, driftwood and shells, for example, which can be stored and displayed in small baskets or bowls. Offer small containers of these tempting things, on a flat surface, and your little one will find it very inviting to play with them. You can make things even more immersive by using a large safe mirror tile as the working surface sometimes. Children might take the loose parts and move, carry, combine, redesign and arrange them in multiple ways. Loose parts are by their very nature materials with no specific set of directions that can be used alone or combined with other materials and will vastly enhance your little one's independent play.

Having a selection of child-friendly tools close to hand will really help them stay with this play for longer than you might imagine too; a magnifying glass or magnifying container, soft tape-measure, pincers or tongs, torches, laces for threading, baskets or bags for transferring, that kind of thing, will give their fine motor skills a good workout, as well as their imaginations.

Let them be surprised

Remind them of some of the great toys and playthings they already have by setting out one or two invitingly in a place appropriate for them to stay and play, then putting them away when interest wanes. For example, you might rekindle their interest in their:

☆ Dolls' house and its dolls
☆ Toy garage and its cars
☆ Puzzles or jigsaws
☆ Toy babies and the things needed to care for them
☆ Box of forgotten toys
☆ Collection of toy aeroplanes
☆ Toy tea set
☆ Wooden fruit and veg and other toy food
☆ Collection of soft toys

Invitations to Create

'Every child is an artist. The problem is how to remain an artist once we grow up.'

Pablo Picasso

Though we might *want* to agree with the statement 'every child is an artist' – in practice it's surprisingly difficult for us grown ups to really recognise them as such. We tend to look for evidence via *end-products*, as we might with an adult artist, because by artist we usually mean someone who uses their imagination, talent or skill to create something original, be it visual, musical, dramatic or literal. We might look at our child's finished painting, sculpture, drawing or performance perhaps, and have serious doubts about this whole every-child-is-an-artist thing. If you've ever been handed a falling-to-bits 'robot' (a cereal packet and two yoghurt pots balanced on top), sat through a group performance in which nobody seemed to be joining in at all, been confused by what you've been shown, *'what exactly is it, dear?'* or couldn't find your child's work amongst twenty identical pictures on display, then you'll know what I mean.

Process not product

However, we needn't give up on the dream that our child is an artist just yet. Work in Early Years research finds that as far as young children are concerned, it's the creative *process* which is at least as important as its products. Once we get to grips with this, we really can begin to appreciate them as artists, and we can even play a part in developing the innate creativity of our toddlers and preschoolers.

Even the current EYFS guidelines, not exactly famous for putting creative concerns first, highlight the need for teachers and carers to focus on process rather than product when it comes to Expressive Arts and Design. It states that young children should be,

> '. . . exploring and playing with a wide range of media and materials as well as . . . being imaginative; having . . . plenty of opportunities and encouragement for sharing their thoughts, ideas and feelings in a variety of activities in art, music, movement, dance, role-play and design and technology.'

Creativity and creative learning

Creativity isn't limited to the artistic areas of learning, of course. Young children use their innate creativity in *everything* they play and do; from understanding their world, in communication and language, to mathematics and in problem-solving. Often, this kind of creativity is called creative learning. Creative learning involves our children investigating, discovering, inventing and cooperating, and has curiosity at its heart – little ones are naturally curious, so providing lots of invitations to play (as in the previous chapter) will definitely foster creative learning. As life coach Joel Brown puts it,

> 'All young kids have creative ideas. They make up imaginary playmates, play with dolls and action figures, bake cookies in imaginary ovens, solve imaginary mysteries when they play detective with the other kids in the

neighbourhood, they sing songs they make up, they dance in free form, and when they draw pictures it doesn't matter that horses aren't purple in real life.'

Creativity, on the other hand, is more about a young child seeing things in a new way and putting ideas together differently to create something new, and has imagination at its heart. Though young children are naturally highly imaginative they often don't have the skills, determination or the time to finish an original creation, so they may not always (or ever) reach the end-product stage of a creative endeavour. This is why it is so important we recognise and encourage the *process* or *incubation stage*, as it's sometimes called, of their creativity.

We can now begin to understand why Picasso believed that every child is an artist. Not because of the great *original creations* they produce, but because young children are:

☆ not inhibited about how the world ought to be
☆ open to possibilities
☆ able to find pleasure in challenge
☆ naturally playful
☆ very responsive to stimulus or inspiration
☆ happy to construct their own personal interpretations of knowledge and events
☆ curious
☆ imaginative
☆ creative

Picasso also made a good point when he saw the problem of how to remain an artist when we grow up; sadly, it tends to be these behavioural traits we lose sight of as we reach adulthood.

Invitations to create are a way to play

I've heard many a parent say they aren't creative enough to think up artistic activities for their little one, or that they don't have any talent for singing, drawing or making. Others tell me their toddler does enough 'messy arty stuff' at nursery or when they're with their child-minder so they don't have to worry about it, thank goodness. We might we feel we've lost our creativity as adults. Maybe it's because we just 'grew up' – somewhere along the way we became more rational, even jaded, about the world; or maybe our need to make money has squelched our creative side – unless we have managed to land a creative job, of course; or maybe it's that we've taken too many standardised tests and have been exposed to there being only one correct answer for a long time.

But fear not, not all creative activities for toddlers and preschoolers need us to feel at our creative best. They needn't be messy and we really don't need to be drama experts, musicians or sculptors to make creativity part of our young child's everyday play. By simply making the home environment lend itself to the creative *process* by using things we *do* have – like time, space and everyday materials, and by tapping into our children's natural imagination and curiosity – we can make it irresistible for young children to engage in some form of creative activity, and be inspired by the world of Expressive Arts and Design. To do this, all we have to do is offer invitations to create.

There is plenty of well-documented evidence of the benefits for young children of participating in creative activities at home. Invitations to create can provide the opportunity for young children to playfully:

☆ develop an understanding of the world and our personal contribution to it
☆ experience and express their ideas and feelings about something in a controlled, safe environment

☆ be inspired by stimuli from the world of Expressive Arts and Design

☆ explore and experience new materials, words, stories, ways to move, and music

☆ record or show their response, ideas, feelings and observations to a stimulus or inspiration

☆ show their own personal interpretations of knowledge and events

☆ find pleasure in challenge

☆ find immersive involvement in tasks

☆ take on problem-solving

☆ develop their self-confidence, motivation and ability to tolerate ambiguity or anxiety

☆ exercise their imagination

☆ experience emotional fantasy in their playing

☆ make choices

☆ dare to do something different, or in a new way

☆ learn about the properties and possibilities of materials

☆ develop gross and fine motor skills

☆ develop hand–eye coordination to manipulate materials and tools

Like invitations to play, invitations to create can be permanent, inviting areas in our homes or temporary provocations – anything designed to tempt little ones to participate in the creative process. Inspiration or stimuli can be taken from the world of Expressive Arts and Design – like listening to a story or piece of music, holding a woven bowl, watching a dance routine or remembering a work of art from a visit to a gallery or museum, for example – but these are in no way essential to every creative experience. Often the materials and tools alone will be tempting enough to spark a young child's curiosity and imagination, and get them started.

Like invitations to play, these provocations do need some preparation; having enough time, space and resources are key to their success. Think about where in your home you might fit in a small creative table or designated floor area, and what tools, materials and resources you might choose to have permanently accessible to your toddler or preschooler nearby. Maybe you're not comfortable leaving out scissors just yet, but what about some low shelving with masking tape (painters' tape), crayons and a few different types of paper and card, stickers, small pieces of fabric and glue sticks, and another shelf with a few pebbles and shells, or a couple of percussive instruments? Here, *less is more*, so just a few well-chosen creative resources on-hand will encourage the most reluctant of artists to help themselves when they need something in their play, and will satisfy the needs of those little ones who love to be making, sticking and drawing – creating – whenever possible. For further ideas on organising your home as a place to play and create, see the Invitation to Create chapter.

Many places to *play* in the home can be used for creative activities too, of course – like the sandbox, the water table, a reading nook, or a sound wall. The difference when thinking about providing invitations to create is to think about how our toddlers and pre-schoolers might use the play spaces and temporary set-ups in the *making* of something – whether it's music, movement, mud-pies or a model – rather than just in discovery play. And remember, we're not aiming for a finished product here, rather it's the *process* of making and creating as a form of play that we are trying to encourage.

Inviting places to create

Different areas of our homes can be adapted, inside and out, to provide static focal opportunities for creative activity. So look around your home for areas that could become inviting areas to create – where a low table might go, for example, or a box of found and recycled materials and a roll of masking (painters') tape, a wall suitable for low shelving to house paper, crayons, glue sticks and stickers which has easy access. Is there a place you could make into a performance area, a place outside to make holes or mud pies, somewhere that could be great for building stuff, or a wall that could be a doodle chalk-wall, or upright blank canvas for mark-making?

Temporary invitations to create

These are set ups which can be changed every day if you like. These invitations to create might be a range of materials and tools set out invitingly, or a deliberate selection of varied materials and playthings to be experienced in combination. You might include inspiration or stimulus from the world of Expressive Arts and Design, or you could set your little one a simple challenge, or pose a question to get them started.

These invitations can be put out on the floor, a low table, on a waterproof tarp or old shower curtain (if messy), a rug or mat, or just about anywhere you like for your child to discover. The complexity and choice of the invitations will of course depend on the age of your child, their specific abilities, interests, their dexterity, their maturity level and the set-up of your home, but here are a few things to bear in mind:

☆ You don't have to set them up every day – having a couple of semi-permanent, inviting places with a few favourite creative materials and tools on shelves and in smallish containers will be enough for happy and busy creative sessions a lot of the time.

☆ Try setting them up when your little one is napping, after they've gone to bed, or are otherwise occupied in independent play. Use toy-rotation techniques for temporary invitations to create: choose from the materials and resources that you've got in accessible storage, and use up those forgotten things you squirreled away months ago.

☆ Combining non-toy playthings with tools and materials is a quick and easy way to make an invitation to create.

☆ They can be suggestive; perhaps they set a challenge or ask a question, or have something to inspire a spark of imagination initially, but don't prescribe an outcome – remember, the journey of the creativity process is open-ended.

☆ As well as supporting the creative process they can tap into every type of play, and can combine more than one play type.

☆ Many invitations to create will be accepted straightaway, and it's a delight to behold, but sometimes they'll be denied until later, sometimes altogether. And some ideas may need you to prompt your child's imaginative thinking.

☆ Some invitations to create will be suited to being left out for a couple of days and will be revisited – creative thoughts quite often need time to incubate. But some may only be used once, and then cleaned up and put away.

☆ Some invitations might need you to model a practical skill using a tool (remember, your hand can be a tool too).

☆ Most creative invitations will need your supervision, and most will work best if you scaffold the activity – more on that later.

☆ If you have more than one tot creating at a time they'll get to practise valuable social skills and engage in communal creative learning – otherwise known as collaboration. Invitations to create are great for trying out sharing, negotiation and problem-solving skills.

Project-managers of the creative process

A parent/carer's role during invitations to create is different to that in other ways to play. We definitely need to find time to supervise more closely here, due to the nature of the tools and materials required, but we need to serve other purposes too – and this is what many grown ups feel worried about. How exactly should we help with a little one's creative play?

Having worked with hundreds of families in creative group sessions, I've encountered every kind of carer/child interaction during the practical activities. From a grown up completely taking over and literally grabbing a paintbrush out of their little one's hand to do it 'properly', to a parent not realising their child was eating the glue – and everything wonderful, interesting and funny in between. I love the French and Saunders' comedy sketch in which they play mummies-on-a-mission to get their offspring engaging in some creative activities at home. They talk about all the fantastic resources they've gathered, and how they are just going to let the kids 'go wild' with them all – how it's all going to be such fun. And then, as the sketch plays out, we see that the reality couldn't be more different, nor the consequences more hilarious. The children aren't given any freedom at all – they are told exactly what to do, when to do it, and how to do it. And when they don't make the cookies correctly or do the painting properly they are judged, scolded and chided. I've shown this video to a few Early Years play practitioners and parents and, although we all cry with laughter at its extremity, it really does illustrate how it's all too easy to inadvertently take creativity completely out of the equation. We might focus on the outcome, whether our child can 'do it properly' or we might worry about the mess so much that the whole thing becomes a nightmare nuisance to hurry up and get over and done with. And, perhaps most distressingly, we might eventually dampen, diminish and ultimately distinguish the joyful creative potential in our children. No wonder we get nervous around this kind of thing!

But we needn't worry that all interactions with little ones during a creative activity might damage their creative potential. For a start, they are pretty resilient at this age; it's not till much later that we really see creativity disappear in many children. As international advisor on Education in the Arts, Ken Robinson argues that young children are the most creative people in the world; it's various outside influences – including school – that will eventually rid most of them of their creative juices. The toddler and preschool years are when curiosity and artistic potential are in glorious technicolour; all we need do is keep our little one's channels of creativity flowing freely and be there to support their creative journeys as best we can – as kind of managers of their creative projects.

There are numerous ways we can successfully project-manage these creative activities. We can:

☆ Pose a very open-ended question or set them a simple challenge to entice them into the activity.
☆ Give children time and space to play and explore materials and tools.
☆ Show interest in their activity but not take over.
☆ Think positive. Give occasional, meaningful encouragement and praise – 'I like how you stuck feathers in that play dough', for example – rather than constant warnings and critical judgement – 'careful you don't make too much mess there' or 'you've not used many colours in your picture, have you?'.
☆ Let them take the lead, and let them express their feelings and ideas about what they're experiencing.
☆ Scaffold their creative experience. This simply means providing structural support to their journey (in whatever direction they choose for it to go). To '**scaffold**' means to provide an external support to a child's

mastery attempts, so they can master something with support that they are currently unable to master on their own. It can mean demonstrating how to use a tool (like an ink-stamp), or modelling a particular skill like drumming or tearing paper. And it can mean initiating a new idea to extend the creative process by asking those 'What if . . . ?' questions.

☆ Model imaginative thoughts – confirming to your little one that one thing can represent another when you use your imagination. Children are great at this from a surprisingly early age but we can encourage and develop their imaginations by picking up on their ideas, supporting them, and extending them. For example, say they pick up a stick and wave it around saying *Abracadabra*, we might comment with something like, 'Oh wow, have you found a magic wand? What magic can you do?'.

☆ Expose them to lots of examples from the world of Expressive Arts and Design – from motifs on mugs, all kinds of music and stories, to examples of traditional crafts like wood carving or pottery, or the print on fabric, and visual art that uses nature – and allow them to respond in their own way. It might be a simple, 'I like that' or 'that's cool', to 'how did they make that?'.

☆ Sharing examples from the world of Expressive Arts and Design with your little one can provide an initial stimulus for an invitation to create – showing young children the properties and possibilities of materials such as paper, wood, metal, clay, plants and textiles, and all manner of handmade or well-designed objects; or of movement with music, or story through drama.

Recap: what is an invitation to create?

An invitation to create is anything that entices a child to engage with the creative process. It can encourage children towards making something original – the incubation stage of creativity. Invitations to create will encourage a child to daydream, think, talk, make music, dance, imagine, role-play, investigate, experience, touch and feel, question, design, explore, assemble, make, mould, tinker, scrunch, tear, watch and mark-make. Whatever the activity, its power is in initiating the desire in children to stop and stay, and participate in some kind of creative activity.

An invitation to create can be an inviting place – inside or outside – where there's space and time and materials with which to create; a whole space, a small area, a table, a rug, a shelf, a mat, a shelter or a tree. It can involve toys and non-toys, a collection of materials and tools, and sometimes, a stimulus from the world of Expressive Arts and Design to inspire and spark their imagination.

Invitations to create tap into and often combine all types of play from construction, imaginative, small world, dramatic and role-play, books and reading, sensory, and those which give our little one's gross and fine motor skills a good workout. This way to play takes a bit of planning and re-thinking our spaces and places at home, so here are lots of examples of invitations to create – to maximise the chances of toddlers and preschoolers unleashing and developing their creative potential, finding joy and learning through meaningful, imaginative and creative adventures at home.

Let them respond to examples from the world of Expressive Arts and Design

It doesn't matter when we expose our little ones to examples from the world of Expressive Arts and Design, just as long as we do. Whether it's a great tune or classical piece you've heard on the radio, to spotting something in the newspaper about a famous artwork, or passing some cool graffiti art, or going to see a show or a visit to a gallery or concert; the source really isn't important, just listen to your little one's response upon seeing, hearing or experiencing these things, and have a chat about them. You will be amazed at their thoughts. They might decide they want to try *doing* or *making* something like that themselves, they might just think it's cool, or they might tell you how it makes them feel. It's all good stuff, and lays the foundation for their future awareness about the creative process, and how to appreciate and be able to talk about performance, music and art.

Let them leave their mark

All toddlers' and preschoolers' scribbling, scratching, drawing, prewriting and painting can be described as mark-making. At this age, children are happy and often wonderfully surprised to see the results of their actions on a surface – it seems they're genuinely impressed that they can leave their mark. At this age, often they will not necessarily be trying to draw anything in particular; on other occasions they may have a very clear view as to what it is they have drawn. The actual marks left will probably be about the same.

Young children's early representations of things and ideas have been widely studied, and from them the development of children, cognitively and physically, can be analysed and tracked. All interesting stuff of course, but what this means for us as parents and carers who want to encourage our child's burgeoning desire to leave their mark is that though they have only a limited dexterity with the tools involved with mark-making, the actual experience is very powerful for them indeed. This is the time to allow them the space, time and resources to play with and explore the hundreds of ways humans can make marks and not worry a jot about the outcome – there need not be anything wall-worthy for it to be a worthwhile activity.

Recently, I worked on an Early Years museum project at the British Museum where little ones got to see cave drawings and inscribed bones from the prehistoric world. The cave people's marks were amazing, often showing an abstract interpretation of the world; definitely art, and truly captivating. Although young children have not yet developed the fine motor skills of their Ice Age ancestors, like those cave artists of thousands of years ago, their frame of reference is wonderfully different to most adults of our modern world. Thus it is a time when they can freely express, explore and make marks that represent their world as they see it or feel it, and their marks often show something other than simply trying to replicate things around them. Interestingly, this is something many modern and contemporary artists strive for too. So, rather than trying to push our children along to being able to draw people, or letters or things, we should tap into their freedom of expression, fresh imagination and creativity by encouraging them to try out techniques, express their ideas, feelings and thoughts by leaving their mark in a variety of ways.

Creative stations – a place to leave their mark

A bench, a low table, or a clearly demarcated floor area with a hard, wipe-clean surface next to a few art supplies on accessible shelving could soon become an established place for your tot to independently visit to make their mark. As they get older you can add more sophisticated tools and materials, but for toddlers and preschoolers – keep it simple. You could have available:

☆ A selection of pieces of paper – just a few sheets of each. Choose from scrap, lined, squared, white A4, coloured A4, tracing paper and thin card in various sizes and colours – whatever you can get your hands on.

☆ Shallow baskets or small boxes of coloured crayons, pencils and washable felt-tips (the chunkier the better for toddlers).

☆ A few large-image plastic or wooden stencils – don't go for those small alphabet stencils just yet, these are way too fiddly and frustrating for most tots.

☆ Dry-wipe pens and a mini 'white' board (or acetate paper).

☆ Chunky ink-stamps and a washable ink pad or two – some stamps cleverly have the ink stored within them, to be released when it's pressed on the paper or card.

This kind of creative station will work best if it is available for your little one to discover independently, but remember you can entice them to start their creating, or you can scaffold their play, by modelling an activity yourself, asking them an open-ended question or setting them a challenge. For example:

☆ What if you use lots of colours to fill in just one stencil?

☆ I see you've chosen some yellow paper. What's going to happen to that?

☆ Can you cover this paper with inky stamps?

☆ Remember our story about Thomas the Tank Engine (or whatever story you've enjoyed recently)? What if you did some drawing about it on this paper?

☆ I've traced the outline of [Peppa Pig, a car, a rocket] here. I wonder who or what will get traced next?

Doodle areas

Some tots go through a stage of making their mark just where you don't want them to, and they can ruin the wallpaper, the lino in the bathroom or even a baby-doll's head (I have particular experience with that last one). Encourage their desire to scribble and draw in the right place by providing them with clearly designated doodle areas, such as:

☆ A blackboard-painted area on a wall or a door (inside or outside) – with a little pot of chalks handy nearby.

☆ A long length of paper from a roll fixed onto a wall with Blu-tack or masking (painters') tape. You could also use parcel paper, the back of some wallpaper (not ready-pasted), a cheap paper tablecloth or a length from a roll of drawing paper – whatever you can get your hands on. Put crayons in a box or basket nearby for some colourful doodles where you're happy to have them.

Again, these designated doodle areas work well if they are open to your child to discover them independently, but be on hand to offer some enticement if need be, for example:

☆ How big can you draw a butterfly? [Or spider, house, magic, cold, or anything else your little one might have seen that day, or be interested in.]

☆ I've started drawing a road with a roundabout. Where will it go next, I wonder?

☆ Can you fill this bit of the paper with [dinosaurs, water, zoom, energy, flowers, zigzags, hearts, fish, smiles, rain, things that are green]?

☆ Put some music on, and invite them to 'draw-along with it'. Change the music and see if this changes the style and manner of their mark-making.

Al fresco mark-making

Whatever the weather, it's possible to encourage your little one to leave their mark. Why not:

☆ Mark out an area on a patio for chalk pavement pictures that will wash away with the next shower of rain, or that can be created whilst it's actually raining.

☆ Leave sturdy sticks and mini-rakes by the sandbox or mud-pit for your little one to try scraping and inscribing marks into a surface of flattish damp sand or mud.

☆ Leave a small bucket of clean water and a clean paintbrush or two by a wooden fence, decking or a post so they can make some temporary marks with watery brush strokes.

If your child is slow to get started, give them a hand with a few questions/challenges:

☆ What if you covered the whole sandbox in stripes?

☆ How many dots can you 'paint' on the wooden post?

☆ What if you used the chalks (on the paving) to show where your hands and feet have been?

Mark-making with temporary provocations

There are so many ways to make marks with different tools and materials that the list is almost infinite. I've chosen just a few of my favourites which I've found to be particularly popular with my own children and those I've worked with in family creative sessions. These temporary invitations will work well if your little one discovers them independently, and you only need set one up every once in a while – just arrange the tools and materials attractively on your creative table, kitchen table or hard-floored area (inside or out).

Let them engrave or inscribe

This simply means giving them the opportunity to create patterns, symbols or pictures by pressing into a flat, hard surface. You could show them some examples from around your home or remind them of something they saw when out and about – maybe in wood, engraved stone or metalwork in jewellery, or a trophy's inscription perhaps. Let them touch the objects so they can *feel* the marks. Here are some simple materials and tools suitable for under-fives:

☆ An air-dry clay slab or flat piece of play dough with scrapers, forks, clean rubber stamps and the like.
☆ A polystyrene tile or a craft foam sheet with a pencil or lolly stick.

Good open-ended questions or challenges here could be:

☆ What if you inscribed some stripes?
☆ Could you make inscribed dots?
☆ What other patterns or things can you inscribe here?

Let them add marks to different surfaces:

Why stick to A4 paper? There are *so* many different surfaces on which to leave a mark. The old masters often painted on canvas, but the famous *Mona Lisa* was actually painted on wood (poplar) by Leonardo Da Vinci in around 1503, and copper was often used as the surface for works of art too. You could show your little one some examples of different marks left on different surfaces – for example, patterns painted on a flowerpot, hand-painted glass or ceramics, canvases with paintings on, hand-painted skateboards or arty graffiti on brickwork. Here are some unusual surfaces and suitable materials on which under-fives might like to leave their mark:

☆ Paint over tin foil (wrap this round a piece of cardboard if you want to make it a little more robust) with poster paints or felt-tips.

☆ Paint on an unglazed ceramic flowerpot or brick, or underside of a tile – water-based acrylics will last but poster paints will give good coverage. You could also use chalks and pastels to leave colour and pattern.

☆ Let them leave their mark on egg cartons and other cardboard things with felt-tips, crayons, poster paints, watercolours – anything you have to hand. If you are raiding the recycling box for this, remember to turn cardboard boxes such as cereal packets inside out first (fix together with a little Sellotape) so it's the non-shiny side that becomes the surface on which to draw or colour.

☆ Find an old piece of sheeting or a plain fabric offcut and let them leave their mark with poster paints, perhaps mixed with glitter, or felt-tips. You could stretch the fabric over an old lightweight frame and fix it with gaffer tape on the back to make a taut canvas.

☆ Acetate sheets or cellophane packaging covered with marks and colour from dry-wipe pens or regular felt-tips are great for holding up to the light when the mark-making is done.

☆ Let them add marks and colour to natural materials like driftwood, bark, pebbles, whittled sticks or leaves with felt-tips or paint or chalks. Add a bit of glitter to the paint for some very sparkly nature.

☆ If you get snow, why not press a spade or two of the white stuff into a tray then let your little one loose with the watercolours?

☆ Brown sugar-paper or old large brown envelopes (inside out if they're a bit shiny) can be scrunched up and flattened again to look like cave walls. Hand over some earthy-coloured pastels or chalks for some Ice-Age art. How will they leave their mark?

☆ Try them with watercolours on wet paper. This gives such a great effect – they'll love leaving their marks and watching them move and change as the paint and water mix and mingle.

You could model these techniques yourself then ask them an open-ended question or set them a challenge:

☆ Can you cover the whole thing in [red and yellow]?

☆ Could you make dots on top?

☆ What other patterns or things can you add here?

Let them print-make with unusual printing blocks

Block-printing is often seen as a kindergarten classic, but professional artists have used the technique of pressing an inked textured block onto a surface to make patterns and pictures for centuries – Japanese block-printing has some of the most beautiful and ancient examples. Rather than spending a lot of time making printing blocks with children, we can offer them some fantastic natural or ready-made versions and let the printing commence.

☆ Those little shop-bought stamps are a great way to introduce young children to block-printing. They often have their ink stored inside, which is very clever, but separate ink pads come in a variety of colours and are usually washable; get the kids' versions to be sure. Add some colourful paper and let them loose with the stamps and inks.

☆ Other, more unusual, printing blocks can be sourced from around the house. Try sponge shapes, corks, the circular ends of cardboard tubes, bubble wrap, cookie cutters, corrugated cardboard shapes or halved fruit and veg – like apples and carrots, peppers (deseeded). Instead of ink, try poster paint. Use the lid of an ice-cream tub or the like and spread out the paint so it's ready to be dipped into for good coverage of the printing block of choice. You could offer a few tub lids spread with paint in a variety of colours.

☆ Hands and fingers make great printing blocks, of course, and if you're feeling brave use the feet. (You might want to do this one outside, or at least have a bowl of soapy water nearby for when they've finished their print-making!) The soles of wellies and crocs and the like leave really interesting prints. Again, one for the garden, try using a flattened cardboard box, or a long roll of paper for the medium on which to run, jump and step the paint.

Demonstrate the techniques yourself if they need help to get started, or ask them an open-ended question or set them a challenge. For example:

☆ Can you cover the whole thing with the pattern from your printing block?
☆ What happens if you use a different colour for your printing block?
☆ What if you print over the top of one you've already done?
☆ What happens if you move the block while you're pressing it down on the paper?

Let them mark-make with the resist/reveal technique

This creative way to leave marks is always very popular with little children because of the surprise *wow* moment when the big reveal happens. You could show your little ones a batik perhaps – which uses wax resist on fabric – but it's going to be the actual doing it themselves that gets them hooked into doing it again and again.

Tape-resist:

Watercolour paper or thin card works a treat because it can handle the tape being peeled off pretty well. Break off lengths of masking tape (painters' tape) and line them up on the edge of the workbench or table ready for your little one to stick them down onto the paper just as they like. Let them colour over the whole thing with watercolours, crayons or pencils before they peel away the tape, revealing their pattern as if by magic.

Wax crayon resist:

Offer a piece of thin card or watercolour paper along with a crayon or a piece of candle wax in a similar or contrasting colour. Let your little one draw away with the wax, just as they like (but pressing quite firmly with the crayon). Once they are happy with their picture or patterns, hand over the watercolours. Because water and oil don't mix, the paint's pigment will be repelled from the waxy markings, to magical effect.

Wipe away wet paint on shiny card:

This is a fun way to leave marks. First coat a piece of shiny card (the backs of old greetings cards work well, though small) in a covering of poster paint. While it's still wet, your child can use their fingers to wipe away paint to reveal patterns and pictures. This is a messy one, so have a bowl of soapy water close by before you start.

Scrape away in a salt-tray:

This technique has been made famous by those mini Japanese Zen gardens; it's certainly a great way to use dry sand or dry salt to leave marks, and maybe some people do find it very therapeutic to work with these materials. Cover a tray with a thin layer of salt or dry sand and let your little one use their fingers, sticks and forks to make marks in the surface. If they get right to the bottom they'll see the tray's surface. For variety you could cover the base of the tray in wrapping paper, foil or colourful paper before covering it with sand.

Once you've demonstrated the various techniques, keep the children interested by asking questions like:

☆ Can you see your pattern or drawing yet?
☆ What other patterns or things can you make?

Let them try making their mark with rubbing

The earliest-known rubbings are Buddhist texts rubbed from wooden blocks in Japan in the eighth century AD. Rubbings are made by carefully pressing paper onto a carved or textured surface and then some kind of pigment block is rubbed over the paper to pick up the detail of the raised parts of the surface. There are lots of other examples of using rubbing as a technique to leave a mark – from rubbing over engraved stonework, and of course brass rubbings – but lots of natural materials have great textured surfaces ripe for rubbing too.

Offer your little one some regular paper and a range of objects they can 'rub'. Colourful chunky wax crayons, without their paper, used sideways, work best for preschoolers. Textures that work really well are basket weave, coins, a sieve, wood carvings, a decorative metal spoon, the sole of a slipper, the underside of leaves or pretty shells and bark. Leave out a selection of intriguing textures for your child to try out.

Model the technique first to get them going, then offer some questions or challenges to keep them engaged:

☆ Can you feel the pattern on the object?

☆ What happens if you rub harder on the paper with the crayon?

☆ What happens if you move the paper while you rub over the pattern?

☆ What happens if you go over it again with a different colour crayon?

Let them try still life

This might seem ambitious for a child under five years old, and while toddlers would certainly find this too challenging, most four-year-olds would love the chance to try to really draw 'what they see'. Arrange something interesting or beautiful and set out some drawing paper along with pencils and maybe some watercolours. A bunch of daffodils, an arrangement of fruit and veg or favourite toys, artfully displayed, are often intriguing still-life set-ups for this age group.

For this activity it might be valuable to show them an example to start with, then get them thinking and doing with some open-ended questions or a challenge. For example:

☆ What shapes can you see in the object on display?

☆ What happens to what you see if you move position?

☆ Can you copy the colours of the objects on display onto your picture of them?

Let them try their hand at portraiture

Some four-year-olds will be beginning to form recognisable faces and figures in their drawings. Give them the opportunity to draw their own likeness by setting up a paint-a-self-portrait workshop. Carefully prop up a safe mirror so they can easily see their face reflected, and give them some good-quality drawing paper and a pencil or crayons. Encourage them to look carefully at their own face, and then attempt to commit what they see to paper. Teddy bears and rag-dolls make great sitters too.

As them a question or set them a challenge to get them started:

☆ What features of your face can you see in the mirror?

☆ What happens to what you see if you move position?

☆ How would you copy the shape of your eyes onto your picture?

Let them use their hands as mark-making tools

Using their hands as mark-making tools is one of the simplest ways to get them stuck in and mark-making confidently. At three, my son was worried about getting his hands dirty, and was rather reluctant when it came to using paints and the like, but showing him how to smudge pastel colours to make skies like Turner, or do finger-dots like Seurat's pointillism technique, for example, showed him that it was okay, in fact necessary, to get one's hands dirty in order to leave his mark sometimes.

Try using a sheet from a colouring-in book along with some thick finger-paints to fill the picture with colourful finger-dots – pointillism on a large scale. Or get them to create some sky pictures using smudgy chalks and chalk pastels in the colours of a rosy dawn, a bright sunny day, a stormy sky above the sea, or a purple-y twilight sky. Let them use their fingers to smudge and merge the colours to create their skies. You could show them some photographs of skies, or take a look at some famous art depictions like those by Georgia O'Keeffe, Turner or Van Gogh. If they need more inspiration, show them an example of your own, or get them thinking with some questions. For example:

☆ What makes all those colours in your sky?

☆ What happens if you put one colour on top of another?

☆ How many colours does your sunset sky have?

Let them try some unusual tools for their mark-making

Why stick to traditional tools for mark-making when there are so many alternative fun ways to do so? In the world of art some pretty extreme and weird things have been used to leave marks, from one artist using their head of long hair as a paintbrush to another using a basketball. However, for our little ones at home, using objects easily sourced from round the house will be exciting enough! Why not try setting out some good-quality paper and some unusual mark-making tools for them to experiment with? Some good tools include:

☆ Cotton buds dipped in poster paints are great for pointillism practice.

☆ Feathers hold poster paint really well, and are great for practising sweeping and swooshing paint onto the paper, leaving interesting marks.

☆ Mixed-up paint-and-water ice cubes will need to be prepared at least the day before, but they do glide beautifully over paper, leaving subtle ribbons of colour in their wake.

☆ Toy car wheels make great tracks when rolled in poster paint (in a tub lid) before being driven around on some paper.

☆ Small rubber balls or marbles first covered in paint (in a tub lid), then rolled around a piece of paper (in a shoebox) can provide a lot of great tracks, and a lot of laughs.

Try asking these questions:

☆ What happens to the marks as the [tool] runs out of paint?

☆ What happens if you add a different colour with the [tool] to the marks already on the paper?

Let them use paint-on-the-move to make marks

This is the territory of Jackson Pollock and the like. It's known as 'action painting', which places the emphasis on the act of painting rather than the finished piece. It challenges traditional conventions by the artist spontaneously dribbling, splashing or smearing paint onto a large canvas on the floor or using hardened brushes, sticks and even basting syringes for applying paint. Right up a toddler's street, yes? These activities are likely to get messier than some invitations to create, so you might want to try these outside or somewhere everyone knows it's fine to be spontaneous, and go for it.

Give your child thinned-down poster paint in a squeezy bottle (an old shampoo or ketchup bottle destined for the recycling perhaps) and make puddles of paint on thick paper or thin card. Give everyone a drinking straw and start blowing the paint to make it move out of the puddle and into different directions. Using the same squeezy bottle of paint again plus a large old sheet or piece of fabric on the floor, allow your little one to squeeze the paint out just as they like. Add further squeezy bottles with other colours for a proper Pollock-type painting.

You could also use regular (or slightly thinned-down) poster paint applied in thick blobs to a piece of card, or get them to tip and turn a thick piece of paper to create some interesting marks; paints will merge and marble and run in some crazy directions. You could try this inside an open shoebox if you want to prevent too much paint travelling off the paper.

Your little ones will find flicking paint great fun (even if the thought of it fills you with horror!). In a part of the room well covered with a play mat or lots of newspaper, let them load up a stiff paintbrush with different-coloured poster paints and allow them to flick the brush to make the paint splat onto a large piece of paper or old sheet placed on the floor. If you don't have much space and the thought of paint flying makes you nervous, do this one outside!

If they need a little push, ask them:

☆ What happens to the marks as the [tool] runs out of paint?

☆ Where on the picture has the most paint? Where has the least?

☆ What happens if you add a different colour with the [tool] to the marks already on the paper?

Let them create something sculptural

Creating something that's 'not flat' – that is to say, something *sculptural* – is often tricky for tiny hands. Unlike mark-making, the changes they manage to make to a substance, or a material, can be unintentionally temporary, so they may not get exactly the same sense of satisfaction as when they've simply left their mark on something. Toddlers and preschoolers are brilliantly imaginative, though, which is why you might get given a plastic fruit box with a cardboard tube inside and told in no uncertain terms that it's a *cash till*, or a *house*, maybe.

As with mark-making, giving young children a chance to engage in the *process* of creating something sculptural is very valuable; we mustn't worry that the outcome isn't permanent, perfect or actually ever realised. It's at least as important to let our children explore and play with the techniques of sculpture. It's all part of the creative process, developing their problem-solving abilities as well as their fine motor skills. Just as there are tips and tricks for holding a brush or crayon effectively in mark-making, so there are ways to make cardboard tubes stand up strongly, balance pebbles, mould clay or play dough into a sphere, or attach two things together. Techniques for creating sculpture can be modelled for little ones just as we might with mark-making techniques but, as project-managers of their sculptural endeavours, it's important to scaffold their experience without taking over.

Sculpting involves the creation of something that has volume, line and plane, and that has texture and colour. Various elements can be played with, explored and talked about when little ones are looking at or making sculpture:

☆ *Scale* – a model of a giant insect, or a tiny skyscraper made of small wooden blocks.

☆ *Balance* – when loose parts are balanced just so to make a sculpture, or when sculptures are made to be symmetrical or asymmetrical.

☆ *Space* – some sculptures are solid, some capture space within them.

☆ *Movement* – some sculptures give the notion of movement, like the aerodynamic-looking wings and nose cone of a Lego spacecraft, or they can have actual movement which is often quite mesmerising. These are known as kinetic sculptures – mobiles are good examples of these.

☆ There are many techniques in sculpture, and your little one can easily experience:
  ☆ Assemblage
  ☆ Carving
  ☆ Modelling

Let them assemble

Assemblage can be described as a sort of collage, but in three-dimensions. For young children we usually see it in the form of junk-modelling; all those boats, robots and rockets made from cardboard boxes, plastic pots, fabric and other bits and bobs you get handed after a visit to playgroup or a morning at nursery – all those were made using the technique of assemblage.

Picasso was an early user of assemblage, making sculpture out of things like a tablecloth and wood, which he glued together and painted. The Surrealists liked to use this technique too – you might know Dali's lobster telephone sculpture? Of course, it's the process of assemblage we should encourage, not the production of exhibition-worthy works, but we can occasionally inspire them with examples from the world of Expressive Arts and Design.

Temporary assemblage

Sculpture is not always meant to be permanent, so inviting your little one to make something temporary is definitely worth it. You can do this when you're out and about or in the garden by gathering leaves, twigs, stones and pebbles and then, like Andy Goldsworthy (famous for his photographs of his natural temporary sculptures), see what they can create. Of course, larger-scale temporary sculptures can be made outside too – long cardboard tubes and boxes, large wooden blocks, or crates are fantastic parts which they can combine, build and balance.

Inside, try offering a few loose parts attractively supplied in a couple of baskets or boxes so your little one can try balancing and arranging things to make slightly smaller temporary pieces. Provide a sturdy flat tray or piece of cardboard to define its base if you like. Loose parts can be anything from large buttons, jar lids, cotton reels, wooden blocks, Duplo, Octons (or other construction toys) – I've used these with my children when they were in the bath – pipe cleaners, large beads, pieces of wood, shells, fir cones or plastic cups. Old things like phone bits and bobs are great for creating 'machines' and inventions. As these sculptures are supposed to be temporary, the loose parts can be used again and again. You could ring the changes by offering just one kind of loose part, or you could sometimes combine several different things. You could occasionally take a photograph before the sculpture is dismantled (or falls down) to keep as a reminder of a particular point in your child's creative process.

You can entice your child into creating a temporary sculpture by asking them open-ended questions or setting them a challenge, and then scaffolding their play and modelling techniques when necessary.

For example:

☆ What can you build with these?

☆ Can you make something tall?

☆ What if you made something funny?

☆ Could you make these things look like something else?

☆ What can you turn these things into?

☆ Remember that [monster, machine, house] we saw in our story earlier? Can you make your own out of these?

☆ Can you make something we can look through to a secret place, or all the way through to the other side?

☆ Can you hide this [toy figure, toy car, flower] with these things? Can you hide them in a different way?

Fixed assemblage

By adding *fixing* materials such as masking tape (painters' tape), play dough, glue-dots, glue sticks, pipe cleaners and the like, it will be possible for your little one to use assemblage to create sculpture with slightly more permanence, or a little more stability at least. By fixing string or thread to at least two elements, children can start to put movement into their sculptures too.

Things from the recycling box, like clean empty milk cartons, juice boxes, drinking straws, cardboard tubes, plastic containers, polystyrene and empty food boxes, can all be fixed together using masking tape. I'm a big fan of this because it's very easy for little hands to rip off the roll, and it can be stuck and re-stuck several times before it loses its power to stick. Smaller assemblage components such as feathers, small plastic cups, buttons, beads and googly eyes can be secured in place with play dough, Blu-tack or modelling clay, and glue sticks are great for attaching tissue paper, googly eyes, sequins or fabric to card or paper.

As with all creative invitations for young children we should try to keep everything very open-ended. We don't have to know what our little one is going to aim to make – they're simply playing with and exploring the materials; their sculpture certainly doesn't have to be finished or kept. Invitations to sculpt are simply that – invitations. Instead we can focus on thinking up different things to offer them to include in their sculptural exploration, showing them some simple techniques as and when they need them and, of course, asking open-ended questions or setting challenges to keep them creating. Such as:

☆ Could you make these things into some kind of [place, robot, machine, monster, building]?
☆ What if these things were to be made into something spiky, or big, or tall, or funny, or special?
☆ What would happen if you fixed these together so we couldn't see through it?
☆ What can you make with these?
☆ Can you make something tall?
☆ How could we make its surface bumpy or smooth, shiny or colourful?
☆ What if you made something funny?
☆ Could you make these things into something else?
☆ What can you turn these things into?
☆ Remember that [monster, machine, boat, castle, forest] we saw in our story earlier? Can you make your own out of these?
☆ Can you make something we can look through to a secret place, or all the way through to the other side?
☆ Can you make a part of it move by itself?

Tips for assemblage sessions

☆ Sometimes the creative vision will come pouring out from your little one and they'll even vocalise their ideas. Sometimes they might not necessarily have the technique or dexterity to realise their vision; they may tell you they want to make that bit stick on this or that bit to turn or dangle, but they won't be able to make it happen.

☆ Most toddlers will be happy with an approximation and will make do with what they can do (imagining the rest). As they reach preschool age, a few ideas and the modelling of technique may need to come from you. Don't worry though, there's not much a bit of sticky tape or masking (painters') tape won't enable to happen here – this is where you can share ideas about how to solve the problem; you might show them a technique for sticking or making something balance or be strong or attached.

☆ Talk to them about what you plan to help them with, but don't take over. And remember that the solution you both come up with doesn't have to last forever, nor does it have to work at all. It's the process of problem-solving and creating that's important here. Sometimes leaving it and coming back to it will allow time for new solutions or a different idea to germinate – that's the magic of the incubation stage of creativity.

Let them carve

Even if we love the idea of Michelangelo saying something along the lines of *every block of stone has a statue inside it, and it is the task of the sculptor to discover it*, carving is a technique that really seems to be completely unsuitable for young children. Alarm bells start ringing as soon as we think about the tools required for cutting and shaping hard materials; chisels, hammers, knives, chainsaws – I think you get the idea. But if we find softer materials than those traditionally used, then the tools needed to find pattern, shapes and design within them are much less scary, and in fact very practical for the under-fives. Of course, we do still need to supervise very carefully with this kind of activity but your preschoolers can have a lot of fun trying out this creative technique, discovering the sculptures within blocks of solid material. They won't necessarily find angels of Michelangelo quality and longevity, of course, but they'll love playing and exploring.

Jelly:

I'm not a huge fan of using foodstuff for play, but since you could definitely eat the jelly sculpture (and the discarded bits) afterwards, this makes it a more attractive option for me. Prepare a jelly or two in a simple mould – such as a mixing bowl or plastic food container – then, once set, turn out onto a clean tray alongside some children's cutlery.

Bread:

This is food again, I know, but of course the discarded crusts could be made into breadcrumbs for future use. Milena Korolczuk is the bread-sculptor *du jour* – she uses squished bread, then moulds and carves it into famous faces. You could show your little ones some examples of her work – currently everywhere online – or just present them with a hunk of bread and see what they can find in it. The best tool for this is their hands – tearing off little bits just as they like – though a chopstick or similar would work well to make holes in the surface of the bread. Bagels and bread rolls are great because they are a bit more robust in texture and shape than, say, a slice of bread.

Wet Sand:

Although toddlers are often highly impressed with the amazing sandcastle Granddad has just made, they usually take great delight in immediately destroying it with their hands, feet or bottom. As they reach preschool age, they will probably get the idea that sandcastles and indeed larger sand sculptures are pretty cool left intact for a while – they can even sit in them if Mummy's made them a full-size sand-car, or similar.

If you'd like to give your preschooler the opportunity to make their own sand sculpture, it's probably best set up outside, even if it's just with a small amount of sand, as it might get a little bit messy as the carving begins. Make your sand as damp as you might be pleased to find it on a beach, then fill a bucket or plastic container with it and compress it, just as you would if you were building sandcastles. Tip the sand out onto a plastic lid or tray – like a kind of sand brick, or, if you want them to think big, add water to a section of your play sand in the sandbox itself and pile it up, compressing it as much as you can to form a mound of wet, compacted sand. Brilliant sand sculptures can be discovered daily on many beaches in the summer – if they need inspiration you could talk to your child about one or two they remember seeing, or you could look up images of sand sculptures on the internet. There are a few world-famous sand sculptors, such as Kirk Rademaker and Sudarsan Pattnaik, and their sculptures are incredibly inspiring and worth showing to your little one.

Let them carve with manual tools such as lolly sticks, kids' trowels, kids' butter knives, tablespoons and drinking straws, an old toothbrush or pastry brush, an old credit card or similar, or a melon-baller to explore the characteristics of the medium and play with creating a sculptural form. Add moisture with a water-spray if the sand starts to dry out too much as they sculpt. Of course, the sculpture may collapse, or they may want to destroy it and make another one over and over again – this is what it's all about; the process of creating.

Snow:

The scarcity of snow in some parts of this country, and the fact that little ones get cold quickly, despite the layers of waterproofs and woollens we wrap them in, means that snow-carving is often an activity that we might not get round to. But, if you do happen to get a good amount of wet snow you could invite your child to carve into a big, compacted pile of it with a small spade or their gloved hands. We've even taken a bucketful of snow inside before now, tipped it out sand-castle style on a waterproof mat, then let the children carve into it using slightly smaller tools – like kids' cutlery. I remember one time seeing a marvellous Planet Hoth being landscaped and then of course the *Star Wars* figurines made an appearance for some wonderful small world play.

Polystyrene:

Polystyrene is a great medium for carving – young children can snap off bits with their hands, dig into it with pencils or lolly sticks, or press golf tees, pipe cleaners or sticks into it to attach pieces together. It is lovely stuff, and often already rather sculptural due to its pre-moulded use. Just confine the mess to a designated making/creative space and supervise carefully. Crayon-colour works well on this surface too, should your little one want to add some colour to their carving.

All of these carving invitations will work well if your little one discovers them on their own but you do need to supervise carefully. Without taking over, you can project-manage their creative endeavours by demonstrating some simple carving techniques as and when they need them, or scaffolding their play with questions and challenges such as:

☆ Could you make this into some kind of [place, robot, machine, monster, building]?

☆ What if you made this into something spiky, or bumpy, or funny, or special?

☆ What would happen if you carved out some [jelly, bread, sand, polystyrene] so we could see inside it?

☆ What other shape can you make this into?

☆ Can you make something beautiful, exciting, interesting, that's different on every side?

☆ How could we make its surface bumpy, or wavy?

☆ What if you made something funny?

☆ What can you turn these things into?

☆ Remember that [monster, machine, boat, castle, forest] we saw in our story earlier? Can you find your own somewhere in this, by taking away some of the [sand, polystyrene, snow] etc?

☆ Can you make something we can look through to a secret place, or all the way through to the other side?

Let them model

In sculpture, the working of clay, or similar modelling material, by hand builds up form. The artist's hands are the main tools, though metal and wood implements are often used in shaping the piece. Modelling is an ancient technique, as indicated by prehistoric clay figurines from Egypt and the Middle East. Often, there are other materials used inside the artworks to add structural strength. You could show your little ones examples of pieces of decorative ceramic art such as pots, wall hangings or figures – they are everywhere once you start looking. Of course, few people have access to a kiln, so your modelling is most likely not going to be fired, so it's the technique of modelling to create shape and form that we're aiming for here – the process. Air-drying clay is widely available, but there are many more materials that can be pressed and pulled and manipulated into three-dimensions. Why not set out some of these and see what your little one does?

Papier-mâché:
This can be quite a messy modelling medium, but if your little one loves gloop and slime then they'll love working with this. Clear the decks and make sure the surface they're working on is hard and easy to clean. I usually put down a cardboard working base-board on which they can build up their sculptures. Fill a bowl with torn news-paper pieces and mix with enough PVA and water (two parts glue; one part water) so that the paper is softened, malleable and, of course, a bit sticky – you might want to leave this for about 10 min-utes for the paper to soak up the wet stuff. Let them take a handful or less at a time and start squishing it and shaping it onto their board, just as they like. Put this somewhere warm for a few days to harden if you want to show them how it changes into a hard sculptural thing.

Play dough:
This has to be one of the most popular modelling media for the under-fives, despite one of my friends once saying that it was, and I quote, 'the work of the devil'. I suspect she'd had a terrible time once, with play dough getting in all the wrong places. Just like a lot of art resources and materials, we really do have to let little ones know where

and when they can use these special things so that everyone, including us grown ups, can enjoy them. You can, of course, buy it, but it is honestly the easiest thing to make, and it lasts for ages in an airtight tin. Also, there is possibly nothing better than working with freshly made, still warm, play dough that's been scented, coloured or is all glittery. I have to admit, I think it's the work of *angels* then (see p.205 for my favourite play dough recipe). Play dough is a wonderful modelling medium because it is so responsive; not only is it soft and malleable, it also keeps its shape wonderfully. It works children's fine motor skills as they roll it, flatten it, stretch it and break it up into pieces.

Let your child work on a flat, washable surface, or maybe a cardboard or plastic board. Add some basic tools to ring the changes, from rolling pins, cookie cutters, sticks and spoons. Small plastic containers destined for the recycling bin or lolly sticks can be used as structural frames to be covered by the play dough, and sculptures can be ornately decorated by pressing into the surface (inscribing or engraving) or if you put out a few extra bits and bobs; our favourites include sequins, beads, pipe cleaners, feathers, small plastic figures and animals, herbs and flowers, wooden letters, Lego bricks and googly eyes.

All these modelling invitations will work well if your little one discovers them on their own but we do need to supervise carefully. Again, as with other activities, we can project-manage their creative endeavours without directing them by asking questions, demonstrating techniques or setting them challenges:

☆ Could you make this into some kind of [place, robot, machine, monster, building]?

☆ What if you made this into something tall, or funny, or special?

☆ What would happen if you added a ball shape to the top of that, how could you stop it rolling off?

☆ What other shapes can you make?

☆ How would you make something beautiful, exciting, interesting, that's different on every side?

☆ How could we make its surface pretty, or bumpy, or dotty?

☆ What if you made something funny?

☆ What can you turn this into?

☆ Remember that [monster, machine, boat, castle, forest] we saw in our story earlier? Can you model your own out of this?

☆ Can you make something we can look through all the way to the other side?

Let them play with different materials, exploring texture, colour and size

There are so many materials young children find intriguing and love to get their hands on. It's simply a matter of us choosing a few different materials to put out in different combinations and see what they come up with. In terms of technique, we're really talking *collage* here, which is where different materials – all kinds of paper (like Matisse and Picasso), plastic pieces, foil, cellophane, photographs, text from magazines, pieces of wood (like Jane Frank), leaves and straw, seeds and pulses, card, ribbon and fabric – are cut to size, arranged and assembled together as a piece of artwork and fixed with glue. This technique grew in popularity in the twentieth century and there are usually good examples of collage, although often printed, in advertisements in magazines if you wanted to show examples to your children.

All manner of tempting materials can be prepared and set out attractively in shallow containers for our little ones to explore and use. They'll be experimenting with scrunching, ripping and tearing paper, bending card, using scissors – perhaps for the first time – to cut paper, plus exploring size and textures of any fabric pieces we might offer as they create.

To get them choosing with purpose, you could offer them a large cardboard base on which to arrange their materials and some PVA glue or a glue stick, or a piece of sticky-backed plastic (sticky-side up, fixed to the table with a little masking tape at the corners) on which to assemble their chosen materials. Then offer them a few of these materials: assorted leaves, different types of paper, pictures and photos from magazines, sequins, tissue paper, cotton wool, craft foam pieces, glitter, stickers, feathers, googly eyes, buttons, ribbon pieces, punchinella, lids from jars and containers, colourful sticky tapes, dried lentils, straw, wood chippings, cellophane pieces or foil pieces.

Exploring and playing with these materials does need careful supervision, though. Again, project-manage them in the usual way, but you could also show them some simple techniques – such as cutting, bending, folding, tearing and rolling – and ask them questions:

☆ Could you arrange these into some kind of picture of a [place, snowman, robot, machine, flower, monster, building]?
☆ What if you made this into something beautiful, funny or special?
☆ What would happen if you added a row of [tissue-paper pieces] to the top of that, how could you get them to stay put?
☆ What other shapes can you make with those ribbons?
☆ How could we make its surface colourful, or bumpy, or like a bird's tail?
☆ What picture can you make out of these things?
☆ Remember that [monster, machine, boat, castle, forest] we saw in our story earlier? Can you make a picture of your own out of these materials?

Let them sing, dance, make music and be dramatic

Toddlers and preschoolers will have the wonderful ability to, as the poem goes, 'Dance like no one's watching, and sing like no one's listening'; it's their default position. In fact, they often don't realise anyone is watching them perform at all, and they certainly don't *need* anyone to watch them to enjoy expressing themselves in this way. They will step into a story or some music naturally given the invitation. At this age it's really about us not putting a stopper in their creative flow, or making them self-conscious about what they're doing.

There are numerous ways by which we can successfully encourage and support expressive activities. We can:

☆ Expose them to lots of examples from the world of Expressive Arts – from music and dance of all kinds, shows and story-telling performances, to telling them stories and listening to audio stories. These can provide powerful stimuli for young children to experience the possibilities of movement with music, or story through drama.

☆ Give children time and space to dance, play and explore instruments and props.

☆ Let them take the lead, and let them express their feelings and ideas about what they're experiencing.

☆ Scaffold their creative experience. This simply means providing structural support to their journey in whatever direction they choose for it to go. It could mean demonstrating how to use an instrument if they're stuck, modelling a particular skill like marching or some fancy footwork, or playing a character; but only if they invite you to join in.

☆ Model imaginative thoughts to demonstrate to your little one that one thing can represent another when you use your imagination. Children are great at this from a surprisingly early age but we can encourage and develop their imaginations by picking up on their ideas; supporting them and extending them. Say your child picks up a block and holds it to their ear like a telephone and says, 'Hello', you could let them know their idea is great by answering with another block and saying, 'Hi, who is it?'

Let them make music, and move to music

☆ Look around your garden for features that might make good musical noise; maybe you have a metal fence or some bamboo screening, both of which make a great sound when tapped with a stick.

☆ Sound walls are easy to create too. Just attach a few different small objects with handles – like a metal colander, a wooden bowl and a metal tray – to a wall or fence at child height and let them tap out some tunes with a stick or spoon to their heart's content.

☆ A few elastic bands stretched over the opening of an empty plastic flowerpot or filled small metallic planters can be plucked like stringed instruments. These garden guitars are great for your little ones to discover, and they may well want to 'charm the snails' with their magical sound, as my daughter does.

☆ Have a few percussive, wind and string instruments accessible in a basket or a box so your little one can help themselves when they feel the urge to join in with a song on the radio, for example.

☆ Occasionally you could set out some instruments, or a few silky scarves or ribbons, and invite them to play along, dance along or sing along with some music. You could use a children's sing-along CD, a themed play list, or a film soundtrack perhaps.

☆ If you gather some pictures of different characters – like a pirate, a spy, a witch, a king, for example – near to some instruments, you could invite your little one to make up music and/or songs for each character.

Some great instruments for preschoolers

shakers (homemade or shop-bought) ☆ tambourine ☆ bongos ☆ triangle ☆ jingle-bells ☆ swanee whistle ☆ small keyboard ☆ thumb-piano ☆ maracas ☆ castanets ☆ chimes ☆ xylophone ☆ hand-bells ☆ child's guitar or a homemade stringed-box ☆ kazoo ☆ drum ☆ wooden scrapers ☆ finger cymbals ☆ monkey drum ☆ harmonica ☆ train whistle

See the Stay and Play chapter for ideas of musical fun and games to play *with* your little one.

Let them be dramatic

You could occasionally set out invitations to create something dramatic. Remember it's the process of this that's important here not the quality of the performance. You will probably not be invited to watch anything, or to take part, especially if there a few little ones creating something together.

☆ Make a bag or box of potential costumes accessible to your little one. You could have a separate container for hats, wigs and accessories, otherwise things do tend to get in a big old muddle. Long fabric rectangles, scarves, thrift or charity shop items work brilliantly because they can be used for so many different characters and situations. Our large piece of lace and faux-fur 'cloak' have been used so many times in dozens of ways.

☆ Props will be gathered by your little one from all over and with their great imaginations they'll improvise if needed. However, you could help them by gathering together things that are often needed in dramatic play. For example, cardboard tubes for wands, walking sticks and, dare I say it, swords (or light sabers), painted sticks for wands (we have quite a selection of these) and a few tote bags, old mobile phones, small blankets or a toy tea set.

☆ A few hand puppets along with a big cardboard box (opened at both ends for a puppet theatre).

☆ After seeing a film or show, gather a few bits and bobs of costume, some toys as other characters and a few props and invite your little one to play *Stick Man, Ice Age* or *Peter Pan*. Let them step into the story and act it out.

☆ Put out a favourite picture book – any story they know and love – along with some soft toys to play characters, some props and costumes, and invite your child to play *Little Rabbit Lost* or *Goldilocks and the Three Bears* or *Lost and Found*, for example. Let them get into the story and act it out.

Make and Take

Crafting *noun*. The activity or hobby of making decorative articles by hand: crafting has emerged as a fashionable form of self-expression.

Before I had children I didn't have much time for crafting or, to use a better-known expression, *making things*. My job was full-time and incredibly full on, and I was lucky enough to often be helping children make things as part of my working day, so I got my crafting *fix*, as it were. As a result, I didn't prioritise, say, baking my own biscuits, or designing birthday cards even though doing this kind of thing always made me happy on the rare occasions I made time to do so. However, it's recently become very fashionable to actually make time to make things. The crafty principle of *'Don't buy it, make it!'* seems to be all the rage nowadays – even for busy people in full-time work. A friend of mine runs a ridiculously cool monthly social event in London's hip Hoxton called The Make Escape. Here, sophisticated grown ups meet and make stuff together of an evening. Apparently, wine is available during these crafting soirees – which make them sound like pretty perfect nights out to me. I should really get a babysitter and go along . . .

The numerous benefits for adults who *make things* are well documented. Professor John Benyon at the Institute of Lifelong Learning, University of Leicester, talks of participation in such activities increasing the happiness and well-being of those involved.

It's said to aid relaxation, encourage self-expression, it can take away stress, promote a sense of pride in learning a new skill, and there's the enjoyment and satisfaction of seeing those finally-finished projects being displayed, used, or, as is deemed acceptable and desirable these days, given as gifts to friends and family. And with more people than ever before openly proclaiming their love of making decorative articles – whether it's through sewing, pottery, baking, painting, knitting, jewellery-making, paper-crafting or wood-carving – it seems set to stay as a popular and sociable pastime for the foreseeable future.

With the recent explosion of eye-candy websites like Pinterest, there is plenty of inspiration out there; all we need do is go online and take a look at literally thousands of images of wonderful and downright cool things people have cleverly made which usually link to websites and blogs, some with very useful online tutorials. Since having children of my own, my love of making things has definitely been rekindled – it's actually one of the few things for which I've made more time since becoming a parent. I've certainly used my little ones as an excuse to get in the kitchen more to bake, to buy lovely craft supplies and to collect random objects for my children not only to freely explore but also for us to intentionally make things together.

I love my art-and-craft store shelves at home – which have only really come into existence since having children – and get a little over-excited at the sight of the fantastic walk-in resource cupboards in the museums where I work. I get such a thrill seeing all those lovely 'things' ready to be used, knowing that children will creatively incorporate them into some making activity or other in the future.

I know not everybody has the same reaction upon becoming a parent – many people, even those who are very creative and crafty themselves – find the prospect of doing craft with little ones unappealing to say the least. It makes them want to run for the hills;

it's a glittery, gluey step too far. For many, taking their children to organised messy/arty/crafty sessions is a much more palatable way to give their little ones a chance to make things; a way of keeping the glitter and glue at bay.

'I am not creative, I don't have an eye for making pretty things, or whipping a lot of pretty paper, beads and glue into a marvellous creation. When it comes to anything artsy-crafty, making pretty things, I leave that to other people. This weekend, we went to Ham House, for a Father's Day tea, and they had a crown-making workshop happening, which both children and I enjoyed. It was short, easy, and uncomplicated, and they both came away very proud of their creations!'

A craft-reluctant mum of two

When teaching make and take activities for little ones in these types of sessions, I hear many parental confessions; some admit they can think of nothing worse than doing arty/crafty things at home; some tell me it actually brings them out in a cold sweat. But I see it all – from those families for whom visits to museum making-sessions are the only way they ever really experience craft, to the family-craft enthusiasts who tell me they cut, stick, make and bake together at home most days. It seems that parents fall into two craft-camps – the lovers and the haters. The parents who hate it often feel they are simply not creative enough to do craft with their kids, or they don't have enough time, or that it's just too messy. Some feel they are too perfectionist, or think their children might be, or that their children don't have a long enough attention span – 'they just won't sit down for that long'. And many parents, who wouldn't go quite as far as saying they hated doing craft with their children, still try to avoid this kind of activity at home if at all possible. What is it that really stops so many people from crafting with their children at home?

Why don't we do craft with our children?

Despite many craft activities featuring on kids' TV programmes, in books, magazines and on the internet these days, many parents and carers still want to leave this kind of activity to the professionals, or at least until their little one's making can take place where it's somebody else's mess. The wonderful images of things to make on the pages of magazines, in books or on screen do inspire everyone – both adults and children – prompting those '*I want to make that*' moments. But, it seems to me, that often this is as far as it goes. Nine times out of ten, it turns out the decorative articles shown have actually been made by talented grown-up artists and beautifully photographed by professionals, and the techniques accompanying the glossy images – if given at all – are often far too tricky for preschoolers, too complicated and take too long. It can put people off even thinking about trying them.

I remember my sister, most valiantly, attempting to make those string egg baskets, as seen everywhere on Pinterest earlier this year, with her two-year-old. I know she didn't manage to get her daughter to help much with it in the end, even though it was labelled as a 'craft for kids'; it left her feeling rather frazzled. She felt that the end product looked vastly inferior to those beautifully-crafted objects she thought she was going to make (actually they turned out great). This kind of way of doing craft – following instructions, trying to make something exactly the same and example – has been called *crafting by rote*, and it leaves many children and adults feeling they 'can't do craft'. They tend to feel dissatisfied with their work. And it certainly doesn't make craft a particularly tempting way to play at home.

As one mum confesses, 'I don't enjoy it, my children get cross with me when we try craft activities, and most of the items I produce end up heading towards the dustbin. I did feel guilty for a long time, and tried to make an effort to be more crafty, and still occasionally linger, looking longingly at the fabulous efforts people put on Pinterest, and at all the hundreds of suggested craft activities for children, but I am over the guilt. Now, we do plenty of other things instead, and I don't think the children are missing out that much.'

Another mum writes about how the internet has made us all feel guilty about not doing craft with our children. She writes rebelliously, 'The crayons will break and it is okay to throw them away rather than save them to make some sort of craft that involves the hair dryer. In fact, I give you permission to not feel guilty about all the crafts you know you will never do.'

And then, of course, there are the craft-kits. Those over-packaged, often over-priced, boxes containing 'everything you'll need to make something', readily available in local supermarkets, craft and toy shops and online. If you have a child who likes to *make*, they always tempt with the promise of 'having fun' and 'creating lovely homemade things' without any need for us adults to do any preparation or have any craft-skill. But how many of these kits actually deliver enjoyable, let alone creative, experiences for our children? How many of them actually make good on their promise that a young child can accomplish the craft activity easily? They rarely say that an adult will need to help them follow every complicated instruction, or take over completely in the end. If I can persuade my child to abandon the instructions and just do their own thing it's always so much more of an enjoyable craft session. If I was more of a radical I would throw away the entire packaging and instructions for many of these kits and simply add their materials to our existing collection of art and craft resources.

Why do craft with kids?

Ideas for what, how and why to make things with young children really are out there; we don't need to rely on the media or kits *all* the time. And we really don't need some kind of crafty gene to provide these experiences for our children. Want to know the best source of inspiration for craft with our children? It's the children themselves.

One of the keys to success at home is to be aware of your child's *call-to-craft*; it's the *why* they might want to make something. Young children's reasons for wanting to get making are many and varied but it's really useful to bear them in mind. It can be easy to miss these moments especially if, like one of my own children, they are few and far between. But this is often the best way to get in and out of a craft situation with success because it all starts with an initial desire from the child, which we can use to carry everyone happily through the whole process.

There are many different reasons why children may decide to make something. Here are some of the key ones to look out for.

They've identified a need and want to make something to meet it:
Like they need a hat, a watch or a rocket. When my three-year-old daughter suddenly announced that she needed to make a guitar, we heard her 'call-to-craft' moment loud and clear. It led on to the most wonderful craft session where she called the shots, but we helped her with the realisation of her vision. I remember how we set up a little making station for her at the table, she chose from the boxes and tubes we offered (from our recycling stash) and we helped her stick them together with strong sticky tape. She told us it had to have three strings, and it had to be orange – so elastic-bands and red and yellow paint were duly found. She helped to fix on the strings then she mixed the two colours of poster paints together and

then, using a nice chunky paintbrush, she covered the whole thing to make it orange, as was her plan. We had to dry it with a hair-dryer in the end, because she was so desperate to use it in a 'gig' straight away.

They've been inspired by a picture book:
After reading *The Shoemaker Extraordinaire* by Steve Light, my daughter wanted to make me some shoes-with-special-powers; totally inspired by the book. When we found we had two empty tissue boxes in our recycling box I was 'measured up' and had a shoe-fitting. The shoes' special powers were, according to my daughter, to make me able to jump very high. My daughter said they needed laces, so we talked about how we might do this. Out came some spare shoelaces; they were red – just the colour I wanted (how convenient) – and the trusty hole-punch. Then we took it in turns to make holes around the opening to the boxes to make all the lace-holes. Some were more successful than others, but it didn't matter – it didn't have to be perfect. Once we had enough holes, my daughter threaded the laces in-and-out, in-and-out then she added a few details with a black felt-tip pen. And my shoes were ready. We kept them on our proper shoe-shelves for ages afterwards. I *loved* my magic shoes.

They've been inspired by something decorative or practical they've recently seen or touched:
It could be something on the TV, in a shop, in a book or magazine, a museum or something on display at home. I remember when my son first started making lightsabers – he was probably about four years old. He'd just seen *Star Wars IV, A New Hope* for the first time, and one of his friends had been bought a plastic lightsaber from a toy shop, so he'd had a go on a 'real' one. When I'd finished a roll of wrapping paper, and the empty cardboard tube was left over, he immediately

saw it for what it was, or had the potential to be. I remember him saying, 'If only this was green like Luke Skywalker's lightsaber.' Well, of course I jumped at his call-to-craft, and explained that we could probably make it green, and turn it into a pretty cool lightsaber ourselves. He said no initially (which is very him), but in the end it was he who asked me if he could actually make the tube into a proper lightsaber. So we set up a little craft-making area on the kitchen table – newspaper down for spills, green paint with loads of green glitter (and a bit of PVA) in it for him to mix into it. He told me he wanted the handle to be black, so we drew a little pencil line to mark where the green would stop. He had a great time painting the tube and in the end he abandoned the brush we'd given him altogether and used his whole hand to smooth the glittery paint all over the tube. My son has always been paint-averse, so to see him getting so messy and so happily absorbed in this making activity made me very happy indeed. We used black felt-tip pen to colour the handle bit and he drew on the buttons. Of course the lightsaber didn't last forever, but then neither did his friend's shop-bought one. And this has become a kind of classic thing to make in our house now. Three years on, my children both frequently ask to make lightsabers and become Padawans for an hour or so.

They know it means 'together time' with a trusted and often well-known grown up:
This is how crafting should really work; traditionally, it was always an elder who passed on the expertise to the young apprentice. When my son was at nursery he came home very sad one day. I really couldn't get him to tell me what had been going on and he seemed so withdrawn. He'd brought home with him a cube-shaped empty tissue box (everyone else had done some junk-modelling with boxes but he couldn't decide what to make with his). I suggested we tried to make

it into a Wall-E (he was a huge fan of this character at the time) as it was the perfect shape for it. He agreed it would make a good Wall-E, and through the making of something together, sticking and painting and so on we had a lovely, natural chat about lots of stuff, and I eventually got to the bottom of the trouble at school. It was positively therapeutic – and his mood had totally lifted by the end of our little crafty together time. Of course, it's not always therapy, but if children know they're going to get you staying and being with them, giving them your attention for a bit of time, it can be a most appealing prospect.

They've spotted some lovely resources and materials they want to 'get their hands on':
One December day I set up a craft opportunity while my children were playing independently, and when they spotted the gorgeous things set out for them to make tree-cone decorations, they couldn't wait to get stuck in. Okay, so on this occasion I *had* put out sugar jelly-sweets, gold paper doilies and pieces of glittery ribbon, so I knew I was onto a winner, but children are drawn to many materials (even non-shiny items), especially if they are attractively and temptingly left out.

They've been shown something handmade and they want to try to make their own:
When I showed my little museum-session children the tickle-bird (actually a mini-feather-duster) I'd made earlier and had taught them a song to help use it, they were all super-keen to make their own versions. This goes for most things I've made an example of beforehand – from giant snowflakes and lanterns to shadow-puppets, badges and bracelets. Of course, you do have to actually find the time to make the thing beforehand, but if it's a simple enough craft for a

little one then it really should only take you a matter of minutes. Alternatively, you could find a picture of the thing you were thinking of. Either way, it can be a really powerful way to awaken a young child's call-to-craft.

They might want to make a present or a card for someone:
This can be a real incentive; children as young as two can hear the call-to-craft when it's to make a gift for granny or a birthday card for mummy. In my museum sessions, and at home, it's just so wonderful hearing the little design features children think up especially for the receiver of the gift or card. 'Oh yes, Papa likes motorbikes, so I'll choose that sticker for him' or 'Nan's favourite colour is blue, so I'm going to use that nice blue fabric there.'

Whatever their reason for wanting to take part in a craft session or, as I call them, make and take activities, we can harness this enthusiasm. It will help give momentum and purpose to any project. And perhaps most importantly, the whole process of making will be positive and fun.

What to make

In my craft sessions at the museum we always take our inspiration for our make and takes from our collection. At home, I try not to look at too many images of beautiful or clever things on Pinterest and the like; I know how unsuitable, unachievable or joyless they can be to actually try at home with small children.

As one mum writes, 'As much as I love Pinterest . . . it perpetuates the notion that parents must do everything perfectly and be the best at everything. I am guilted into thinking we should [. . .] make our own finger paints and sew pillowcase dresses. No. No. No.'

There are specialised pinboards now, where tried-and-tested ideas for making things have been pinned by people who actually know what they're talking about, and the websites from which the images come usually give brilliant and child-friendly instructions. Try *Kid Blogger Network Activities and Crafts board* at www.pinterest. com/playdrmom/kid-blogger-network-activities-crafts/ if you're not one to feel overwhelmed; there is an awful lot out there, even for me – who loves a bit of mess and making.

When it comes to actually deciding what to make, it may sound obvious, but if we are using the internet or other media for inspiration we should always look hard at the practicalities behind the glossy images of those super-cool things. If they look too good to be true, they probably are. Always choose things which have super-simple techniques and that use materials you have around the house or that can easily be obtained, or substituted if need be. Above all, choose things that you are interested in making. If you think it's a pretty lame idea, then chances are it won't work out too well.

There are so many sources of ideas for making stuff with our children. We needn't be chained to the computer to find inspiration for crafting projects. Here are my top ten sources of inspiration:

1. The seasons
2. Things you made when young
3. Ideas from your child
4. Special days and occasions
5. Needs (of your children, your home, yourself)
6. Picture books
7. TV and movies
8. Your child at play
9. Family outings and walks
10. Interesting found objects and packaging

How to lead make and take sessions

We really don't need to be professional craftspeople to make craft part of our young child's occasional play. We just need an idea of what to make, a reason for making something (even if it is because we want to have a bit of fun with our children), some space, everyday materials and a little time for preparation and to do the activity itself, then we can tap into our children's natural imagination and capability of finding pleasure in a challenge to make it irresistible for them to engage in some form of making activity and be inspired by the world of craft.

Try going to an organised family craft drop-in activity if you are unsure about how to start doing craft at home. You can see how your little one likes to go about their making and you can dip your toe into crafty waters without having to buy loads of stuff or clear up any mess yourself. Parents tell me that they often go on to replicate the activities we do in the museum craft sessions back at home, and that they feel more confident about helping their little one with something similar at another time after they've attended a few such group sessions.

Here are my top tips for setting up successful make and take activities at home:

☆ Make space in your home for a go-to making area – for little ones it can be the floor, of course. Just make sure that when you set up for a crafting session you cover the surface with something tough and that you don't mind it getting dirty. This will invite them in, and keep the mess contained. Not all craft activities involve glitter, but many of them are a little messy.

☆ Time it right. If your little one is tired, hungry or really needs to be out and about running around, then this is not the best time to embark on or persevere with a craft project, however simple it is. Leave it till another time.

☆ This might sound obvious, but always make sure you and your child are wearing appropriate clothing. Not all craft is messy, but it's such a shame if you feel you have to curtail their wild-but-happy attempts at stirring or sticking because you're worried about them getting a bit of cookie-dough or glue on their clothes.

☆ Planning and preparation is required. From cutting suitable lengths of ribbon or getting out all the bowls, spoons and ingredients for those biscuits, to cutting up small bits of tissue paper. Whatever you can do beforehand to enable your little one to jump in right to the actual *making* part of craft or baking, the better. They'll be tempted in to the activity by those attractively set-out, intriguing, ready-to-use materials too, but will lose interest if they have to wait while the grown ups run around fetching and prepping things.

☆ As with traditional crafts, where the elders pass on their expertise by demonstrating to the apprentices, crafting with children is all about staying around, not merely supervising, but by being a kind of tutor. By demonstrating some of the techniques used in the particular craft, or by making one of your own alongside, help them make theirs when they need a hand; now's not the time to try and make your own batch of greetings cards or decorative cupcakes though. First and foremost, you're in the role of expert/teacher – but it is the most gentle and informal form of teaching I know.

☆ Make and takes are definitely stay and play activities, which means that they are *shared* adult and child experiences, and as such are great opportunities for some together-time. (See more about the benefits of stay and play activities on page 216.)

☆ You don't have to have any great skill in a particular craft, it's more important to think about how to get a really simple technique across to your little one, to help them achieve the decoration or shape or feature they want, in an accessible and fun way. If you can't think how they might manage it, even with a bit of adult help, then it's probably better to think of something simpler to do.

☆ You need to consider how to tap into a little one's favoured learning styles (which you'll quickly find out if you don't already know it). Maybe your child is a visual learner – in which case they'll want you to *show* them how to make something. Maybe they're a tactile learner and they'll want to get their *hands* on all the stuff straight away. Maybe they're an auditory learner and want you to *tell* them how to make it. Try different ways of sharing techniques and methods, and see which work best for your child.

☆ The simpler the craft, the better time everyone will have participating in the activity. Of course you want your children to learn or develop some skills, but if it's too fiddly, too delicate, too heavy or too darn tricky for them to be able to even try the techniques, then it will put them off, and it will discourage you too. You know your child and their abilities – there's a fine line between something being a fun challenge and it being a frustratingly horrible experience. Stay on the side of *easy* whenever possible.

☆ The shorter the session, the sweeter it will be. Sometimes parents are surprised how little time it takes for their child to make something. It's okay; sometimes it really is that quick and simple – it doesn't make it less worthy because they haven't struggled over it for hours. If you want to stretch the activity, you can always encourage them to look at it again, and see how they could make it bigger, or fuller, or better, or whatever is appropriate. Just be careful what you wish for though – you might get them covering the whole colourful thing in black paint if you ask them to add a finishing touch. Of course, some children do rush, and some children do lose interest. You know your child, and depending on their maturity and personality they'll approach crafting differently.

☆ Putting on some background music sometimes helps indicate to the little ones that this is time to stay and make – and you can have great fun finding relevant music to accompany craft sessions.

☆ Sometimes, having a few pictures to show ideas for how to make something is fun – and is a great way for little ones to begin to learn how to follow instructions.

☆ Occasionally, having an example or a picture of what you're actually aiming to make close at hand is a great way to inspire them. Of course they will want to put their own spin on it – and that should be encouraged.

☆ Make it fun! Tell them the techniques for the craft so that they appeal to their playful nature – from tickling the flour to sprinkling sequins, to counting to ten when sticking something on with glue, to making up little phrases or rhymes to help with certain techniques. For example, if they are working with small balls of scrunched-up colourful tissue paper, perhaps sticking them on something for decoration, you could teach them a little rhyme like 'Scrunch and stick, scrunch and stick, pick another colour and scrunch and stick'.

☆ If you have more than one child, a baby as well as a toddler, say, you might want to use the baby's nap times to do a little simple craft with the older one. Crafting with an older sibling with baby on one's lap is possible, though, and works out okay as long as the baby has some part to play in the making – perhaps enjoying the sensory experience of an age-appropriate material like a piece of ribbon, or crunchy cellophane, or a piece of tissue paper to rip up, etc. They will definitely want to be a part of the activity; you just have to offer them something to explore rather than make.

☆ Always allow for your child's ideas to be an important part of the design of the article. Let them choose colours, the final touches or the style of it, for example. Crafting-by-rote is not going to work with most little ones – they are the most imaginative and creative people on the planet, remember, so while they'll want to make something *like* the thing you showed or described to them to a certain extent, they'll definitely want to make it in their way, with their own twist; their creative juices will skyrocket as a result of you allowing them to do so.

☆ Celebrate what they've made by displaying it (just for a little while, anyway) – or by giving it as a gift to someone. I honestly don't know anyone who won't be deeply touched to receive a handmade something if the person who made it is under five. Heart-strings plucked, anyone?

Here are some tried-and-tested make and takes we've had fun with at home. Of course you can adapt them according to the age of your child, their specific interests and abilities, their dexterity, their maturity level, their call-to-craft moments and whatever materials you can get hold of easily, but I hope they give you some ideas for getting started, and really *enjoying* crafting and baking with your little one.

The seasons

It's spring; let's make blossom branches

Materials:

☆ A few small, leafless, windfall branches

☆ A hand-sized piece of hard polystyrene packing or a small flowerpot containing damp sand or soil

☆ A large sheet of tissue paper in pink, white or light green

☆ A glue stick

What you'll need to prep:

☆ Stick the bottoms of the branches into the polystyrene or pot of sand so they stay upright without being held.

☆ Cut the tissue paper into pieces about 2cm x 2cm and put them in a shallow container.

☆ Have the glue stick at the ready.

Optional: Show your little one a photo of a tree in blossom to inspire their craft, or if it's a nice spring day, make this outside near some trees in bloom.

How to make blossom branches:

☆ Let your child choose a tissue-paper piece and wipe the glue stick across it so it's sticky.

☆ Show them how to pincer grip the sticky tissue-paper piece around part of a branch, crushing it slightly so it looks like blossom.

☆ They should hold it there for a count of five before letting go; perhaps with a 'Ta Dah!'

☆ Continue with this until the branches have transformed from winter into spring.

☆ Display in a vase, or tie with a piece of ribbon to give as a spring gift.

Let's make a sun-catcher

Materials:

☆ A couple of small sheets of cellophane in at least two colours, or a handful of colourful cellophane sweet wrappers

☆ A paper plate

☆ A piece of sticky-backed plastic about the size of the paper plate

What you'll need to prep:

☆ Cut the cellophane into small pieces, none bigger than 2cm across, and place in a shallow container.

☆ Use the paper plate as a template. Lay it on the backing of the sticky-backed plastic, draw around it then cut along the line to create a circle of plastic the same size as the plate.

☆ Cut away the centre of the plate using scissors so you're just left with its fluted rim; like a circular picture frame.

☆ Remove the backing of the plastic and fix the clear film to the *underside* of the plate, pressing it firmly to the back of the rim so you've got a kind of window (albeit sticky). The underside doesn't have to look neat at all.

Optional: look at a photo or two of some stained glass with your child to get them thinking about translucency and sunlight.

How to make a sun-catcher:

☆ Lay the paper plate window sticky-side up on a flat surface.

☆ Let your child choose a cellophane piece and press it down onto the sticky window.

☆ Continue with this process, letting them choose different-coloured pieces of cellophane, until the window is totally covered with beautiful jewel-like colours.

☆ Try saying 'Pick and stick, pick and stick' to get a little rhythm going with this bit. Show them how to hold the window up to the light to see how the light shines through the cellophane.

☆ If they wish, they can cover the rim of the plate with cellophane too (a glue stick will work for this), or decorate it with crayons.

☆ Display the sun-catcher by attaching it, with a little Blu-tack, to any windowpane likely to catch some spring sunshine.

It's summer; let's make meadow bangles

Materials:

☆ A selection of summer meadow nature; daisies, grass, fallen petals, buttercups and clover

☆ Some wide masking (painters') tape

☆ You can do this craft sitting on your back lawn or in a meadow, of course – just remember that masking tape.

What you'll need to prep:

☆ Simply tear off a length of masking tape and wrap it loosely around your child's wrist like a bangle; maybe make one for yourself too. The important thing to remember here is that the tape should be sticky-side out.

How to make meadow bangles:

☆ Show your child how use their pincer grip to gently pick a daisy, a piece of grass, a fallen petal or a leaf.

☆ Demonstrate how to carefully transfer petals and leaves to the bangle by pressing them carefully but firmly with your fingers, or the palm of your hand, onto the sticky band of tape.

☆ Encourage them to keep turning their bangle as they stick so that every bit is covered.

☆ You could sing some flowery songs while you work – like *Daisy, Daisy* or *Ring-a-ring o' Roses.*

☆ The bangles' beauty is ephemeral, so enjoy them while they epitomise the nature of a summer meadow – as fresh as a daisy.

Let's make fresh fruit ice lollies

Materials:

☆ An ice-lolly-making tray

☆ A small selection of summer fruit – raspberries, strawberries, blueberries, grapes or cubed melon (whichever fruit your little one loves)

☆ A favourite fruit juice

☆ A small jug

☆ A tea tray

What you'll need to prep:

☆ Prep the fruit by washing it and chopping up anything that's larger than bite-size. Put enough fruit for about 3 or 4 pieces per lolly into a shallow container.

☆ Put the ice-lolly-making tray on the small tea tray, to catch any spills, and on a flat surface.

How to make fresh fruit ice lollies:

☆ Each lolly needs some fruit. So let your child divvy it out fairly, between the moulds, just as they like. You could get a little rhythm going here by saying something like, 'One, two; some fruit for you. Three, four; have some more.'

☆ Then fill (and refill if necessary) the small jug with the juice, letting your child practise their pouring by filling each mould up to the top as best they can.

☆ Let them place the lids gently on top.

☆ Check you have a free spot for the lollies before you attempt to transfer them to the freezer! Then freeze the lollies overnight, and prepare yourself for squeals of excitement when you announce that it's time to cool down with one of *their* fruity ice lollies.

☆ Run the moulds under a hot tap for a few seconds to free the lollies with ease.

It's autumn; let's make a fallen-leaf garland

Materials:

☆ About twenty newly fallen, big, interesting and colourful autumn leaves gathered when out and about or from your garden

☆ Some really cheap moisturising cream

☆ A plastic embroidery needle

☆ About 1.5m of embroidery thread (in an autumnal shade, if possible)

What you'll need to prep:

☆ This might sound a bit crazy, but the first thing you need to do is to moisturise the leaves. Your little one may want to help you with this but try to get a few done in advance. You could even do this a few days before making your garland as the hand-cream will keep the leaves supple for ages.

☆ Arrange the moisturised leaves invitingly on the floor, or on a tray, to make selecting them tempting to your child.

☆ Thread the plastic needle with the embroidery thread.

☆ Attach the other end of the thread to the leg of a table or a door handle to stop any leaves being threaded too far and slipping off the end.

How to make a fallen-leaf garland:

☆ Let your child choose a leaf.

☆ Push the threaded needle in and back out of this leaf to make a big stitch in its centre – too near the edge and the thread will split the leaf.

☆ Once the leaf is threaded on, keep hold of the end with the needle and pull the thread taut.

☆ Let your child pull the leaf *gently* along the thread to the far end.

☆ Repeat this process until all the leaves are on the thread with a little gap in between each one.

☆ You can make this very playful by imagining the leaves are like trains on a track – with train noises and all. Toot-toot!

☆ Your garland should last for weeks – hang it by both ends wherever you need a pop of autumn colour.

Let's make a spiced apple warmer

Materials:

☆ Apple juice (any variety, but cloudy, pressed juice tastes most like apple pie)

☆ Honey

☆ Cinnamon powder

☆ Hot water from the kettle

☆ A small jug

☆ A cup

☆ A teaspoon

☆ A cinnamon stick (optional)

What you'll need to prep:

☆ Set out all the ingredients and equipment on a low table or bench.

☆ Half-fill the small jug with apple juice.

How to make a spiced apple warmer:

☆ Let your child measure out 1 teaspoon of honey from the jar and drip it into their cup. This may take some time . . .

☆ Then, showing them the pincer grip, allow them to add a pinch of cinnamon to the honey.

☆ Let your child pour the juice from the jug to half-fill their cup.

☆ Pour a little hot water (but not boiling) from the kettle into their cup; it should make the drink warm but not hot.

☆ Let them stir everything together with the teaspoon or a cinnamon stick, if you have one. You could help them keep their stirring steady by saying together 'Stir, stir, stir and stop. Stir, stir, stir and stop.'

This delicious warm drink is autumn in a cup, and will help soothe a sore throat.

It's winter; let's make everlasting snowballs

Materials:

☆ White poster paint
☆ Silver glitter
☆ PVA glue
☆ Water
☆ A4 paper (one sheet makes one snowball)
☆ An old washing-up bowl or similar
☆ White scrap (or kitchen) paper

What you'll need to prep:

☆ Set everything up where you don't mind things getting a bit messy; maybe put some newspaper on the floor or on your low table too.

☆ Lay out some white kitchen paper on a large tray where you can put the finished snowballs to dry.

☆ Prepare a bowl or sink of soapy water for you and your child to wash your hands after you've finished making your snowballs.

☆ Mix a cup of white poster paint, a good sprinkling of silver glitter, a cup of PVA glue and half a cup of water in an old washing-up-sized bowl and place on your work surface.

How to make the everlasting snowballs:

☆ Show your child how to take one sheet of white A4 paper and soak it in the glittery paint and glue mixture for a count of ten.

☆ Then lift the soggy paper out of the paint and glue and, keeping it over the bowl, show your little one how to scrunch it and squish it into a snowball shape with your hands – squeezing out all the excess liquid back into the bowl.

☆ Put the finished snowball on the kitchen paper to dry.

☆ Now let your little one have a try. Remember to let the paper soak for a count of ten, then help them to squash and squish it into a snowball by saying 'SQUEEEEZE.'

☆ Allow the snowballs to dry on the white paper. They might stick to the paper a bit, but as it's white it shouldn't show.

☆ Once dry, the snowballs can be used for a game of inside target practice – young children will love to throw them into a box, basket or even into a big woolly hat. Lots of snowball fun, without any melting.

Let's make magic icicles

Materials:

☆ Transparent, rigid, thin plastic (raid your recycling box for soft-fruit containers and the like)

☆ PVA glue

☆ Glue brush

☆ Silver glitter

☆ A hole punch

☆ White cotton thread

What you'll need to prep:

☆ Set everything up somewhere you don't mind things getting a bit messy; maybe put some newspaper out on the table where you'll be working.

☆ Lay out some newspaper on a large tray where the finished icicles can dry.

☆ Cut the transparent packaging into manageable, flat-ish pieces like icicles – any size and shape you like, making sure there are no sharp corners.

☆ Set out the glue in a shallow container with a small glue brush.

☆ Sprinkle plenty of silver glitter onto the lid of an ice-cream tub or something similar.

☆ Have the hole punch and cotton thread to hand.

Optional: show your child some images of real icicles, or take a look at some if it's cold enough where you are.

How to make magic icicles:

☆ Let your child help with punching a hole in the top of an icicle. Then show your little one how to apply glue in patterns to just one side of the plastic, using the small brush.

☆ Let them press the gluey side of the plastic into the lid of silver glitter, hold it there for a count of three, then lift it off with a 'Ta Dah!'; the glue patterns should be totally covered in glitter.

☆ Place the icicle, glitter-side up, on the tray to dry.

☆ Repeat this process until your child has made as many icicles as they like, or until you've run out of plastic. Encourage them to make different patterns with the glue for each icicle.

☆ When the glittery ice sheets are dry, thread a doubled length of white cotton through each hole and pass the two ends through the loop. Knot the ends of the thread together.

☆ To display, hang the glittery icicles from the branches of an inside plant, or near a window, where you can watch them magically spin and twinkle.

Things you made when young

Let's make paper snowflakes

The classic fold-and-snip method is really too tricky for little hands. Try this toddler-friendly way to make beautiful paper-plate snowflakes instead.

Materials:

☆ White or silver paper doilies

☆ Children's scissors

☆ A white paper plate

☆ Some silver glitter or sequins

☆ Scissors (optional)

☆ A glue stick

What you'll need to prep:

☆ Set out the paper doily along with the scissors.

☆ Have the paper plate and glue stick close to hand, as well as a small shallow container of a little glitter or, even better, a glitter shaker.

Optional: show your child some images of snowflakes under the microscope; so amazing they'll definitely be impressed and inspired.

How to make a giant snowflake:

☆ Let your little one loose with their scissors to cut up the doily to look like a snowflake. It doesn't matter if they end up with lots of separate bits. If scissors are not appropriate for them, let them tear the doily into shapes and strips.

☆ You could sing this little song together while they snip or rip,

One little snowflake glistening bright ♫
Swirling and twirling, making the world white

Two little snowflakes glistening bright
Swirling and twirling, making the world white . . .

[continue to ten little snowflakes]

☆ When your child has finished cutting, put all the doily pieces to one side while they wipe glue over the front of the paper plate.

☆ Now they can add the doily pieces, just as they like, to make it look like a snowflake.

☆ Show your little one the pincer grip to pinch a bit of glitter or some sequins and then sprinkle them over the snowflake to cover any uncovered gluey areas, and to add a little sparkle.

☆ Display it on a wall using a little Blu-tack, or attach a stick to the back of the plate with some strong tape; your little one can then hold it while they dance around being a swirling snowflake.

Let's make Chinese lanterns

Another classic craft activity here; most people remember making these delightful paper lanterns when they were little. Why not make some to celebrate Chinese New Year? Use a red light ideally; the colour red is found everywhere during Chinese New Year because it symbolises good fortune and joy.

Materials:

☆ A4 coloured paper

☆ Scissors

☆ A pencil

☆ Some sticky tape

☆ Sequins, shiny tape or stickers to decorate the lanterns

☆ A back bike light (the red one) for each lantern

What you'll need to prep:

☆ Fold the paper in half lengthwise.

☆ With the pencil, draw guide lines – about 1cm apart – running from the folded seam to about 5cm from the other edge.

☆ Set out the scissors, sequins or stickers and shiny tape.

How to make a Chinese lantern:

☆ Let your child use their scissors to snip along the guide lines.

☆ Unfold the paper and bend it width-wise to form the lantern shape. Secure the join with some sticky tape.

☆ Let your little one decorate the lantern with sequins, shiny tape or stickers, just as they like.

☆ Display by placing the lantern on a flat surface and pop the red bike light inside. Turn down the other lights and enjoy the magical red glow of your Chinese lantern.

Ideas from your child

Let's make scary skittles

We took care of some silly night-time monster-worries by making and then knocking down these scary skittles.

Materials:

☆ 6–10 large plastic water or soft drinks bottles rescued from the recycling (we used green bottles for extra spookiness)
☆ Coloured paper
☆ Googly eyes
☆ A dark-coloured crayon or felt-tip pen
☆ A glue stick

What you'll need to prep:

☆ Remove the labels from the bottles.
☆ Pour a couple of inches of water into each bottle (for extra wobble when hit), then screw the lids on tightly.
☆ Set out the coloured paper and googly eyes.

How to make a set of scary skittles:

☆ Show your child how to tear the paper to make crazy monster-ish shapes. You could make a few for each bottle.
☆ Let your little one stick on the googly eyes just as they like. Some monsters will definitely have one eye, some more than two.

☆ Your child might like to give their monsters some mouths using a felt-tip pen or crayon.

☆ You could ask your child to make up a different monster noise for each one.

☆ Show your little one how to wipe glue onto the back of their monsters.

☆ Then they should stick the paper shapes to the outside of the bottles by pressing them firmly with the palm of their hand.

☆ When every bottle has at least one monster on it, you can set it up for a game of scary skittles. You could use the traditional formation (1-2-3) if you have six skittles. Use beanbags or soft small balls to take those monsters down.

Let's make a play scene

Both my children love playing imaginatively with small toy figures. We've made lots of different play scenes over the years – from a dolls' house, a swimming pool and stables, to a countryside scene, a cityscape and a hospital. If your little one loves small world play, they might like the idea of making an actual place for their toy characters to visit and have adventures. The secret of success with this craft project is to keep it very, very simple – and wait till your little one *asks* to make a school for their Sylvanian Family rabbits, or a landscape for their toy dinosaurs to wander around in.

Materials:

☆ A cardboard box no smaller than a shoebox, but as big as you like

☆ A pencil

☆ Collage bits and bobs; tissue paper, wrapping paper, foil, shredded paper, cotton wool, fabric scraps

☆ Scissors

☆ Glue

☆ Sticky tape

☆ Poster paints with a little PVA mixed in (optional)

What you'll need to prep:

☆ Choose your box and prep it accordingly. If it's a kind of diorama, dismantle it so it makes a backdrop and sides or, if it's to be the inside of a building, make sure it's got at least one side open for easy access; you may have to remove a few of the box's flaps.

☆ Have the collage bits and bobs close to hand along with scissors, sticky tape and a pencil.

☆ Pour a little PVA into a small pot with a glue brush or spatula nearby.

☆ If using paint, choose just a couple of appropriate colours and put them into small containers. Mix the paint with a little PVA to stop the paint peeling off. Have ready a chunky paintbrush for each colour.

How to make a play scene:

☆ Have your child bring the toy figures who will be interacting with the play scene to the making area, so they're part of the whole thing.

☆ Chat with your child about what features they'd like the scene to have. Keep the list as short and simple as possible.

☆ Start by making the background. Maybe it's an outside scene, so think sky and ground. Maybe it's an internal space, so think about how the walls, ceiling and floor might look.

☆ Help your child paint the background inside the box just as they like, or cover it in decorative, colourful paper. If covering the inside surfaces with paper, use the outside surfaces of the box as templates; draw around them on the paper, then cut along the lines – then they should be the right size. Let your child help with all the cutting and sticking.

☆ Once the background is done, spend a little time adding a few finishing features; maybe clouds of cotton wool and a yellow paper sun, some green paper shreds glued on as grass, and some pebbles or sticks if it's an outdoor scene. Or if it is indoors, stick a foil window to one of the walls, or a fabric blind, curtains or a rug. To make this playful let your little one consult with their toy figures about what they need, or how they would like it to look. And keep it simple.

☆ Once everything is dry the figures can move in and explore their new world.

Special days and occasions

Let's make a greetings card

Whether you are wishing somebody to get better, happy birthday, or saying thank you, there aren't many occasions when giving a card is inappropriate. I started making cards with my two children when they were about three years old – it's always a really good excuse to get out some lovely crafty things and let them whip up something brilliant for someone. Young children are never short of ideas.

Materials:
☆ Good-quality A4 card in a variety of colours
☆ An envelope that fits the card when it's folded in half
☆ A box of old greetings cards; don't put anything in there that's too special or poignant to cut up
☆ A pencil
☆ Scissors
☆ A glue stick

Other optional materials:
☆ PVA with glitter sprinkled on top
☆ A glue brush

☆ Felt-tip pens
☆ Stickers
☆ Sequins
☆ Letter stencils (optional)

What you'll need to prep:

☆ Make a card-creation station; invitingly set out your materials and equipment on a low table or floor so your little one can access them.

How to make a greetings card:

☆ Decide who you are making the card for, and why.
☆ Let your little one choose the colour for the card itself – do they know their friend or auntie's favourite colour?
☆ Help your child to fold the card in half and decide where the fold should be. To the left? Or along the top?
☆ Once this has been decided, let them browse through the old card collection and choose motifs and bits of design from a few cards to feature on theirs.
☆ Once these have been selected, draw a pencil line around the particular bit of the card they wish to use and let them cut out the desired sections. You may need to help with this if they are finding it a bit hard; share it out if you have more than one pair of scissors.
☆ Let your little one arrange the cutouts just as they like – you'll be impressed by their reasoning and decisions about this.
☆ Then let them wipe the back of each cutout with the glue stick and press it firmly down just where they like, counting to five then letting go with a 'Ta Dah'!
☆ Final touches are needed now; let them add stickers or sequins or a bit of gluey glitter just where they like.
☆ Let the card dry before writing the message inside it. Your little one will be very proud to give their uniquely designed card to that special someone.

Let's celebrate Valentine's Day

Try making a hearts-and-hugs necklace each and then exchanging them as a little gift to each other. They're incredibly easy to make and, even better, they're edible.

Materials (per necklace):

☆ Six small, healthy, baked pretzel snacks (the hearts)

☆ Six healthy, looped cereal, potato rings or corn rings (the hugs)

☆ About 90cm of thin ribbon (plasticised paper or fabric)

☆ A piece of sticky tape

What you'll need to prep:

☆ Put the loops and pretzel crackers in a clean little bowl.

☆ Tape one end of the ribbon to the far side of a low, clean table to anchor it while the threading takes place.

How to make a hearts-and-hugs necklace:

☆ Make sure you and your little one have clean hands.

☆ Show your child how to take a pretzel and thread the ribbon through one of its holes. If they've done threading before they may be able to manage returning the ribbon through another hole in the pretzel, so the heart lies flat against the ribbon.

☆ Slide the pretzel cracker towards the taped end of the ribbon with a resounding 'MWAH' – well, it is a kiss.

☆ Then take a hoop (or loop) and thread it through the ribbon towards the pretzel. You could make up your own sound for a hug of course.

☆ Continue with this pattern – kiss and hug, kiss and hug – or whichever order your child wants the pretzels and hoops or loops.

☆ When finished threading, remove the sticky-taped end of the ribbon from the table and tie both ends securely with a knot.

☆ Swap necklaces, and then snack away for Valentine's Day.

Let's make a little lamp for Halloween

Even if you don't mark Halloween so much – it can be pretty scary for very young children, after all – this little lamp will evoke a slight spooky-house atmosphere after dark.

Materials (per lamp):

☆ A clean and dry jam jar

☆ Double-sided sticky tape

☆ A cotton wool ball

☆ 30cm of white or grey wool

☆ A small piece of black card or paper (about 5cm x 5cm)

☆ Scissors

☆ A battery-operated, or regular, tealight, or a front (white) bike light

What you'll need to prep:

☆ Remove the label from the jam jar and make sure the jar is clean and dry.

☆ Cut off about 20cm of double-sided sticky tape and wrap it top to bottom, sticky-side down, all around the outside of the jar, in a kind of swirl. It doesn't have to be neat or precise at all. Keep the backing on the other side of the tape – you don't want it sticky just yet.

☆ Set it out along with the ball of cotton wool, the black card, a pencil and some scissors.

☆ Prep the wool by cutting a few short lengths – each about 5cm long.

How to make a little lamp:

☆ First your child will need to make a small spider to live on the lamp. To do this, give them the black paper and ask them to draw their spider on it so it takes up most of the card.

☆ While you are cutting this out (good luck with all those legs!) your little one can tease out the cotton-wool ball so it looks like wispy bits of dusty cobweb. Show them how to do this using a pincer-grip and pulling the cotton wool gently away from the ball.

☆ When the spider is ready, offer it up to one end of the tape on the jar and peel away enough of the backing so the spider sticks to the tape. Now the whole spider's web can be revealed. Help your child peel away the rest of the tape's backing.

☆ Now finish the lamp by adding the cobweb. Show your child how to press little bits of wispy cotton wool and the other pieces of wool onto the tape, just as they like.

☆ To display, pop a bike light or tealight into the jar and put on a windowsill or mantelpiece.

Needs (of your children, home, or yourself)

Let's make dried petal pouches to help Mummy sleep

Materials:

☆ A tablespoon of dried lavender

☆ A tablespoon of dried rice or pulses, like lentils

☆ Some lightweight fabric

☆ A teaspoon

☆ An elastic band

☆ Two or three contrasting ribbons

What you'll need to prep:

☆ Cut the fabric, with pinking shears if it's prone to fraying, into a square of about 15cm x 15cm.

☆ Put the dried lavender petals and the pulses into separate small containers.

☆ Cut the ribbon into lengths of about 20cm each and put them in a container.

☆ Have the elastic band and teaspoon to hand.

How to make a dried petal pouch:

☆ Lay the square of fabric, patterned side down, on a flat surface.

☆ Let your little one help themselves to their petals and pulses, spooning them into the centre of the square. You could try singing a little song while you do this,

Lavender's blue, dilly, dilly, lavender's green, ♫
When I am king, dilly, dilly, you shall be queen.

☆ Help them gather up the corners and then all the edges of the fabric to make a pouch to enclose the scented filling.

☆ You should secure it with an elastic band, but let your child check it still smells fragrant through the material. Let them squish it a bit to release its perfume.

☆ Now, to cover up that unsightly elastic band; let your little one choose two or three pieces of ribbon to wrap around it. Help them secure the ribbons with a couple of knots.

☆ We've needed these in our clothes drawers to keep them smelling sweet, and I've used mine under my pillow as an aid to sleeping.

Let's make a shiny frame for this photograph

Materials:

☆ An empty tissue box

☆ A glue stick

☆ A sheet of shiny foil wrapping paper

☆ Scissors

What you'll need to prep:

☆ Dismantle the tissue box, then carefully cut away the top and bottom faces. These two pieces are going to form the front and back of the photo frame.

☆ Remove any plastic from the tissue-dispensing hole, and if it needs to be made a bit bigger to show off that photo, now's the time to adjust its size; carefully cut away to make the hole just slightly smaller than your photo.

☆ Prep the shiny foil wrapping paper – you'll need pieces about 5cm x 5cm.

How to make a decorative photo frame:

☆ Lay the front of the frame on a flat surface, shiny side down.

☆ Wipe the glue stick over about a third of the card's surface.

☆ Show your little one how to take a piece of the foil wrapping and pat it down, somewhere on the sticky part of the frame.

☆ Continue this process until the whole frame is covered in foil wrapping-paper pieces.

☆ Any pieces of foil wrapping that overhang either the hole or outer edge of the frame can be folded around to the back and stuck down with a bit of extra glue.

☆ When dry, put the photo in place and, lastly, attach the back of the frame with a little glue in the corners.

☆ Display on a wall with some Blu-tack, or make a little stand for it from the remaining tissue-box card.

Picture books

We have been inspired to do some making or baking by so many lovely children's books over the years. One of our favourite ever crafting sessions came after reading *Sharing a Shell* by Julia Donaldson. It's such a fun story, starring a hermit crab, a bristle worm and a sea anemone. It's full of glittery and shimmery rock-pool pictures and, after we'd read it for the hundredth time, the children were really keen to make their very own rock pools.

Let's make a paper-plate rock pool

Materials:

☆ A blue paper plate as the rock pool

☆ Shredded paper for seaweed

☆ A4 paper for pebbles

☆ Craft-foam shells, fish and sea creature stickers

☆ Pipe cleaner bristle worms

☆ Watercolour paints, plus brush and water pot

☆ Lots of silver glitter mixed with PVA glue

What you'll need to prep:

☆ Cut out some pebble shapes from the A4 paper.

☆ Put a little PVA into a small container and sprinkle generously with silver glitter.

☆ Have the watercolours close to hand along with a little brush and a small pot of water.

How to make a paper-plate rock pool:

☆ Imagine the paper plate as an empty pool of water.

☆ Ask your child what they think should go into the pool to make it like the one in the story *Sharing a Shell*.

☆ Let them choose from the materials to fill the pool – pebbles, seaweed, a bristle worm, and various sea creatures – then stick them onto the plate with the glittery glue.

☆ Chat about the story with your child while they choose and stick. Do they have a bristle worm like in the story? What about pebbles? What about a crab?

☆ Add some colour to the pebbles or the seaweed using the watercolours.

☆ Give everything a final flourish with the glittery glue and then let it dry.

☆ Display by sticking the rock-pool plate to a wall with a little Blu-tack, just like a souvenir plate from the seaside.

TV and movies

Let's make bug or butterfly wings

After seeing the movie *A Bug's Life,* my children were very keen to be bugs themselves. Here's a very easy craft to turn *your* little ones into beautiful bugs too.

Materials (per set of bug's wings):

☆ 2 x A4 sheets of thin craft foam in the same colour

☆ Chunky felt-tip pens (metallic pens look great, but they're not essential)

☆ Some neoprene shapes and offcuts

☆ Scissors

☆ Double-sided sticky tape or glue-dots

☆ 2 x paper clips per child

What you'll need to prep:

☆ Trim just two corners, top and bottom, of one craft-foam sheet to make a semi-oval; this is one of the bug's wing cases. Use this as a template to cut out the other foam sheet so that the two wing cases are symmetrical.

☆ Lay the wing covers next to each other, straight edges towards each other, on a flat surface ready for decorating.

☆ Set out the felt-tip pens.

☆ Cut some contrasting colours of craft foam (if you don't have any pre-cut shapes) into smaller pieces for decoration; wide stripes, big dots and other, randomly shaped offcuts look great too. Don't make anything too small as it will all get too fiddly to stick.

☆ Have the scissors and double-sided sticky tape (or glue-dots) to hand.

How to make bug or butterfly wings:

☆ Listen as your little one tells you about how they would like their bug-wing cases to look. If they've seen A Bug's Life they will have lots of ideas.

☆ Help them find long bits of foam for stripes, circles for dots – or any other shapes they like. You can layer up a few shapes to make very interesting wing-covers.

☆ As they begin their designing, help them stick their craft-foam dots, stripes and patterns on to the wing cases with double-sided sticky tape.

☆ Let them loose with the felt-tip pens if they like – to add spots, swirls or any other fine detail.

☆ When finished, simply fix each bug wing case to your child's clothing at the shoulder or neckline with the paper clips. A pair of deely-boppers as antennae would complete the look.

Let's make Strictly Come Dancing bangles

Strictly Come Dancing or SCD has been a firm TV favourite in our household since the children were really tiny. My daughter was inspired to make these during one of the shows but my son soon wanted his own bit of bling. Everyone on the show wears something sparkly round their wrists, and we still put our bangles on when it's time to watch the show.

Materials:

☆ An empty cardboard toilet roll tube

☆ Sparkly sticky tape

☆ Star stickers and metallic markers (optional)

☆ Scissors

What you'll need to prep:

☆ Cut the cardboard tube into two equal pieces to make two bangles.

☆ Set out the shiny tape invitingly (plus any other materials you're offering).

How to make SCD bangles:

☆ Let your child cover the cardboard tubes with strips of shiny tape at the edges or all over, just as they like (you may need to help cut the tape).

☆ Fill in any gaps left by the tape with metallic felt-tips and star stickers.

☆ If you'd like to have some too, snip through each bangle to make cuffs that can slip on and off easily.

☆ Pop them on, and 'Keep Dancing!'

Your child at play

If your children are Formula 1 fans, or even if they just love playing with cars and tracks, here's how they can make their own champion's trophy at home.

Let's make a trophy to treasure

Grand Prix trophies are brilliantly designed for recreating at home. They are usually silver, so aluminium foil (a kitchen-drawer staple) is perfect.

Materials

☆ A small plastic circular container – from your recycling box

☆ A thin piece of card – from a cereal box or a paper plate

☆ Some aluminium foil

☆ Some sticky tape

☆ Scissors

☆ Pencil

What you'll need to prep:

☆ Cut a slit along the centre of the bottom of the circular tub.

☆ Set out the card, pencil and a sheet of foil.

☆ Have the sticky tape to hand.

Optional: show your little one some images of F1 trophies; the geometric and sculptural designs will definitely inspire them to make their own.

How to make a racing car trophy:

☆ First, let your child decide the main shape for their trophy – encourage them to keep it simple; they might choose a triangle, a circle, an arrow or a diamond, for example.

☆ Help them draw their shape, no bigger than A4, and then help them to cut it out.

☆ Work together to wrap the shape tightly in foil so it's all covered and looks very shiny and special.

☆ Then wrap the plastic tub in foil. This is going to be the base of the trophy. Using a pencil, find the slit in the tub beneath the foil, and push the point of the pencil through to reveal it again.

☆ Slot the shiny shape into the base and secure it underneath with some sticky tape if it looks a bit wobbly.

☆ The trophy can, of course, be displayed somewhere prominent, but not before it's been held aloft by the champion. Cue cheers!

Make your own play dough

I always use the same recipe for my children's play dough because I know it by heart, and it works every time. Of course, I vary its colour and its scent according to how they want to play with it, but the real beauty of this recipe is that it's very easy and enjoyable to make with a little one; it's a bit of a kitchen classic.

Materials:

☆ 2 cups flour

☆ 1 cup salt

☆ 1 tablespoon vegetable oil

☆ 2½ teaspoons cream of tartar

☆ 2 cups cold water

☆ A teaspoon and a tablespoon

☆ A saucepan

☆ A wooden spoon

☆ Plastic bag or container in which to store the play dough

☆ A few capfuls of food colouring

Optional: 5 drops of lavender oil or peppermint oil, two tablespoons of cocoa powder or cinnamon powder, or a good dose of glitter

What you'll need to prep:

☆ Set out all the ingredients and equipment.

How to make play dough:

☆ Let your little one help you measure out, into a medium saucepan, the quantities of flour, salt, vegetable oil, cream of tartar, water and cocoa or cinnamon (if using) and food colouring if you want it all the same colour. If not, wait to add the food colouring until after it's cooked; divide the dough into the number of colours you'd like, then add it by kneading it into the warm dough.

☆ Let your child help you mix the ingredients together until smooth.

☆ Cook the mixture, uncovered, over a low to medium heat for about 5 minutes. Stir constantly until the dough is the consistency of really lumpy mashed potatoes.

☆ Turn the heat right down and keep working the mixture until it forms a ball of dough.

☆ Remove the saucepan from the heat and tip the warm dough-ball onto a clean kitchen surface. Knead it for a minute or two to cool it down and to work up its elasticity. It will feel incredibly warm and lovely – as fresh dough should.

☆ Divide the dough into small portions if you want to add different smells, extra colours or glitter. Let your little one help work any extra things into the dough once it has cooled down a bit; it doesn't take long.

☆ The play dough will last a long time if you keep it in an airtight container. But it's always good to find an excuse to make a lovely new fresh batch.

Family outings, walks and holidays

Let's make bird-feeders

My children first made bird-feeders like these at a local Apple Day event. Here's a simplified version – perfect for tiny hands – that one can easily make at home.

Materials:

☆ A windfall apple

☆ An apple corer or sturdy screwdriver

☆ An apple peeler

☆ A handful of sunflower and pumpkin seeds

☆ A metre of garden twine

☆ A sturdy stick – about 12cm long (for a perch)

What you'll need to prep:

☆ Take the apple and roughly core it with a sturdy screwdriver or apple corer.

☆ Use the peeler to remove the skin in three strips around the apple – at the Equator, the Tropic of Cancer and the Tropic of Capricorn.

☆ Set out the other materials, putting the seeds into a shallow container.

How to make a bird-feeder:

☆ Let your child push sunflower seeds and pumpkin seeds into the peeled sections of the apple randomly or in a pattern. Show them how to push the seeds in halfway so the birds can easily get them. You could set up a little rhythm with this by saying, 'Pick and push, pick and push. Pick another seed and pick and push.'

☆ Help your child to fasten the smallish stick – the perch for a bird – to the garden twine, at its centre; wrap it round a few times and secure with a knot.

☆ Help them thread the other end of the twine through the bottom of the apple; it may need a little encouragement.

☆ Hang the bird-feeder as high as possible on a branch of a tree or hanging from a bird table. Make sure it is in a safe place for the birds – not too close to where cats might lurk, for example.

Found objects and packaging

We're always on the lookout for a bit of packaging, or an empty box or bottle to transform into something. I remember a shower-cream bottle being eyed-up for weeks before it was even empty. It was an EVE-in-waiting apparently, to go along with our Wall-E model. Here are a couple of other great things to make from found things and empty containers.

Let's make orange-peel boats

Materials:

☆ Large pieces of orange or clementine peel

☆ A few cocktail sticks

☆ A sheet of A4 paper

☆ Some crayons

☆ A pair of scissors

☆ A little Blu-tack or modelling clay

What you'll need to prep:

☆ Choose some of the largest pieces of peel to be the boats' hulls.

☆ Cut the A4 paper into small rectangles for the sails.

☆ Set out the crayons.

☆ Have the scissors, cocktail sticks and Blu-tack or modelling clay
   close to hand.

How to make orange-peel boats:

☆ Let your little one design patterns for the sails by letting them loose
   with the crayons. Both sides of the sail could be decorated.

☆ When the sails are ready, carefully push a cocktail stick in and out
   again to make a kind of big stitch in the sail.

☆ Push the sail up towards one end of the cocktail stick (the mast) and
   carefully push the other end through the very middle of the orange
   peel hull so you can just feel the point through the bottom.

☆ Let your child make the boat watertight by letting them press a small
   amount of Blu-tack or modelling clay around the base of the sail's mast
   inside the hull. This should make the sail a bit more stable too.

☆ When you've made a few boats, half-fill a washing-up bowl or a basin
   with water and carefully float the boats. Try blowing gently to put some
   wind in the sails.

Let's make a milk-bottle owl

Materials:

☆ An empty and clean plastic milk bottle – the type with a handle and
   scooped-out side

☆ Double-sided sticky tape

☆ A selection of craft foam, tissue paper and/or patterned wrapping paper

☆ A pair of googly eyes

☆ A few pebbles

What you'll need to prep:

☆ Cut up the craft foam, tissue paper and/or wrapping paper into small pieces about 4cm x 2cm and put them in a small shallow container.

☆ Cover the bottle in horizontal stripes of double-sided sticky tape, and peel off the backing so the owl is ready to get its feathers.

☆ Have the googly eyes to hand.

Optional: Show your little one some pictures or photographs of owls for feature familiarisation and inspiration.

How to make a milk-bottle owl:

☆ Pop a few small pebbles into the bottle so it won't get knocked over while your child is decorating it.

☆ Let your little one cover the whole thing in pieces of craft foam or paper feathers. You could set up a little rhythm here by saying, 'Pick and stick, pick and stick. Choose another feather and pick and stick.'

☆ You could add two larger pieces of paper or craft foam as wings. You'll need two semi-circles of foam or paper, or they could be teardrop shapes. When you're happy with your wings, put a bit of double-sided sticky-tape to the top of each and press them to the owl's sides.

☆ Leave the handle and the scooped-out bit behind the handle feather-free.

☆ When the owl is be-feathered (and be-winged) add some finishing touches; stick on a googly eye either side of the handle – in the scooped-out bit.

☆ Lastly, transform the handle into a beak by covering the front of it with a piece of foam or paper in a contrasting colour of your child's choosing. Help your little one to cut it into a beak shape (a long and pointy triangle works well) then put a little double-sided sticky-tape on the underside and press it firmly onto the front of the handle. You could practise your owl impressions here; HOO-HOO, or the classic TWIT TWOOO.

☆ To display, fill with a few more stones or some sand to make it into a doorstop. Or remove all the pebbles and pop a mini-torch inside. After dark, the torchlight will glow warmly from its big eyes; an owl night-light.

Stay and Play

'What do most Nobel Laureates, innovative entrepreneurs, artists and performers, well-adjusted children, happy couples and families, and the most successfully adapted mammals have in common? They play enthusiastically throughout their lives.'

Stuart Brown, Institute of Play

Permission to play

In the chapter Invitations to Play, I touched on the idea of how, as we reach adulthood, the amount of time we spend *playing* diminishes significantly. Recently, I read a fascinating article related to mental health about this very subject. It suggested that by the end of adolescence we have often exchanged the very notion of play for *work* and *responsibilities*, and if we do manage to glean any leisure time in our busy lives, we're more likely to zone-out in front of the TV or computer than engage in creative, brain-stimulating or physical play. Indeed, some adults believe that they have actually forgotten how to play all together. Adults in this category are not likely to think about their work as play, nor do they consider play as a respite from their work; they probably think of it as a luxury rather than a necessity – as something *just for kids*. But this article – aimed at people who believe they have really forgotten how to play – explained that taking the time to replenish yourself through play is one of the best things you can do for your career. It sighted some of the benefits as helping to keep you functional when under stress, refreshing your mind and body, encouraging teamwork, helping you see problems in new ways, triggering creativity and innovation, increasing energy and preventing burnout.

Finding the time and having the inclination to play with other adults at work or during our leisure time – giving ourselves permission to play, as it were – will, according to many psychologists, give us the opportunity to learn, to create, to feel challenged, to pass time, to calm and focus ourselves, to be a spectator watching others play, to be competitive, to banish loneliness and to experience the joy of play. Their view is that when we fully engage in some sort of play it's possible to experience feelings of delight, clarity, confidence, serenity, timelessness and motivation just as children do when *they're* in the full flow of play.

'Play is simultaneously a source of relaxation and stimulation for the brain and body. A sure (and fun) way to develop your imagination, creativity, problem-solving abilities and mental health is to play with your romantic partner, officemates, children, grandchildren and friends.'

Bernie DeKoven, *author and fun theorist*

Even if we are alive to the idea of *playing* per se – taking part in games, sports, craft or quiz nights with other adults, for example – we might still feel uncomfortable, or unfamiliar, with the idea of actually playing with children. And if we have fallen out of the habit of play altogether, it can be a bit of a harsh wake-up call if we find we are in charge of, or in the presence of, a child or two – the *experts* of play. If you've not had much exposure to children under five during your working day or in your domestic life up till now, you might feel absolutely daunted or, at the other end of the scale, rather over-excited by the prospect of staying and playing with little ones. But let's not wind the kids up just yet . . .

It might be a relief, if not a surprise, to hear how *little* Early Years teachers and nursery workers actually *play* with the children in their care. That is not to say that play doesn't happen, of course, it just means that they rely heavily on setting up lots of opportunities for children to be engaged with independent and free-play. This is how children of this age should be spending a large proportion of their days. We don't need to stay and play with our children all the time. We are not their peers, and we don't need to be their full-time play-mates. As I'm an advocate of play, people often make the mistake of thinking I play with my children all day long. Of course this is far from accurate. The majority of my time 'playing' with my children is, in fact, *facilitating* their play; setting things up, then supervising – with a bit of *scaffolding* or *project-managing* on the side.

As established in the chapter Invitations to Play, children find playful opportunity in almost everything around them, so, even if we think we have totally lost the ability to actually play ourselves, it is still possible to 'feed *their* fun', most of the time, by seizing on this wonderful characteristic of childhood. All we need do is recognise and provide environments in which children can find their flow, and then let *them* play, by offering 10-second set-ups or invitations to play; there are plenty of ideas for these on pages 46 and 86. In these scenarios we are not particularly required to play, as such – but rather to inspire and enable children's playtimes. This is a very rewarding role as it encourages independence and creativity in our children, and is especially useful if we aren't feeling particularly playful ourselves.

The art of play

Some people, however, are absolute naturals when it comes to play-ing with children. You probably remember the grown up who, when you were small, would always mesmerise you with a new trick, or another who would always be up for playing tea-party, or another who was happy to tell you a fabulous story or play a game of I-spy. When a baby arrives somewhere sociable there's always someone who won't be able to resist playing Peekaboo with them, or making silly faces. This urge to interact playfully with little ones is definitely instinctive in some grown ups. These are the people who *haven't* for-gotten how to play; they are the stars of stay and play and they're reaping all those psychological rewards of playing when they do so – even if they're unaware of it.

When nursery and Early Years teachers play with the children in their care they do so for a number of reasons. It might be to deliberately find out something about the children, or to motivate or excite them. It might be to quieten them down or to focus them, or it might be a way to develop a particular type of learning or skill. It's often much less spontaneous-seeming than, say, Granddad making everyone laugh with a hanky on his head, but actually it involves many of the same elements. Whether it's a funny game, a story told, a dramatic moment, a bit of role-play or a song sung, they're all ways to stay and play; to engage with young children for fun or learning – and sometimes both.

Stay and play

To engage in play – to stay and play – with young children is all about sharing the joy and power of play. It is supposed to be fun. But it can't happen on an even playing field; it is not, I believe, a *pure* play experience for us adults. For example, it is not about trying to play a sophisticated game that's way beyond the skill-set of the child with whom you're playing – that game of chess or strict offside rule in football will need to wait a few years. It is not about entering into a game with an intention of winning – in fact, competitive games are just one way to stay and play with young children and certainly need to be handled with care. It is not about giving yourself over as some kind of plaything to be hit and climbed and tortured. It is not about having to don a fake straw hat and attend a tea party as Mrs Nesbitt, like poor old Buzz Lightyear in *Toy Story*, if you're not into that kind of thing. It's not about teasing and winding-up the children to a wild frenzy or until *Noddy comes to cloddy* (a great phrase my mum used when things got out of hand, and someone got hurt). It is not about twirling a child round and round on a swing until they are about to vomit and then passing them back to their parent, thank you very much, person-who-will-remain-nameless.

So that everyone involved comes out the other end smiling, we need to stay in the role of grown up and make certain concessions when we stay and play with little ones.

We should, for example, always model the best characteristics of someone at play; like good sportsmanship, winning gracefully or losing calmly (if it's that kind of game). And we should always be generous with how the play pans out, how long it lasts, and bend or even change the rules according to the age and maturity of the child, or children, involved. We should keep in mind the rules of Improv by saying '*Yes*' as much as possible during our time playing with our little ones. If we keep saying, 'No, it won't work,' or 'That's impossible,' or 'Nope, we can't do that,' then it's not going to be much fun playing with us. We should try to take what play the child has created and add something to it by saying '*Yes* **and** . . . '

When we stay and play with a small child we need to be aware of the experience from their perspective. But it doesn't mean we can't still be our natural self; our most playful self. And even with a few concessions, we can still reap many of the benefits of play.

Why we should make time to stay and play

Saying to a child, *Okay, I will play that with you,* when they've asked so nicely or, dare I say it, even *suggesting* playing something with them, can't and needn't happen all the time. But it should happen sometimes, and even though we might internally groan at the prospect of playing yet another sub-standard game of Hide and Seek, most grown ups have to concede to never really regretting saying *yes* to playing with their children (or grandchildren or nieces and nephews). Here are a few of the benefits of making time, sometimes, to stay and play with our little ones.

For us grown ups, playing with our children means we can:

☆ be in the moment; phone off, and away from our emails, or the TV or newspaper
☆ enjoy spending time with our child
☆ be with them in their most natural state (of play)
☆ strengthen our bond with them
☆ not be in charge of transition – that is to say, the person who's saying it's time to do something, or be somewhere
☆ not be the provider – we are not the feeder or the nappy changer when we are playing
☆ see the child, or children, in a different way

☆ learn surprising things about them

☆ be a teacher, fostering the learning of all kinds of skills – including verbal and non-verbal communication, concepts, social and emotional literacy – in a gentle, fun and nurturing way

☆ be a role-model for social and emotional behaviour

☆ model imaginative and creative thinking

☆ experience their imaginative and creative thinking

☆ have a genuinely good time, and a laugh, with the little one

☆ be relieved of stress and get distracted from other worries

☆ be connected to the child, or children, and the world around us

Benefits of playing with an adult for young children might include the following:

☆ they are in the spotlight of a grown-up's attention – and for a great reason

☆ they might get to be the expert – they could teach you a game they've learned at nursery, for example

☆ they get to see you in a different way

☆ they see how you lose or win (if it's that kind of game)

☆ they learn new skills and vocabulary

☆ they learn social skills in the give and take of play

☆ their verbal communication and body language skills get a good workout

☆ they will learn about safety and danger

☆ they will learn about freedom and boundaries

☆ they will learn about cooperation and teamwork

☆ they get to show you their amazing imagination and creative thinking

☆ they will get to have fun with you, which they'll remember forever

How to stay and play

I asked parents of young children, via social media, to tell me about their early-childhood memories of grown ups who were keen to stay and play with them. It was great how many people could remember exactly who played with them and what they played. I heard about party games, sporty competitions, makeshift fun with packaging, and games when walking home from nursery. There were paper-craft sessions, simple card games and tricks, very dramatic stories told and times when they were allowed to give granddad a crazy hairdo. And, of course, there were the rough-and-tumble tussles and the 'classic' uncle-dressing-up-and-scaring-the-bejeebers-out-of-all-the-kids-by-chasing-them-round-the-garden type games. I think it's pretty amazing how these little pockets of time spent staying and playing with a grown up make such precious, powerful and lasting memories for so many people.

While some adults are more than capable and very willing to play with little ones, others are more reluctant. They seem uninterested, or they're always too busy or too daunted to consider it. Some are all too eager to play with the kids but tend to wind them up and over-excite them. So how exactly can we successfully stay and play with children? How can we 'get out alive' and without tears? And how come some grown ups are so good at it and even claim to enjoy it?

I have to admit to being one of those people who really, genuinely enjoys staying and playing with children. No, I don't do it all the time; I simply can't; I'm a busy parent for goodness sake, with rarely the chance to go to the toilet uninterrupted let alone be the in-house entertainer. But give me a choice between playing fun games with the kids or making small-talk with the grown ups at a party, say, and I'll be straight out to where the kids are at, and if they're up for it I'll definitely start up some game or other. I just think they are simply the best people to hang out with. I know not everyone feels this way, and you certainly don't have to feel as purely enthusiastic as I do to successfully stay and play with young children. But there are certain things you can do to become really good at it; enjoy it even.

Check before you play

The key to success, if you're at all worried that you might 'do it wrong', or that it will all end in tears, is to first do a super-quick test to think about the appropriateness of your, or the child's, idea. You can then appear to be totally spontaneous when you announce what the game or play is going to be, because this little thought-process only takes a few seconds. Honestly.

I've come up with *gazillions* of fun things to play with lots of different children in my time and grown ups are often amazed at how I apparently seem to know just what to play. It is no big secret; I actually don't always know exactly what the game is going to be (we'll often make it up as we go along) – but the children won't know this. What I *do* know is that the game will be appropriate, because I always use the little test before I suggest or agree to any stay or play. This is really all you need to consider beforehand, and then you can improvise the finer details along the way. The one thing you can rely on with little children is their absolute enthusiasm to play something, anything, with a grown up. As long as it's fun, it will be irresistible.

So, when considering what is appropriate to play with a little one or group of little ones, consider:

☆ the time of day
☆ the situation
☆ their clothes (say they're dressed up for a wedding, are you really planning on playing something so rough-and-tumble?)

☆ the time available

☆ the environment

☆ the materials and resources you've got to hand, if any

☆ the age and particular interests of the child or children concerned.

Then – whatever the game or play is, make it fun – that, after all, is what stay and play should be all about. Here are a few tips to make this time with little ones a roaring, or a quiet, success.

☆ Keep it simple – often games will need to be got into straightaway before a little one's interest wanes or the time to play runs out. Choose an activity that needs little or no preparation and don't spend too long finding equipment, resources and materials. Children can be employed to fetch a ball, or go ask to borrow a bunch of keys, but if the materials are too difficult to source quickly, think of something else to play.

☆ Many games don't need any equipment at all – just a bit of space. Check the environment is suitable for the game– are there good, safe places to hide close by for Hide and Seek, say, or is the ground suitable for lying down on for a game of Dead Lions?

☆ Try playing something you've enjoyed playing before (or that you remember playing when you were little) if this is a new thing for you – you'll soon have a range of go-to stay and plays that little ones will repeatedly request.

☆ Leave space, and be open to, the children's ideas to feed into the play or game; leave room for improvisation.

☆ Make the games' techniques or skills fun and playful.

☆ Remember, traditionally competitive games can be adapted so that they're not about winning or losing at all. You can ensure everybody wins, or that there is some common goal. Competition usually divides rather than unites, especially when children are very small.

☆ Acknowledge the end of the game in whatever way is appropriate – a fun 'formal' shake of hands, or a high-five, an elaborate bow and round of applause if it's a song/performance type game, or a dramatic 'The End!' at the end of a story or book-reading.

☆ Stay and play fun and games can last from just a couple of minutes to much, much longer. It all counts as quality playtime; nourishing and benefiting everyone's well-being.

☆ It's always good to give everyone a heads-up when the stay and play is coming to an end – for whatever reason – from it naturally finishing or time running out, to the food arriving at the cafe or it getting too dark to see the ball. You can give gentle signifiers that it's nearly time to finish the game so it's not too bumpy a stop – like, 'We've got time for three more rounds', or 'let's see if we can get to 10 points and then it's the end of the game', or 'this is the last scene', or 'let's sing about five more animals before we finish'; that kind of thing. Otherwise you can find you're stuck in a loop of stay and play for what seems like forever and no one will think of taking over because you'll be doing such a 'good job' of entertaining the kids.

☆ It's often useful to make sure you can say what might happen after the game has finished. Sometimes young children will simply accept that the game is finished and they'll wander off and find something else to do, but it's so much easier if they have a mission. Perhaps they could go and get a drink, or maybe you could suggest finding a favourite toy. Again, think of what is appropriate, necessary or tempting for them to do next and give them a heads-up, so there's a clear and smooth transition from the stay and play mode to something else.

Stay and play in practice

When my sister and her husband were trying to pack up and load their car at the end of our holiday recently, I offered to play with their two young children (plus supervise my own) so they could get on with the task relatively uninterrupted. The three older children were playing nicely and independently together, so I sat on the lawn with the baby (8 months old) who was happily playing on the picnic rug. Of course, when the older kids spotted me with the baby, two of them came running over and wanted to play with us. I decided to seize the moment and stay and play. So I did my little test:

☆ the time of day – *mid-morning*
☆ the situation – *need to keep the kids away from the busy grown ups packing*
☆ their clothes – *holiday play clothes*
☆ the time available – *about 20 minutes*
☆ the environment – *lovely sunny day, we're outside on a smooth flat lawn on a picnic rug*
☆ the materials and resources you've got to hand, if any – *none (difficult to go and get anything because I need to keep close to the baby)*
☆ age and particular interests of the children concerned – *8 months, 3 years and 7 years old. (My son, aged 8, is happily reading by himself.) Interests; very creative, full of beans but not over-excited, they like songs and dancing and have great imaginations*

So, I decided to play Sleeping Bunnies with them. This is one of my go-to stay and play games. If you don't know it, it involves a repetitive, but tuneful, song where the children join in with the singing and actions; lying down asleep, then jumping up and hopping around. It goes something like this:

See the little bunnies sleeping 🎵
Till it's nearly noon
Shall we wake them
With a merry tune?
Oh, so still
Are they ill? No
Wake up soon
Hop little bunnies – hop, hop, hop
Hop little bunnies – hop, hop, hop
Hop little bunnies – hop, hop, hop.

Now, that could have probably gone on for about five minutes – the baby (now sitting up on my lap) was both mesmerised and delighted to be part of the game, but to extend it, and make it more interesting and less repetitive for me, we started to change the kind of animal that was being sung about. I made a few suggestions, then they started offering their own ideas; so we had lions roaring, frogs leaping, snakes slithering and fish swimming. You get the idea. Their unerring enthusiasm for each new animal was inspiring, and their impressions of the animals 'doing their thing' were hilarious; I mean, carefully crafted. We had a great time, and the baby loved it too. When I got the signal that the car was full, I told them we'd have time for three more animals. When we got to the last one, I told them what we'd be doing next to help them finish the game happily. At the end we gave each other a big round of applause (the baby too, of course – he's very advanced) and that was that.

Now, I know not everyone likes singing (I happen to love it) but of course these stay and plays don't have to be singing games. There are so many other ways to stay and play – you just need to choose something that *you're* comfortable with and that's appropriate. Just do that little test to check, and it'll be great.

What to play

If you're not the kind of person who wants to start a singing game like Sleeping Bunnies or maybe perform a spontaneous trick with a handkerchief, don't worry, stay and plays exist in all shapes and forms; you're bound to find a few with which you feel comfortable. There are word games, number games, search games, parlour games, outside games, physical games, sporty games, arty games, party games, drama games, relaxing games and team games; all of which can be successfully and joyfully played with young children. And don't forget that you can stay and play with your little one when carrying out household chores too, see the Chores: not Bores chapter; and when you're crafting and baking with your child – see Make and Take.

So, here are some ideas to help you stay and play – some classic, some of my invention. Try one out when you've got even the smallest amount of time to stay awhile with a little one. You'll soon spot those that suit you and your personality; they *all* have the potential to have a positive effect on both you and your child, or children. Just remember to do that little test of appropriateness before embarking on any game or play, and above all have fun; even a little bit of play can go a long way to boosting our happiness. Everyone should give themselves permission to experience the magic of play every once in a while.

Games to develop skills or concepts

For learning about numbers, letters, emotions, size, shapes, colours or developing language.

Let's play . . .

Toy sort

What you'll need:

☆ lots of soft toys

Gather all the soft toys together on a rug or bed. Choose some categories to sort them into. It could be groups of big and small, patterned or not, tailed or not, by number of legs, those with long ears, short ears, no ears. You can play as many rounds as you can think of ways to sort them. Just start the game by saying, 'Ready, Set . . . SORT!'

What you'll need:

☆ lots of toy cars and vehicles

Sort through a collection of toy cars and put on a car show. Which cars will be shown? How will they be shown? You might have categories like Sporty Cars, Red Cars, Big Cars, Little Cars, Trucks and Buses. Have fun displaying them. Perhaps they'll be in rows, in formal formations or in circles. You choose.

Colour collect

What you'll need:

☆ a basket, box or bag for each player (or for each team)

First choose a colour to collect. Then, with players holding a basket or bag or box, the collecting time can begin. The challenge is to find items of that colour and bring them back to base when the time is up, or when, say, five items have been loaded into their container. The items have to fit in the bag, box or basket, of course – then they can be examined together to check they fit the bill.

Jumping Jack says . . .

What you'll need:

☆ chalks, a paved surface

In chalk, write the digits 1–9 in a circle. The player stands in the centre of the circle (Home) and waits for Jumping Jack to call out which number they need to jump on. The caller shouts out 'Jumping Jack says jump to . . . 5!' and the player jumps on to the chalked number 5 – calling out 'Five!' as they jump. The game continues like this, with Jumping Jack calling out different numbers. Jumping Jack can also ask the player to 'Jump Home!' Then the player has to jump back to the middle of the circle, calling out 'Home!' If there is more than one player, Jumping Jack can address individuals to jump in turn.

What's up?

What you'll need:

☆ a hand-held mirror and some photos or pictures of people showing different emotions. Mr Men, Little Miss, Thomas the Tank Engine and Friends books or any children's books with a face on the front cover work well. You'll need at least five different expressions

Lay out the books on a flat surface so all the faces can be seen, then take it in turns to pick an expression to copy. Check in the mirror to see if it's right. Call out 'What's up?' to be shown the expression and then make a guess by pointing to one of the images.

What's that smell?

What you'll need:

☆ a few things that have a scent; try houmous, Marmite, soap, chocolate, strawberries, rosemary and coffee

Hide a little of each chosen food in foil-topped, fork-pricked pots. Put the pots on a tray and muddle them up so no one knows which is which. Sniff and share the different aromas – descriptions of the *type* of smell should be encouraged. Make a final guess as to the contents of each pot before peeling off the foil to reveal its identity.

Guess what

What you'll need:

☆ a collection of something. It could be a box of jewellery, a bag of hats, a basket of balls, a cloth of patchwork pattern, a selection of shells, photographs, some toy dinosaurs or cars, pebbles or leaves; whatever you've got to hand

Spread the collection out so everyone can see the items. One player chooses an item for the other to guess, but keeps it top secret. The other player asks questions to work out which one they chose. Is it stripy? Has it got blue on it? It is not allowed to simply point and ask 'Is it that one?' until you make your final guess.

With a take-a-look book

What you'll need:

☆ a book that can be shared, explored, and talked about, together. It should be full of visual detail. *You Choose* by Pippa Goodhart & Nick Sharratt, the *Where's Wally?* books, *Curious George's Big Book of Curiosity*, Usborne's *1001 Pirate Things to Spot* or *1001 Things to Spot on Holiday* are brilliant take-a-look books

Find somewhere cosy and comfortable to enjoy a take-a-look book together. Who knows what you'll spot and talk about, but I guarantee it'll start a thousand interesting conversations.

Shape shop

What you'll need:

☆ wooden, plastic or beanbag shapes, a small bag (optional)

Take it in turns to be the shopkeeper of the Shape Shop. The shopkeeper sets up the shop, displaying all the shapes, just as they like, saying 'Shop's open!' when it's ready. The customer can buy as many shapes as they like but there should be a lot of sales banter about the features of the various shapes.

Easy-peasy pairs

What you'll need:

☆ a set of pairs cards

Fully formed pelmanism (Find the Pairs) is too tricky for toddlers, so try setting out just five or six pairs from your set for young children. You could play with the cards face-up to start with; make sure it's just challenging enough. Help each other find and collect all those pairs – working towards a common goal can be exciting.

Screen-time play

Most screen-based technology is designed to be completely intuitive in its use these days, so while you should be impressed with your two-year-old being able to swipe and scroll and tap, it's not really different to them being able to hold a pencil and mark-make, or tear paper. Although young children may be able to handle an iPad with dexterity and speed, they may often try scrolling and swiping on other objects, as they might draw on the sofa or rip up your mail.

What's important here is that any screen-time is supervised. Without our presence they could go on and on playing the same game over and over again. Looking at a screen instead of interacting with the real world for too long can't be good for developing their understanding of it, let alone their impression of it; there aren't nearly as many crazy colours or silly sound effects in the real world, for example. We don't really want them thinking reality is actually a bit boring compared to the virtual, do we?

Using computer websites and Apps with your little one can be a great way to develop their letter, colour and number recognition, to make music or 'interact' with favourite characters. And most of these will be in the form of games. This is why screen-based play should be a stay and play. Share the games together, enjoy what skills and concepts they develop and then be strong and turn it off when the game is done.

Parlour Games

Traditionally, parlour games were played indoors when the family was all together in the parlour – hence the name. Parlour games don't require much equipment beyond a few basics that might be found in any living room. They tap into all types of play, to challenge and stimulate everyone, and can be adapted especially to suit young children.

Animal charades

This is a simplified version of the classic parlour game. Instead of miming words and syllables of films, books and TV shows, this pre-schooler-friendly game has each player taking turns to mime an animal. Everyone watches each silent impression carefully and the first person to get it right has the next turn. Or, if that causes trouble, take more formalised turns – try 'youngest goes first'.

Honey Bear

What you'll need:

☆ a small pot, at least three players (but soft toys can play too)

The youngest player is usually Honey Bear first. They 'go to sleep' in the middle of a circle of the other players, who need to be sitting down. The small pot of 'honey' is placed next to the bear's head. Everyone chants, 'Go to sleep, Honey Bear; don't peek, Honey Bear.' As the bear sleeps, someone from the circle is chosen to steal the honey pot. They must creep to collect it then return silently to their place, hiding the pot behind them. Everyone in the circle puts their hands behind their backs, and then shouts, 'Wake up, Honey Bear. Your honey's not there!' The bear sits up and has to guess who stole the honey. The players show their hands if an incorrect guess is made, saying, 'Not me!' The player who stole the honey pot is the next Honey Bear.

Tray takeaway

What you'll need:

☆ a tea tray and a clean, light but opaque piece of fabric which is big enough to cover the tray. A tea towel usually works well

Choose five to ten items from around the living room and place them on the tray. Lay the tray on a flat surface in front of the players and talk through what's there. Lay the tea towel on top of the tray, hiding all the items. While one person takes one item away and hides it behind their back, the other player covers their eyes – no peeking – and says:

Cover my eyes, so I can't see
One will be missing, which will it be?

When told to do so, the person hiding their eyes opens them, whips the fabric away from the tray with a flourish, and looks hard at the items to try to work out which one is missing. There can be as many rounds of this game as you like – it does get easier the more you play. Keep taking turns to be the person taking the article away and the person hiding their eyes.

Magic tricks

What you'll need:

☆ a pen

Parlour game tricks don't really involve magic, of course; they're just fun illusions. But young children are usually wowed by a grown up showing off their best party tricks; even more so if they're shown how it's done.

'Disappearing Birds' trick:

Draw a basic bird face – just two eyes and a beak – on the pad of each of your index fingers. Holding up your index fingers only, sing:

Two little dickybirds sitting on a wall, ♫
One named Peter, one named Paul
Fly away Peter, fly away Paul.
Come back Peter, come back Paul.

When you get to the line about them flying away, make a grand sweep of each of your arms to suggest Peter and then Paul flying away; change fingers quickly out of sight, returning your hands to the starting position but showing the pads of your middle fingers instead of your index fingers. These are, of course, bird-less. When you get to the next line about them flying back, do that movement again, but return to holding up your index fingers; Peter and Paul are back.

Rubbing your head and patting your stomach at the same time:

Ask your little one if they can pat their head. They'll show you they can do it, especially if you demonstrate. Then ask them if they can rub their stomach. Again, demonstrate. Then try doing both things at the same time. A little one will not be able to do this very well, but you'll both have a chuckle trying.

Party games

You don't have to wait for a party to enjoy a classic party game. Here are a couple that work very well as parlour games.

Pin the tail on the donkey

What you'll need:

☆ a couple of pieces of paper – the bigger the better but A4 would be fine – a few felt-tip pens or crayons, scissors, a blob of Blu-tack, a scarf or similar to be a gentle blindfold

First decide which animal or character will feature in the game. It certainly doesn't have to be a donkey. We've had a hat pinned on Santa, a moustache on a cowboy and a snout on a piggy face before. Draw the animal or character on the paper, as large as possible. Remember to leave out the item you're going to pin on. Then draw the thing to be pinned on a separate sheet and cut it out; add a blob of Blu-tack to attach it during the game. Take it in turns to try to attach the nose, tail, hat, or whatever it is, to the animal or character. See how many turns it takes to get it in the right place; having a common goal is great for young children.

Spin, spin, spin

What you'll need:

☆ an empty plastic water bottle

The players sit in a circle (soft toys make great participants if you're a bit short of people) and the water bottle is placed in the middle. The youngest player spins the bottle first. As the bottle spins, say 'Spin, spin, spin. Who will win, win, win?' Whoever it points towards when it stops spinning has to accept a simple challenge. It could be doing a star jump, or touching their toes, or running around the circle and back to their place. That person decides the challenge the next time the bottle stops spinning.

Board games and card games

These are often not really suitable to play with young children. Even if they find the dice, board, cards and counters appealing, often the stress of competition, and the devastation at losing – even just a point – can be too much for some three- and four-year-olds. It can take every effort to bend the rules and fudge results to let the game progress without tears. Even if we are modelling graceful winning, and calm losing, it won't be until children are well over five years old that they will really be able to emotionally handle any proper competition. So unless you are willing to bend the rules a bit, or a lot, I would really wait till they're a bit older before embarking on those types of games. Instead, I would try specialist preschool games. These tend to be a little bigger visually, and often there's a physical aspect to the game which young children find thrilling. Games like Mousie-Mousie, Burst the Telephone Box, Ker-plunk, Elefun, Hungry Hippos,

Jenga or bingo-based games are a safer bet for a tear-free and giggle-fuelled stay and play session.

Completing a jigsaw or puzzles together

Jigsaws can independently occupy and absorb young children very well, of course, but sometimes it's wonderful to sit with your little one awhile and work on a puzzle together. Don't get your 1000-piece jigsaw out, though, stick with one of theirs, and let them show you how they go about it. Enjoy the pleasure of a shared challenge, and a job well done when the picture is complete.

Outside games

Let's play a relaxing game

When outside, your little one may be a zooming little machine most of the time. But young children can be still – especially if they have the undivided attention of an adult, and there's a cool game to stay and play.

Making daisy chains

What you'll need:

☆ an obliging summer lawn that's covered in daisies

Little hands will find the technique for making a daisy chain way too fiddly, but give them the chance and they'll happily trot around picking daisies for you. Show them how to pick them close to the root (to get the longest stem possible) and see how many they can collect. Split the stem with your thumbnail and post through the stem of the next daisy and show your little one how the chain grows. Why not make bangles and headdresses for everyone?

Do you like butter?

What you'll need:

☆ a buttercup

This classic little game is one of the sweetest things you can teach your child. Show them how to see if you like butter by picking a buttercup and holding it close, but not touching, the underside of your chin. If they see a yellow glow from the flower on your skin, then you do. There's always a glow, of course, but apart from that, it's a great test. Your little one will love the repetition of the game, asking the question, 'Do you like butter?' again and again.

Looking at the clouds or stars

What you'll need:

☆ somewhere to lie down comfortably looking at an expanse of sky

Night or day, you can entice your child to play this game by starting it yourself, announcing when you've seen a shooting star, or a satellite, or the most brilliant dragon shape in the clouds. Some skies are better than others for this game, of course, but when you've got a good one, there's no better game of I-spy.

Grass-blade blowing

What you'll need:
☆ a long blade of green grass

I learnt to do this trick when I was about ten years old, but it's something I remember my father showing me when I was really little; I thought it was so clever. You can impress your little one too by selecting a long blade of regular green grass and doing an impression of Mr Punch. Just put the blade of grass tautly between your two thumbs – like a reed – and cup your hands around it to make a soundbox. Then blow through your thumbs and talk at the same time, 'That's the way to do it!' Try saying your child's name or a little rhyme – it will all sound pretty funny to a two- or three-year-old.

Look for a four-leaf clover

What you'll need:
☆ a grassy bank to search

You can entice your little one into this game by starting the search yourself – counting and saying, 'One, two, three. No. One, two, three . . . '. Explain how most clover plants have three little leaves, but how every once in a while you can find a really special one that has four. They'll be joining in the search in no time – helping you look for that lucky fourth leaf.

I hear with my little ear

What you'll need:

☆ somewhere comfortable to sit and listen

This is a very easy game to play – much easier than I-Spy. Just encourage your little one to sit or stand still with you and listen carefully to all the sounds around them. When anyone hears something interesting they can say 'I hear with my little ear' – and then guess what made that sound.

Let's get moving

For many grown ups the most instinctive way to interact with a young child, and have a bit of a run about, is by starting a game of tag or 'It' – brilliantly exciting for the children – or, if there happens to be a ball close at hand, an impromptu kick-about. The following games are all based on the principles of these two basic stay and plays.

Games with a soft large ball

Get to Ten

Roll or kick the ball back and forth to each other, counting up to ten. Then do it again.

Goal!

One person's the goalie, who stands, legs apart, to make a goal. The other is the striker, aiming to kick the ball through the legs of the goalie, who shouts 'Goal!' when it happens.

Wall-ball

Little children think it's very funny to watch a bouncy ball rebound off a wall. There won't be much catching here but a lot of laughter. Take it in turns to throw the ball to the wall and let the other player retrieve it. Then it's their turn to throw the ball to the wall. Can you do it ten times?

Caught-it, missed-it

My Nana has played this with all her great-grandchildren, and her grandchildren before them. It's a lovely and gentle ball game for younger toddlers and sets up a lovely lilting rhythm of rhyme. Sit or stand close to one another and roll, or gently throw, a soft ball to each other. When a player catches it, say 'Caught it,' and if not, say 'Missed it.' Simple as that.

Games with things other than a ball

Balloon keepy-uppy

Work together to keep an inflated balloon in the air. Use heads, use hands, use elbows and knees.

Parachute

You do need a few grown ups and children to play with one of these satisfactorily, but it does encourage everyone to stay and play. Try games like Up-and-Under, where the grown ups waft the parachute up, a caller shouts out the name of one child who then runs to the other side of the parachute before it wafts down again. Or play Colour-Touch, where the children gather under the parachute in the centre, and when the caller shouts out a colour they all have to jump up and touch that colour. Add difficulty and giggles by getting the grown ups to walk the parachute in a circle during the game.

Tin-can alley

Grown ups and children alike can't resist the lure of a tin-can tower to knock down. Use beanbags as the projectiles to aim at a tower of between five to ten cans for some fun target practice. Help each other knock it down. Can it ever be knocked down in just one go?

Hide-n-Find

Hold up the treasure to be hidden – make it something pretty big like a hat, a teddy or a ball, so it's relatively easy to spot. Tell the players to hide their eyes while you hide the treasure. How hard you make it is up to you, but be prepared to give clues, or help with 'hotter, colder' comments as they race around trying to find what's been hidden.

Bubble trouble

There's nothing like a grown up bubble-blowing to attract a crowd of children. You can get them to 'help' you pop those pesky bubbles as the beautiful spheres try to escape. Can they catch them all? Ring the changes by challenging them to pop them with their elbows, noses or by clapping them away. Watch out for the floor getting slippery though – carpeted or outside surfaces tend to stay pretty non-slip.

Let's dance

Pop on some tunes (yes, you can dance outside) and simply say 'Let's dance!' My children would often evolve this into a *Strictly Come Dancing* scenario whereby at the end of each tune we'd have to judge each other's moves in the manner of Craig or Bruno; hilarious. Try alternately starting and stopping the music for a round of Musical Statues.

Games without a ball, or anything at all – just a bit of space

In and out the dusty bluebells

This is a classic that can be adapted for just two players. The first verse is sung while the little one follows the grown up, who moves away from them in zigzags (in and out).

> *In and out the dusty bluebells, in and out the dusty bluebells,*
> *In and out the dusty bluebells, you shall be my partner.*

The leader then lets the little one catch them (with a bear-hug), crouches down so their shoulders can be reached (from behind). The child tippy-taps the grown up's shoulders gently during the next verse.

> *Tippy-tappy, tippy tappy on my shoulder, tippy-tappy, tippy tappy*
> *   on my shoulder,*
> *Tippy-tappy, tippy tappy on my shoulder, you shall be my partner.*

What's the time, Mr Wolf?

The caller (the wolf) stands with their back to the players about twenty paces away. The players call out, 'What's the Time, Mr Wolf?' The wolf turns round and tells them a time (on the hour). Whatever time it is the players have to take that many steps towards the wolf. So, if it's three o'clock, they take three steps. The wolf turns back away from the players, and the play continues like this until the wolf turns round and answers the question, 'Dinner time!' At which point the players run back to the start as the wolf chases them. If the wolf catches them then of course, this results in a bear-hug. There will be squeals and screams, so bear this in mind.

Let's play hide-and-seek

This classic game becomes very popular when children are about three. Their skills at hiding, and seeking for that matter, develop much later. So be prepared for them to 'hide' in the same place over and over, and for that place to be totally in view. You'll often see them with their eyes shut, thinking that will help with the whole invisibility thing. Make your seeking quite showy; verbalise where you're looking. 'Are they hiding here? No. How about here? No. Hmmmn. Where could they be?'

Helicopters and horse-y-backs

These stay and plays, where the grown up is engaged as a kind of 'ride-giver', are tricky to summarise because, from my experience, they tend to evolve from *spontaneous* moments of play with a parent. Little children adore being held up in the air, spun round, bounced on a leg or lap by a close adult, and these physically vigorous games are an important part of bonding with us, and for developing language like, 'faster', 'more', 'up', 'down' and 'stop'. Whatever game you play it is more important than ever in this one to establish a clear beginning and ending. I've seen far too many dads winded by an unexpected leap onto their stomach by a toddler who really thought the game of 'Spidey Clutch-on' was still going on. Let them know when it's the last one, and don't leave them hanging. You've got to think of something pretty tempting to move them on from the intensity of such joyful, exuberant play.

Hello sunshine

If you want to stretch and include a bit of yoga in your day, then try this simple sun salutation. Young children will love to join in with the words and mirror your poses.

Tadasana (Mountain or Standing Pose)

As you move from pose 1– 2 say, 'Hello sun'

 Urdhva Hastasana (Upward Salute)

As you move from pose 2–3 say, 'Sunshine everywhere'

 Uttanasana (Standing Forward Bend)

As you move from pose 3–4 say, 'Hello everyone'

 Lunge, left or right leg back (or jump back)

As you move from pose 4–5 say, 'As strong as a bridge'

 Plank Pose

As you move from pose 5–6 say, 'Down in the lift we go' *[make a 'going down' noise]*

Chaturanga Dandasana (Four-Limbed Staff Pose)

As you move from pose 6–7 say, 'Here's the little dog ' *[make a high yap]*

Urdhva Mukha Svanasana (Upward-Facing Dog Pose)

As you move from pose 7–8 say, 'Here's the big dog – uh-oh; hold on to her lead' *[make a gruff bark]*

Adho Mukha Svanasana (Downward-Facing Dog Pose)

As you move from pose 8–9 say, 'Look out, Grasshopper' *[make a 'jumping' noise]*

Lunge, with opposite starting leg forward (or jump forward)

As you move from pose 9–10 say, 'Bottoms up!' *[make a 'going up' swanee whistle noise]*

Uttanasana (Standing Forward Bend)

As you move from pose 10– 11 say, 'Goodbye sun'

Hastasana (Upward Salute)

As you move from pose 11–12 say, 'We are done'

Tadasana (Mountain or Standing Pose)

With hands to heart centre in anjalai mudra.

Let's play when we're out and about

Whether you're on the move or staying put, stay and plays are a great way to make an outing memorable for everyone.

Pooh Sticks

What you'll need:

☆ a carefully selected stick per player

This classic stay and play made famous by Winnie-the-Pooh never fails to delight young children. You need to be on a footbridge over a flowing stream. Each player drops their stick into the water, from the side of the bridge that's upstream, after a count of three. The players run to the other side of the bridge to see the sticks emerge.

Who's at home today?

If you're lucky enough to be on a beach with rock pools, at an aquarium, near a pond or another watery habitat, then you'll need to stay with your child for safety reasons. You can dial up the fun and keep them focused by playing 'Who's at home today?'. Just posing this simple question will be enough to start some careful searching of the watery nooks and crannies to see who's at home and where they're hiding.

Stay and play at the seaside

Making sandcastles

What you'll need:

☆ a bucket, spade, pebbles and shells for decoration

If you're on a sandy beach with a toddler or preschooler, it's a great excuse to immerse yourself in some good old-fashioned sandcastle-making. You'll be the absolute expert in their eyes, and they'll love helping you. Try not to be too ambitious, though; if you need a blueprint for your grand design, they'll most likely have wandered away before you even get started. Some children may not be beyond the knocking-it-down-immediately-it's-made stage – so be prepared for this.

Pebble shop

What you'll need:

☆ a beach with pebbles, some watercolour paints

Set up a little painting workshop for pebbles by collecting some smooth light-coloured stones, bringing them back to the workshop and painting them just as you like. When they're done, why not display them in your 'pebble shop'?

Pebble kingdom

What you'll need:

☆ a beach with pebbles, some felt-tip pens

If you're on a beach where there are lots of pebbles, it's possible to use them as small-world figures and scenery. Use felt-tip pens to add required detail, like a face or a crown for example, and work together to pile up other pebbles to approximate rooms in a castle with thrones and the like.

Stay and play when out for a walk

Collecting nature

What you'll need:

☆ a bucket or basket or little bag for the collection

Young children adore collecting things during a walk. Give them a vessel and they will fill it; they'll let you contribute to the collection too. You can have rules like only collect fallen nature or maybe just leaves or sticks, for example. Toddlers may not want to keep their collections for the duration of the walk, so be prepared for them to tip it out and start again. Preschoolers will probably like to keep their finds for closer examination back at base.

Who can find the biggest leaf, tallest tree, best seed, best wand (stick)?

These are great questions to ask during a walk; it gives everyone a playful purpose and helps us to focus on particular things as the walk progresses. It's competitive, but only in a most gentle way. Make sure the little ones in the group know they are finding really good stuff.

Walking on the sunny side of the street

Introducing a fun rule to a walk can help the whole outing become much more playful for everyone; from a rule about only walking on the sunny side of the street, to having to jump in every pavement puddle (correct footwear for all, of course) as you pass them, or looking for the best Christmas tree in town, for example.

Let's explore

This is a really useful phrase to get your little one to understand. It can put a playful spin on visiting a new park, neighbourhood, museum gallery or an inviting-looking lane or path.

Let's be Thing-Finders

Pippi Longstocking is probably the most famous Thing-Finder out there. Even if your little one hasn't heard of Pippi yet – a literary inspiration in my view – it's still possible to become official Thing-Finders. With young children, it's a good idea to decide what 'thing' is to be sought before you set off. Keep the search brief – just a walk around the block or up to the park and back will be enough for most novice Thing-Finders. We've looked for lizards, ladybirds, blue cars, icicles, frost, footprints and cracked paving slabs before now. They'll get completely excited when they come across an example of the Thing you're trying to find.

Let's sing with actions

If your child goes to nursery, chances are they'll already sing you the songs they've learned there. From traditional nursery rhymes and songs to teach specific concepts and skills, to songs to help them get ready or motivate them or that signify lunchtime and home-time – there's a whole lot of singing going on in a preschool setting.

At home, we can use songs to help those daily routines run smoothly too – babies, toddlers and preschoolers are incredibly responsive to music and they're famous for having no inhibitions when it comes to joining in. See Chores: not Bores and Sanity Savers for some very useful and fun songs to try with your child at home.

If you don't know many traditional nursery rhymes, find a book and CD as soon as possible; it's our responsibility to pass on these wonderful songs to the next generation; and the earlier in our children's lives we do this, the better. There's a relatively small window of time when, for our children, these rhymes and tunes have the power to motivate, teach and encourage enthusiastic self-expression through joyful singing.

With this age group, there doesn't always have to be a reason for singing. As a stay and play, singing is all about the joy of it; simply sharing a musical moment with your tot. They don't mind if you're out of tune, they certainly will be, so don't hold back. Sing like there's no tomorrow and make up some actions, just as you like, to bring the songs to life. Here are a few of our favourites:

I see fireworks (to the tune of Frère Jacques) ♪

I see fireworks, I see fireworks
Sparkling bright, sparkling bright
Multicoloured starbursts, multicoloured starbursts
In the night, in the night

I hear fireworks, I hear fireworks
Whoosh, whoosh, fizz. Whoosh, whoosh, fizz
Crackle-crackle, bang-bang. Crackle-crackle, bang-bang
Wheee, pop, whizz. Wheee, pop, whizz.

Head, shoulders, knees and toes ♪

Head, shoulders, knees and toes,
  Knees and toes.
Head, shoulders, knees and toes,
  Knees and toes.
And eyes, and ears, and mouth,
  And nose.
Head, shoulders, knees and toes,
  Knees and toes.

Place both hands on the parts of the body as they are mentioned. On the second time, speed up and get faster with each verse.

Zoom, zoom, zoom ♪

Zoom zoom zoom
We're going to the moon.
Zoom zoom zoom
We're leaving very soon.

If you want to take a trip,
Climb aboard my rocket ship.
Zoom zoom zoom
We're going to the moon!

Five, four, three, two, one,
Blast off!

One potato, two potatoes ♪

One potato
Two potatoes
Three potatoes
Four!
Five potatoes
Six potatoes
Seven potatoes
More!

Five currant buns in a baker shop ♪

FIVE currant buns in a baker's shop,
Round and fat with a cherry on top.
Along came a boy with a penny one day,
Bought a currant bun and took it away.

Five little speckled frogs ♪

FIVE little speckled frogs,
Sat on a speckled log,
Eating some most delicious bugs – yum, yum!
One jumped into the pool,
Where it was nice and cool,
Then there were FOUR speckled frogs – glug, glug!

[repeat until there are no speckled frogs left on the log]

Five little monkeys jumping on the bed ♬

Five little monkeys jumping on the bed.
One fell off and bumped his head.
Mama called the doctor and the doctor said,
'No more monkeys jumping on the bed!'

[repeat until there are no more monkeys left on the bed]

Jack-in-the-box ♬

A great singing game to play if you've got a big cardboard box handy
[One person curls up small in the box . . .]

Jack-in-the-box
Still as can be
Lift up the lid
What do you see?
It's a . . . Jack-in-the-box!

[Jack pops out of the box, arms waving, saying 'Boo!']

Then hide other characters in the box. For example, there could be a car-in-the box, a piggy-in-the-box or a kitten-in-the-box. Practise the sound and action of the thing-in-the-box before each turn.

Choose an instrument you can play

Set out all of your percussive instruments for this wonderful musical game. Sit near the instruments and pass, back and forth, a small trinket – a bit like pass-the-parcel – as you sing:

(to the tune of London Bridge is Falling Down) ♫

Choose an instrument you can play
You can play
You can play

Choose an instrument you can play
What's your favourite?

Whoever is holding the trinket at the end of the song picks up an instrument and plays along to the next part, stopping as instructed.

You can play and play and stop
Play and stop
Play and stop
You can play and play and stop . . .
That's my favourite.

[Repeat until all the instruments have been chosen at least once]

Wind the bobbin up ♫

Wind the bobbin up,
Wind the bobbin up,
Pull, pull, clap, clap, clap.
Wind it back again,
Wind it back again,
Pull, pull, clap, clap, clap,

Point to the ceiling,
Point to the floor,
Point to the window,
Point to the door,
Clap your hands together, 1, 2, 3,
Put your hands upon your knee.

Let's pretend

Young children can slip incredibly easily into the world of let's pretend. Not only can they readily imagine they are inanimate objects, plants, animals or characters, but they can also play a game in this mode. So, they could be a building, a tree, or a tiger and 'go-to-the-shops' or 'take on the baddies' quite happily. Unlike our three- and four-year-olds, though, we may not feel nearly as comfortable with 'being a tree' but, as with *singing* with our children, it's really good for us to join them in a bit of let's pretend every once in a while. If they say, 'Let's be puppies' we shouldn't always say, 'No'; sometimes we should say, 'Yes', and even 'Yes, and . . . ' to add something to the improvisation. It's usually more comfortable for us adults to play along if the let's pretend is in the form of a game. Such as:

Let's be . . .

In the chapter Chores: not Bores, I mention getting little ones to help tidy up or to clear the table 'in the manner of' somebody else. To dip your toe into the water, why not join in with that kind of 'make it fun, get it done' game? Having a 'job' to do whilst in character suddenly makes the whole thing less daunting for many grown ups;

fun even. Clearing up 'in the manner of Superman', for example, can feel most liberating.

To play an actual game of 'Let's be . . . ' you don't need anything but a little bit of time and space. Have a few ideas of what you can 'be' up your sleeve, and let your little one make suggestions. You only need to play each round for about 30 seconds or so but if it really takes off, you could give it longer. Say 'Freeze' to stop the action. And then, 'Now, let's be . . . ' for a new role. Try being cats, superheroes, aeroplanes, statues, balloons, giants or elephants.

Let's have a story

Reading or telling stories to your child is one of the best ways to enter the world of let's pretend because by storytelling you're letting their imaginations take them to different places and times, and to the lives of make-believe characters, exploring their feelings and actions.

With very young children, start simple. There are some fantastic picture books out there, but you don't need to stick religiously to the text. Let them look at the pictures – they'll get so much of the story from those – and above all tell the story like it's brilliant. Build up *any* drama and give the characters voices if you can. Step out of the text and ask your child what they think is going to happen next. Most good stories have at least one point of 'high drama' – make sure you don't miss it. And then, of course, they all live happily ever after. We might think this is a bit predictable, but actually for little children this is a really important and comforting story device – so don't gloss over it.

Let's be in the story of . . .

Many three- and four-year-olds will have their favourite stories. Whether it's a classic fairy story or a story from a picture book, they can be used to take imaginations up a level, dramatically, if you play 'Let's be in the story of . . . '

Spend a couple of minutes gathering your props. Encourage approximations; young children are renowned for being able to imagine a colander as a space helmet or a banana as a telephone. Choose which characters everyone's going to be; you might have extra characters played by your child's soft toys; they're generally great at this; they don't steal the limelight or pad their part. Then act out your story; you could be the narrator, either reading from the book, or telling the story in your own words. Or just let your little one take the lead, and be a character as and when invited.

Books we've enjoyed acting out – many times – include Julia Donaldson's *Room on the Broom* and *Tyrannosaurus Drip*, Harry Horse's *Little Rabbit Lost*, *Little Red Riding Hood*, *Cinderella* and Phyllis Root's *Lucia and the Light*.

Let's pretend we're somewhere else . . .

This stay and play scenario is often reasonably palatable for grown ups to engage in because often we're allowed to be ourselves; it's just the place that's imaginary.

There are so many places our child will imagine being when engaged in independent play, but sometimes we'll be invited to join in. If this happens, we shouldn't always say, 'No'; sometimes we should say, 'Yes' and even, 'Yes, and . . . ' to add something to the improvisation.

So, enjoy being pampered at the 'hairdressers', waited on in their 'restaurant', sharing an afternoon tea with them at the 'cafe', being educated in their 'school' or being measured up for a new pair of sandals in their 'shoe shop'– it's a wonderful opportunity for your children to enjoy themselves, and for you to enjoy them.

Let's play an art game

Let's show each other shadows in the sunshine

If you get the opportunity, take a few minutes to make some shadow shapes on the walls or the ground. Take turns and work together to see how many different shapes and patterns you can make.

Let's paint each other's faces

What you'll need:

☆ a few face-paints plus soft brushes, wipes and a hand-held mirror

Face-paints aren't particularly expensive, and most little children love being transformed by a touch of pattern and colour to their face. You don't have to be an artist to have a go, and if you're feeling particularly brave you could let them loose with the paints on your face too.

Let's draw by taking turns

What you'll need:

☆ paper and pencils or crayons

Draw a person or object by taking turns to add to the picture. For example, you could say 'Let's draw a house' then take turns to add an element or feature to the drawing until it's done – like walls, roof, windows, door and so on.

Let's play a word game

These are great for playing in the car or on the bus or train. You don't need any equipment, just to be able to give them your attention for a round or two.

Say banana

Ask each other questions; the answer is always 'Banana'! Try and trick your opponent into giving the real answer.

Tongue twisters

These are great fun to practise together. Our favourites are:

Red lorry, yellow lorry
Tie twine to three tree twigs
She sells seashells on the seashore
Peter Piper picked a peck of pickled pepper

I-spy

Make this classic word game easier by giving the mystery item to be spied a clue other than what it begins with. So, for example, 'I Spy with my little eye something that's blue'.

Let's take something apart

What you'll need:

☆ a small broken or unwanted electrical item or machine, a selection of tools like a screw-driver set and some pliers

For the keen mechanics or technical-whizzes out there, inviting a child to help you take something apart to see how it works or to mend something together is a wonderful stay and play opportunity. Having a grown-up 'expert' show a child how to look inside an old plastic clock to see how it works, or how that old kettle was made is something they'll remember for a long time; they'll definitely be curious. You can build up the excitement of unscrewing things, or removing parts to see what's underneath – they'll love it.

Sanity Savers

'Rose: *Do you love him, Loretta?*
Loretta: No.
Rose: Good. When you love them they drive you crazy because they know
they can.'

Moonstruck (1987)

If you've ever been amazed at the way nursery teachers and child-minders seem to be able to get umpteen children simultaneously coated and shod, toileted and hands-washed, listening intently, sharing and taking turns nicely, napping or eating stuff without a fuss, you may have asked yourself, 'What on earth is their secret?' This may be particularly pertinent if getting your little one to do anything at home has involved tears or a tantrum recently, but you hear they're happily complying and 'doing as they're told' at nursery. How do the teachers do it? Well, the answer is actually very straight-forward; it boils down to the fact that the kids in their care are *not their own children*; simple as that.

As an experienced teacher and Early Years practitioner myself, I know how it is. When I'm teaching lots of little ones I can pretty much get them to do what I need them to do, when I need them to do it, and they are usually very happy and keen to do so. As with most teachers and childminders working with this age group, I am an advocate for making *playfulness* a daily habit; making children *want* to cooperate with simple routines, songs and games to make transitional parts of the day run smoothly, and with plenty of playful tactics to get them to listen well, or want to join in. There are so many fun rules for sharing and turn-taking too – they cannot resist them. If play is the language of children, then I'm fluent in it – or at least I aim to be. It's these playful tricks and tips that this chapter is really all about.

I can also spot a tired, stressed, shy or hungry child in a moment; and if they are unhappy, or someone else is making them unhappy, or they are behaving in a way that I want to change, I've got plenty of strategies to help them out before things get, let's say, messy. But it's also important to reiterate that it is often easier and clearer to read what a little one needs, and get them to happily cooperate, if they are other people's children. The question is, why?

It's a love thing

As a parent, having unconditional, unerring, constant, endless amounts of love for our children is what makes it complicated. Love can be both the powerful and wonderful heart, beating the rhythm of the way we are with our children, *and* the spoke in the works; it's this *love thing* that's the reason it's only our *own* children who can truly drive us crazy. It's why our children *can't* drive their nursery teachers mad. I quote the film *Moonstruck* at the beginning of this chapter because I think the wise-but-cynical character Rose really hits on something when she expresses her relief at Loretta not loving the man she's due to marry because, in her experience, when you really love someone, they drive you crazy because *they know they can*.

I believe this applies to the love between us and our children – that is to say, they can drive us parents absolutely *crazy*. Unlike adults, though, very young children don't *know* they can, and they certainly don't *mean* to; but they can and they often do. Because of love.

What really pushes our buttons?

As our children grow from babies to toddlers we will undoubtedly witness some very surprising, and not so pleasing, behaviour at some point. And what's more, we might think we are the only one around who has to deal with such a terrible problem. 'How come I get the biter, the clingy-one, the grabber, the head-banger or the child who doesn't want to poo?' we might ask ourselves. 'Why is my child doing this?' Or perhaps in darker moments, 'Why is my child doing this *to me*?' We tend to take these things very personally because we love our children, and the more frequently or longer they behave in this way the more emotionally we react to it – we might let these unwanted behaviours push our buttons or grind our gears. Our kids drive us *crazy* with their apparent 'naughtiness'.

Here's one mum's story: 'There isn't a single day when she doesn't have a tantrum about something (usually something very minor as well) or do something that gets her into trouble (e.g. antagonising her big sister or tormenting the cat). Her immediate and loud tears drive me nuts. I've lost the ability to tolerate it. There was an incident in the car yesterday which caused her to scream loudly and distract me so I ended up totally screaming back at her. This morning I lost the plot too and shouted incredibly loud and slammed my hand onto the table. This is not how I want or like to parent and it makes me feel that I'm not a fit parent if I can't keep my temper. I ended up in tears too this morning. It's just in her nature to be like this and I am at an utter loss in how to cope and as a result I'm struggling to keep my temper and more often than not I'm losing it and end up really shouting at her. When she is in a good mood (and she can revert to a good mood in minutes / seconds after a tantrum, as if nothing ever happened) she is like having a ray of sunshine in the house. She's got genius comic timing and delivery and often has us all in stitches. She sings all the time. She also knows how to behave because she confirmed that she would never throw a tantrum like she does at someone else's house.'

This mum isn't alone in being at her wit's end. Here are some more behaviours and habits of young children that parents are concerned about. Some are clearly more extreme than others, but the whole list certainly makes for quite a startling read:

tantrums ☆ hits others ☆ bites others ☆ over-excitability ☆ cries and screams ☆ defiance with back-chat or shouting or pouting ☆ throws things ☆ head-bangs ☆ body-rocks ☆ shouts ☆ grinds teeth ☆ has grabby hands ☆ picks nose ☆ holds off a bowel-movement or holds onto a full bladder ☆ sucks thumb ☆ won't sleep or stay in bed ☆ runs off ☆ naughty ☆ stubborn ☆ doesn't let me help, ever ☆ holds breath ☆ doesn't eat ☆ won't share ☆ won't take turns ☆ doesn't play nicely with others ☆ sulks ☆ clings ☆ ignores people ☆ whines and whinges ☆ won't follow instructions – like getting dressed

It doesn't make for a glowing report of early years' behaviour, does it? However, it might be comforting to know that all of these examples are not actually considered particularly worrying. Paediatricians and psychologists tell us that most of these behaviours are usually just phases of many a child's development, and are perfectly normal.

Our child does not start behaving in this way to deliberately annoy or test us either – they aren't simply 'being naughty'; on the contrary, according to the experts, these behaviours are usually *coping strategies*. Our children will revisit them when they are stressed, tired, frustrated, unhappy, insecure or falling asleep, or because they are dealing with some big emotions that they cannot cope with in any other way just yet.

Emotional and social development in under-fives

If we take a look at the typical emotional and social development in our children – this summary, adapted from *PBS Parents* is very clear – not only can we see the kind of behaviours we might expect them to be exhibiting at different ages but, more importantly, we can see where the gaps are – the things that they probably won't be able to deal with. It's in these gaps of social and emotional development where we often witness unwanted or what we might think of as 'bad' behaviour – usually in front of the neighbours or in the middle of the supermarket, naturally. Of course, this is a very basic guide, and your little one will develop different emotional skills at different rates and in different orders to this list.

At age two-plus children will:

☆ Enjoy playing alongside other children, but usually keep to themselves.

☆ Need adults to step in when conflicts arise to prevent aggression and teach appropriate behaviours.

☆ Begin to expand their understanding of what others' feelings mean (e.g. look at expressions) and label feelings that they recognise in themselves and others.

☆ Find controlling emotions difficult, so frustration may trigger emotional meltdowns or tantrums.

☆ Like comfort objects like blankets or teddy bears which help them cope with new situations or strong emotions.

☆ Extend trusting relationships to other adults and to children with whom he or she plays frequently.

☆ Show a strong sense of self as an individual (e.g., say, 'No!' to an adult's request, simply to assert their individuality).

☆ Increase their understanding and use of language related to emotions.
☆ Show awareness of others' feelings and may try to give basic help to others who may be sad.
☆ Look to adults for comfort when conflict happens.
☆ With much adult support, begin to develop some strategies for resolving conflicts constructively.

At age three-plus they will:

☆ Need familiar adults nearby for security as they explore and play.
☆ Begin to have real friendships with other children.
☆ When conflicts arise with peers, typically seek adult assistance.
☆ Be learning to recognise the causes of feelings.
☆ Give simple help, such as a hug, to those who are upset.
☆ Be better able to manage their emotions, but may still fall apart under stress.
☆ Begin to develop and express a sense of individuality and personal preferences.
☆ Label their own feelings and those of others' based on their facial expression or tone of voice.
☆ Understand, at least on a basic level, that feelings have causes.
☆ Show progress in expressing feelings, needs and opinions in difficult situations or conflicts, without harming self, others or property.
☆ Show an interest in other children and copy what they do. They will also play cooperatively with another child for a time.
☆ Give simple help to peers who are in need, upset, hurt or angry. Such attempts to give aid may not take into account the other child's characteristics or needs.

At age four-plus they will:

☆ Continue to learn what causes certain feelings, and realise that others may react to the same situation differently.

☆ Have learned to better manage intense emotions with coping strategies like talking it out, drawing a picture or through playing it out.

☆ Show further progress in their social interactions with peers, such as by smoothly joining in a group play situation, being sympathetic to others, or suggesting ways to resolve conflicts.

☆ Uses adults as trusted role models.

☆ Be better able to tolerate the absence of familiar adults; cope with distress through the use of language, drawing, etc.

☆ Increasingly express a sense of self in terms of abilities, characteristics, preferences, and actions.

☆ Compare themselves to others.

☆ Successfully enter the existing play of a group of children.

☆ Begin and sustain pretend play in a cooperative group.

☆ Show further progress in developing friendships with peers, even if a bond is formed with just one other child, and begin to try to please other children.

☆ Respond more appropriately and sympathetically to peers who are in need, upset, hurt, or angry.

☆ Suggest solutions to problems with other children, while continuing to seek adults' help (www.pbs.org/parents/childdevelopmenttracker/four/socialandemotionalgrowth.html).

Often, it's when a child's lack of developed social and emotional skills bump up against a new situation or one that is too complex, too stressful, or when they are over-tired or hungry that we see them exhibit something from that list of unwanted behaviours. It is then that we, obviously, need to step in to help them. This is easy when they're babies because we're in charge of their every situation, but as they become toddlers they'll get more adventurous and so they'll experience a lot more new, complex and stressful situations, even in familiar settings. It doesn't mean we shouldn't allow them all these experiences, it just means there needs to be a lot of adult intervention during the early years; and that means a lot of supervision.

The more extreme behaviours – those that our children need to *stop* immediately because they could be harming another child, us, an object, or be putting themselves in danger – can be called *red-light* behaviours. These behaviours are always exhibited for a reason, but our immediate priority should be to stop them before trying to analyse the cause. *How* we stop them is important, though. It is when our children exhibit the more extreme behaviours that we are most likely to yell, or worse, because we are mortified, scared or embarrassed by our child. This can result in us sending all kinds of unwanted messages to them. It's precisely at these times when we need to think calmly, professionally almost; take a couple of deep breaths before stepping in and stopping the behaviour without having our own emotional outburst. We can think about *why* our child acted in such an inappropriate way a little later.

One of the main advantages of professional carers, in circumstances like these, is that they can remain healthily detached and clear-headed as they guide, comfort and resolve such situations – because they are helping *other people's* children. We parents, however, are in danger of having our emotional 'buttons' pushed when we see things going wrong or our little one is not coping with a particular situation – 'Oh no! He's not doing this *again*, is he?' we might say to ourselves, or we might be embarrassed at our child's meltdown, their aggression towards another child or their rudeness towards us while in front of others. We might take what they're doing as a personal affront and imagine that our children are doing this in some way *on purpose*, and they will end up as horrible grown ups. Or we simply may not have *time* for this right now; we might need to get to an appointment or get home, or deal with another child.

Removing those emotional buttons

Rest assured, our young children do not do this to deliberately annoy us, but they will quickly absorb *how* we react to certain behaviours and store that information away. Psychologists and family counsellors tell us that if young children always see that our buttons get pushed when they throw a wobbly, scream or hit out, or we give them attention (albeit negative attention), or end up giving them what they want because of their meltdown – then yes, it will eventually make negative lasting connections between their behaviour and ours.

But as Dr Laura Markham of *AHA Parenting* understands it, children misbehaving-in-the-extreme are mainly asking us to *help* them; they are not coping with a particular situation so they need us to intervene. So we must be calm and caring; we must listen and understand; we must help them resolve the situation and help them move on from it – not add fuel to the flames. That's really all they want. Dr Markham reminds us that it's up to *us* to remove our emotionally-charged 'buttons', not be embarrassed at who might be looking, and remain clear-headed and calm as we step in and sort out the situation. They need our help to find their *way back home*.

In these situations, if we can *fake-up* some professionalism we, like preschool teachers and childminders, really can be super-soothing problem-solvers, and truly save the day, respecting our children and helping them through the social maze on the way to behavioural maturity.

When and how we intervene with *less* extreme but still unwanted *amber-light* behaviour is also important. If kept positive, respectful and calm, our interventions will help our children towards their social maturity – so they can be happy, understood, get along in a group and interact positively with other individuals in most situations as they approach the age at which they might start school.

If an *amber-light* behaviour feels like it's becoming a habit, though – perhaps they are regularly running off, or they always seem to be grabbing everything, for example – then we might feel we can't just keep stopping it, or ignoring it, again and again. We might want to target our help to specifically help them with the habitual nature of the behaviour; to:

☆ be there for your child while they go through the phase of whatever coping mechanism they're falling back on by simply acknowledging their behaviour, knowing they will not revert back to it forever;
☆ encourage them to replace the unwanted behaviour with something appropriate;
☆ offer carefully considered rewards for that particular behavioural issue, like a sticker chart or marbles in a jar, to show their successes at keeping to an appropriate behaviour;
☆ notice when they are exhibiting the behaviour we want and praise them for it. Nothing sustains the behaviour we want and shapes what they're going to do next like a well-timed bit of praise.

However, during the toddler and preschool years, for the majority of our time supervising our children, we should be on the look-out for opportunities to help them to learn certain skills rather than simply stopping those *red-* or *amber-light* behaviours. These are emotional and social skills, and sooner or later will include them:

☆ being able to share
☆ not being too timid, nor too assertive/aggressive or bossy
☆ learning some basic manners
☆ enjoying basic social interactions with grown ups and peers

☆ learning to wait their turn without tears or pushing in

☆ getting adult attention without whining, clinging, crying, screaming or throwing things

☆ being a leader, and sometimes a follower

☆ being able to listen, to follow a two or three step set of instructions, and to not ignore us

And to help with their emotional skills like:

☆ understanding others' feelings

☆ increasing positive thought patterns

☆ managing conflict without tears, trouble, a tantrum or aggression

☆ understanding and playing within rules

☆ gaining self-control

☆ acquiring problem-solving skills

☆ gaining the beginnings of resilience

☆ the beginnings of patience in order to practise something

If this all sounds rather complex and somewhat daunting, just imagine having to help twenty or so preschoolers – all at different stages of social and emotional development – with these skills, as nursery workers do in a busy classroom setting. As a parent you won't have to deal with nearly as many.

Good behaviour as normal behaviour

As a child advocate I agree with parenting expert Juliet Neill-Hall of *Teaching Expertise* who says that children have an inborn desire to please the people they love and care for, and seek approval from them. And this means I believe that we should always start from an *expectation* of good behaviour in our children – or *green-light* behaviour as some people call it. From this expectation we can build a firm foundation and structure of normal-behaviour-is-good-behaviour in which our children can become responsible, resilient and moral, with emotional accountability. As parenting expert, and family councillor, Dr Sears says, 'Parents who don't *expect* good behaviour, generally don't get it.'

Here's an example of a parent for whom the 'bedtime routine' is a chore to be endured. A journalist wrote about his experiences in an article for the *Telegraph* newspaper, where he revealed the 'bad' behaviour of his children.

'I then have to persuade all four children to get undressed, get into the bath, get into their pyjamas, do their teeth, get into bed and turn out the light. And they are not merely reluctant. They are hell-bent on resistance. As far as they're concerned, asking them to perform any of these tasks – rather than, say, letting them watch television or play video games – flies in the face of natural justice. They puff themselves up with moral indignation, outraged that I should have so little regard for their feelings, even though this has been the ritual every day of their lives. The phrase "herding kittens" doesn't do it justice. It's like trying to herd a group of tiny lawyers, all convinced that "herding" is a breach of the European Convention on Human Rights.'

Reading this made me wonder how things got so bad in their household. Why was he trying to 'herd' his children? They aren't sheep or cows. He was obviously struggling with his children's downward-spiralling negative behaviour – their rebellion against his demands. But there was also no *expectation* of good behaviour – and, it seems, no framework in which it might have been able to exist.

The framework in which good-behaviour-as-normal-behaviour, or *green-light* behaviour, exists doesn't magically appear; it is parent-made – and is usually built from us:

☆ modelling good behaviour
☆ making rules
☆ helping our children to keep within limits
☆ helping them to not go beyond boundaries
☆ developing their social-emotional skills

It's where all those adult common sense and common courtesies are born.

Encouraging good behaviour as normal behaviour – with play

These rules, limits and boundaries can be – and I believe *should* be – fun, light, positive and playful – especially when our children are toddlers and preschoolers. This is how nursery workers and Early Years teachers keep their classrooms happy and calm; normal behaviour is good behaviour, good behaviour is *green-light* behaviour, and *green-light* behaviour is fun. Using similar techniques at home, we can steer well clear of:

☆ most flashpoint furies
☆ regular resolute resistance
☆ many a meltdown moment

If the journalist had started from a more *playful* position, making those routines his children were resisting more positive and fun, then they would have been enthusiastic about getting ready for bed – happily in the *green light* – and a million miles away from being 'hell-bent on resistance'. How refreshing it would be for him to exploit the language of children – *play* – and experience the harmonious busy-buzz that comes from playful banter, fun challenges and little games to help young children get ready for bed.

By weaving *playful* moments into our family's rules, limits and boundaries and finding fun ways to motivate our little ones, we can truly connect with our young children and establish this firm structure in which good behaviour exists as normal behaviour. As play is the language children really understand, I believe using playful tactics is *essential* to keeping a young family's life rolling smoothly along – on a *green light* as it were.

If *most* of your days (and nights) are like this already, then you are definitely doing something right. I bet you model great behaviour and have lots of fun rules, games and rituals to happily get through the day – even if you hadn't thought about it like that before. And I bet you don't need to offer rewards or bribes either – because in your family *green-light* behaviour is just normal, usual, behaviour.

Sanity savers

Sanity savers will keep toddlers and preschoolers in the *green light* as much as possible. They can keep us from nagging or yelling, feeling exasperated, handing out rewards, having to repeat ourselves or tearing our hair out; losing our sanity. With these playful techniques we really can promote good-behaviour-as-normal-behaviour.

These ideas involve modelling good behaviour, communicating clearly and positively, and weaving fun rules, irresistible games and challenges into the fabric of family life. They use a toddler and preschooler's natural desire to play and be playful, and their love of routine and ritual to *get on*, *move things along* and *get things done*.

I asked parents via social media about when their family's day got most *challenging*. Mealtimes, getting out of the house and being in the supermarket seemed to be most problematic. But other pressure points were mentioned too, and some of these are listed below:

mealtimes ☆ cleaning teeth ☆ washing hands ☆ getting dressed ☆ using the potty or toilet ☆ washing hair ☆ bedtimes ☆ when it's time to leave ☆ getting in pushchair or car-seat ☆ in cafes and restaurants ☆ crossing roads and walking along nicely ☆ in the supermarket ☆ travelling in the car ☆ travelling by train or bus

As all these examples are things that might happen if not every day then quite frequently, wouldn't it be great if they weren't pressure points at all but, instead, opportunities to get our children practising those social niceties, good manners and appropriate behaviours? This is where sanity savers come in; fun rules, rituals and routines that *prevent* instead of *cure* unwanted behaviour; that take the confrontation and tense negotiation out of the equation, getting your children enthusiastically and happily playing along and behaving well, as a matter of course, most of the time.

Getting ready

The drive to be independent and to do things for themselves, using self-help skills, is a healthy part of normal child development. It can emerge strongly and early in some toddlers – way before their gross and fine motor skills are up to it, and everything gets very messy and slow for a while. If we try to take over and do things for these little ones, it usually results in them being outraged and even more determined to see the job through without any help from the grown up.

Other children don't develop the drive to be independent till much later, in which case we can find ourselves doing everything for them until we realise that they should and really could be doing these things for themselves.

It's important that we either allow the feisty independent ones, or encourage those for whom the independence-drive hasn't kicked in yet, to take responsibility for themselves whenever possible. By practising personal chores such as feeding and dressing themselves, not only do they hone those motor skills but they also gain confidence in their ability to try new things, they'll build their self-esteem, learn to accept help and begin to take pride in their independence.

Here are some playful ways to inject some fun, silliness, momentum and structure into personal chores, helping your little one to become independent and self-reliant in their own time, without pressure or negativity; keeping it all in the *green light*.

Washing hands

Ensuring young children wash their hands is the best way to prevent the spread of germs but, of course, they won't see it like that, and they certainly won't be motivated by that. Instead, encourage them to scrub and rub with water and soap for at least 20 seconds before snacks and meals and after using the toilet by modelling the correct way to do it yourself.

You could try singing the *ABC* song, or *Twinkle, Twinkle Little Star* together while they wash their hands, or make up your own song that lasts about 20 seconds. You might like to try this one, which also helps to flag up the correct order of doing things:

The hand-washing song (sing to the tune 🎵
of In and Out the Dusty Bluebells)

Wash our hands
With lots of soap now
Wash our hands
With lots of soap now
Wash our hands with lots of soap now
Can you see the bubbles? YES!

Now it's time
To rinse our hands clean
Now it's time
To rinse our hands clean
Now it's time
To rinse our hands clean
Can you see the bubbles? NO!

Dry our hands
On the towel now
Dry our hands
On the towel now
Dry our hands
On the towel now
Do we have clean hands now? YES

Brushing teeth

Most young children like the idea of cleaning their teeth – having their own brush and little tube of paste makes them feel very grown up. However, the fine motor skills required to squeeze the correct amount of toothpaste out of the tube, to apply it to the toothbrush and then to brush effectively don't come without a lot of practice. They will watch you cleaning your teeth with fascination – so try to model this activity whenever you can, and every once in a while let them try brushing your teeth.

☆ Try getting your little one to squeeze a pea-sized blob of toothpaste onto a little plate or plastic lid rather than directly onto their toothbrush – it's a much bigger target. Then they can pick up the paste with their brush from there.

☆ Your little ones might like to practise their toothbrushing through role-play. Use an old (but clean) toothbrush and any hand puppet with a jaw. We have a horse puppet that is very bossy about how he likes his teeth cleaned, and he makes sure the children brush every tooth in his mouth – they love it. You could even make some pretend teeth out of a small plastic circular lid (like from a pot of fresh soup or custard). Bend it in half to form a kind of jaw and *voilà* – it's a mouth ready to be cleaned. You could make a pink paper tongue and stick it to the inside of the 'mouth'. You can make it talk to your little one as they practise their brushing technique.

☆ Try singing a tooth-brushing song – once as they brush, and again for you to take a turn – if you need to make sure their teeth are clean. The classic 'This is the Way We Brush our Teeth on a Cold and Frosty Morning' is a good one to start with, but why not make up your own to any tune you and your child know well?

A favourite of ours is sung to the tune of Alicia Keys hit, 'New York':

We are brushing 🎵
Brushing all our teeth, they're so shiny
And ever so minty

We are brushing
Brushing them to make them so bright
And very white
We are brushing
(brushing . . . brushing . . . brushing . . .)

Getting dressed

The simpler the clothes are to put on the more likely your child is to be able to get dressed with minimal help so, when buying clothes for toddlers, try to choose items that don't have poppers, zips and other fastenings; maybe save clothes with these for special occasions. If your child likes to choose their clothes, put out a few options (which all coordinate, if that's important to you) that are appropriate for the day's activities, so that he or she feels they are making the final decision. But be prepared for some crazy combinations – don't worry – a preschooler can get away with most things and look brilliant – it's one of their special talents.

☆ Start by encouraging them to get undressed by themselves; this is a much easier skill for young children to master. Most little ones love the challenge of seeing how quickly they can strip off ready for a bath. They'll soon get the order in which garments need to be removed.

☆ When they're attempting to get dressed themselves, help your child avoid the pants-over-the-trousers look by setting out their clothes in the order they need to be put on. You could have fun with this by deliberately getting it wrong – your little one will soon catch on and be looking for your silly mistakes. Try putting a halved sticker in each of their shoes. The halves should match up if they get their shoes on the right feet.

☆ Try setting out your child's clothes on the floor in a fun action-shape – like a running pose, or in a star jump. Challenge your little one to get the clothes into the same position once dressed in them – it's a wonderful motivational carrot.

☆ Try using a rhyme to help break down the order of putting on items of clothing, and to help orientate them correctly. For example:

Easy as one, two, three 🎵

What's on the front of your top?
Where should the label be?
Pick it up; pull it over your head
Make sure you can see.
POP! (as their head comes out)

What's on the front of your top?
Where should the label be?
Post your arms through each sleeve
It's as easy as one, two, three!

Let your toddler try the more manageable parts of the dressing process – you can always sing a song to help the job along without stepping on any independent toes:

Keiri is pulling up his pants ♫
Keiri is pulling up his pants
Hey there everyone
Keiri can do it
Keiri is pulling up his pants

Mia is putting on her top
Mia is putting on her top
Hey there everyone
Mia can do it
Mia is putting on her top

Leo is finding both his sleeves
Leo is finding both his sleeves
Hey there everyone
Leo can do it
Leo is finding both his sleeves

Reemna is putting on her socks
Reemna is putting on her socks
Hey there everyone
Reemna can do it
Reemna is putting on her socks

Going to the toilet

For toddlers and young children who are just starting to make the transition from nappies to pants, going to the toilet is a time when having one-to-one interaction with you is very important. At this stage it's necessary to respond to their needs, often very quickly, in a sensitive way. Accidents will happen, so it's important to remember that the way we react when they don't quite make it, or it gets a bit messy, gives children powerful messages about themselves and their bodies. Using the toilet is a rather complex process. It has several steps, all of which require skills that children need to learn, often with a lot of support and a lot of praise, initially. These include:

☆ recognising the need to use the toilet
☆ pulling down pants
☆ sitting on the toilet or potty and keeping balance
☆ wiping their bottom
☆ getting off the toilet or potty
☆ pulling up pants
☆ flushing the toilet
☆ washing and drying hands

They will also watch you go to the toilet with avid interest so, if you're comfortable with this, occasionally explain what you're doing and get them to help with flushing the toilet or tearing off the toilet paper.

Try using a song to help break down the order of tasks necessary for toilet or potty use. For example:

The going to the toilet song ♪

Davy is pulling down his pants
Davy is pulling down his pants
Hey there, everyone, Davy can do it
Davy is pulling down his pants

Evie is doing a wee. Weeee!
Evie is doing a wee. Weeee!
Hey there, everyone, Evie can do it
Evie is doing a wee. Weeee!

Henry can tear off some paper
Henry can tear off some paper
Hey there, everyone, Henry can do it
Henry can tear off some paper

Celine is wiping herself dry (or clean)
Celine is wiping herself dry (or clean)
Hey there, everyone, Celine can do it
Celine is wiping herself dry (or clean)

Fred is flushing the loo (whoosh)
Fred is flushing the loo (whoosh)
Hey there, everyone, Fred can do it
Fred is flushing the loo (whoosh)

Practise the more complex toileting skills with toys and games, and light-hearted rules:

☆ Hand over a metre length of clean toilet roll for tearing along the serrations practice. See how many squares of paper they can separate without ripping. (The paper could be returned to the toilet area for use later, so as not to waste paper.)

☆ Put a little marker on the wall to show them how far down to pull the toilet paper from the roll.

☆ Let them play with teddies and dolls, helping the toys use the (toy) potty or changing their nappies.

☆ Put a positive spin on reminding them about going to the toilet in time, and when there's opportunity. For example, before you go out you might all have a Make Sure wee, then there's the Bedtime wee and the Just Up wee. Your little one will soon enjoy checking you visit the toilet at these times too.

Mealtimes

By the time children have reached toddlerhood, their *habits* of eating have already started to take shape. Whether you've spoon-fed them since they began to take solid food or you've gone for the self-feeding approach (or for a combination of the two), mealtime habits will have become part of your little one's everyday routine.

Making mealtimes happy, positive and sociable occasions should be our aim from as soon as they are eating solid meals throughout the day. The easiest way of making them so is to *model* the kinds of mealtimes you'd like yourself. Maybe you don't want to have your main meal with your little one just yet, but there will be at least two other opportunities in your day when you can join them for a meal, and show your child the good habits of mealtimes – from happy chat and a pleasant atmosphere, to sitting up 'nicely', eating healthily and eating independently with developing manners or, if with help, then without *biting the hand that feeds*.

Yes, mealtimes will be messy for a few years yet, but that doesn't mean they have to be miserable. Get your little ones enthusiastic about mealtimes, keep their interest during the meal and give them time to enjoy their food and the sociable nature of the occasion by:

Encouraging enthusiasm

☆ Look for some fun children's cookbooks at the library and let your child choose a recipe every now and again.

☆ Encourage interest in what's on their plate. When you have finished putting on all their food, point to each item and say what it is. Make up some silly ones too – that'll keep them listening and laughing. For example, 'So, we've got some fish there, two potatoes there, two hats and a slice of glove there.'

☆ Try different foods as a positive and exciting opportunity. For example, having tapas like Nan loves, or spaghetti with cheese like their friend Jake enjoys.

Give them time

☆ Give your little ones a clear heads-up when a meal is approaching – let them know they'll have time to do one more thing before lunchtime, for example.

☆ Be playful when calling them for dinner; call the parrots to the birdtable for their seeds, or the cheeky monkeys for their bananas. Or let them ring a dinner-gong or bell telling everyone (even if it's just them) that it's time to eat.

☆ Give your little one time to eat. Pass the time with gentle chat about this and that, including some talk of the food, but don't just talk about the food.

☆ Keep mealtimes short and sweet. If they need to stretch their legs between courses, let them.

Keep their focus

☆ Focus their attention on the table by letting them help you check everything's ready. 'Spoons?' They could reply, 'CHECK!' 'Forks?' 'CHECK!' 'Glasses?' 'CHECK!' And so on. You could add a few silly ones to keep them interested; 'Toothbrushes?' 'CHE . . . Whaaa . . . ? NO!'

☆ Have some fun with the meal sometimes. Arranging their food in a simple picture – a face, a truck, a person and the like – on their plate can help them keep focused. 'Look, I am eating the wheels!' they might announce, as they pick up a slice of cucumber.

☆ Have a few little competitions along the way. For example, find out who can make the noisiest crunch when biting their carrot baton, or who can give the broccoli the craziest haircut.

☆ Invest in a table-top bookstand, then choose a book (large, take-a-look books work really well) and if your child becomes restless or loses interest during the meal, you've got something close at hand to talk about and look at without it being in your hands or theirs.

☆ Sometimes, bringing a favourite soft toy or toy figure to the table is a good way to keep them focused. For example, 'Let's see if *Spiderman* would like some mashed potato too – I heard it was his favourite.'

☆ Get imaginative. If it's a hand-held morsel – like a slice of pizza or a sandwich – try playing a little game where whenever a bite is taken you take it in turns to decide what the shape looks like. 'It's a dress!', takes a bite, 'Now it's a cloud!'

☆ Get singing. Try a few food-themed songs while the plates are being filled, or between courses.

Try *One potato, two potatoes* (see p.250) or

On top of spaghetti ♫

On top of spaghetti all covered with cheese.
I lost my poor meatball when somebody sneezed.

It rolled off the table, it rolled on the floor,
And then my poor meatball rolled out of the door.

It rolled in the garden and under a bush,
And then my poor meatball was nothing but mush.

So if you eat spaghetti all covered with cheese,
Hold on to your meatballs and don't ever sneeze.

Bananas in pyjamas ♫

Bananas in pyjamas are coming down the stairs,
Bananas in pyjamas are coming down in pairs,
Bananas in pyjamas are chasing teddy bears,
'cause on Tuesdays they all try to catch them unawares!

Five fat sausages ♫

Five fat sausages sizzling in a pan
one went pop the other went bang.

Four fat sausages sizzling in a pan
one went pop the other went bang.

Three fat sausages sizzling in a pan
one went pop the other went bang.

Two fat sausages sizzling in a pan
one went pop the other went bang.

One fat sausage sizzling in a pan
one went pop the other went bang.
No fat sausages sizzling in a pan.

Hot cross buns ♫

Hot cross buns,
Hot cross buns,
one ha' penny,
two ha' penny,
hot cross buns

If you have no daughters,
give them to your sons,
one ha' penny,
two ha' penny,
hot cross buns

☆ Make sure the TV is switched off. If it's all a bit too quiet, try putting on a CD of nursery rhymes or gentle, child-friendly songs, to listen to during the meal. This will make for a pleasant atmosphere without distracting you or your child from the meal like TV can.

Surprises

☆ Why not try having the food like a character from a children's book; you could try making Milly-Molly-Mandy's lid-potatoes or Pippi Longstocking's pancakes, or Lola's (of Charlie and Lola fame) moon-squirters. Why not read them the part of the story in which the food features beforehand to build up the excitement?

☆ Try having a few dishes from which children can serve themselves; make it even more fun by naming the food imaginatively – perhaps with an explorer theme – with houmous for quick-sand, cucumber batons cut in half, almost but not quite, lengthwise for crocodile jaws, and breadsticks for tree trunks – that kind of thing.

☆ Surprise them with a friend popping round for a meal, preferably a good eater, and see the sociable side of mealtimes blossom.

Bath-time and washing hair

Helping your toddler learn to love a bath usually paves the way for similarly blissful times in the tub when they become preschoolers.

Come on in, the water's fine

☆ Add different and unexpected things to the water before your child gets in – not all at once, of course. Ring the changes and keep surprising your child with 'What's in the bath tub today?' Try glow-sticks, Duplo or Octons or any other waterproof blocks, stick-on craft-foam shapes, waterproof books, or go low-tech with tubs and containers from the recycling box.

☆ Pop in a balloon whisk, a plastic measuring jug and some small containers for 'milkshake' or 'cupcake' making.

☆ Add plastic sea creatures, the rubber ducks, waterproof figures or a few plastic cars.

☆ Natural materials work well in the bath too; try adding rose petals, a few ice cubes, some clean leaves, some wood bark or some orange peel.

☆ Colouring the water blue, with just a spot of blue food colouring, will make it look like the sea.

☆ Offer a little plastic bucket containing shaving cream, plus a soft paintbrush; let your little one get creative with some 'painting' in the tub.

Now it's time to wash their hair

☆ Above all, we need to be calm and positive. If we look nervous, they'll definitely get the fear too.

☆ You could give them a choice about when their hair will get washed – some little ones feel better when they have a choice. Will they wash their hair before or after dolly today?

Then make it fun:

☆ Let your child wash a dolly's hair in the bath. You might even be allowed to wash your child's hair at the same time. Make a game of it, so you're keeping up with dolly's progress.

☆ Try putting an acrylic (safety) mirror at the end of the bath to help your little one make shapes with their shampoo-covered hair. We've had spikes, ice cream, rabbit ears, horns and Elvis hair before.

When it's time to rinse:

☆ If you're using a showerhead to rinse away the suds, let your little one have a chance to judge if it's the correct temperature. Test it out on their hand and then their knee, then their back. Slowly, slowly, they'll find that it's lovely, and will accept it on their head.

☆ Looking up can be encouraged by putting fun stickers or a mobile on the ceiling above the bath so they have something to look at.

☆ Cover their eyes if they don't like the water running into them – a dry facecloth usually does the trick. They could hold it on themselves – it might be a magical facecloth that lets them see all kinds of places when it's over their eyes. Ask them what they can 'see' today.

☆ Sing a special hair-washing song – the noisier the better, so that they can join in and not worry about the whole hair-washing thing. We like:

I had a little turtle ♪
His name was Tiny Tim
I put him in the bath tub

To see if he could swim
He drank up all the water
He ate up all the soap
And now he's gone to bed
With a bubble in his throat!

Or:

Look at the stars 🎵
See how they shine for you
And everything that you do
Goodbye to you, shampoo

I wrote a song
I wrote a song for you
And everything that you do
Goodbye to you, shampoo

☆ If they favour the lying-back-in-the bath technique of rinsing hair, make a lot of it being relaxing, or that they're a water fairy, mermaid or sprite. Their hair will waft and wave in the water as they imagine they are floating in the shallow waters of a magical lagoon. Keep things as calm as possible here; a moment or two of serenity.

Their bath-times may be so good that they are reluctant to leave the tub:

☆ Give them a heads-up that it will soon be time to be an enchilada (i.e. wrapped in their towel). In the winter, you could put their towel on a radiator to warm through – for a hot enchilada. When they get out, wrap them tightly in it, asking them what's in the enchilada today.

☆ The promise of something when they're dry is an example of using when/then positively. For example, 'When you're out and dry, then we'll have a story', or 'When you're out and dry, then Daddy will put on the twinkly-star nightlight', or 'When you're out and dry, then we'll have a cuddle'.

☆ Or create a little challenge. 'I bet you can't get dried before all the bath water runs out,' or 'Can you get dried by the time Mummy counts to thirty? Can it be done?'

Bedtime

If we want our little one's bedtime routine to be free of resistance, rebellion, procrastination and shenanigans, it is up to us to make it so. We have to bear in mind that it all happens at the *end of the day* and this is when *we* will have little left in terms of energy, resilience and patience. This is the main reason why we should decide on a simple bedtime routine that suits us and our child, and then stick to it. If we keep chopping and changing it, adding to it with requests for this and ideas for that, we'll soon have a complicated and stressful route to bedtime on our hands; no good can come of that. Golden Slumbers is what we're after – not Gold Medals for stamina.

Make sure they're tired enough

☆ If you feel your little one might still have some puppy wriggles to get out, make sure you factor in some bouncing on the trampette, or instigate a run around in the garden, or maybe put on some lively music for some dancing at least an hour and a half before bedtime.

Start the wind-down at least an hour before bedtime

☆ Don't initiate any tickle sessions or rough-and-tumble games. If you're just in from work and want to spend some time with your little one, pick something calm to do with them, like sharing a book or building with bricks together.

☆ This isn't the time to put on the TV or let them have any screen-time in fact. It can really have a negative effect on your little one's ability to fall asleep.

☆ Turn down the lights a little, and if you have any music playing, change it to something a little softer.

☆ Give your little one a gentle heads-up that it will soon be time for 'the night-time jobs' to begin.

The route to bedtime begins

☆ Start the routine gently but clearly, and certainly positively, with the first 'night-time job' on your list. Your little one may know what this is – perhaps it's Tidy-up Time (see p.18 for ideas of how to make this fun), or perhaps it's putting on their pyjamas. Set them a challenge like, 'You couldn't get your pyjamas on by the time this song finishes, could you?' or by laying out their PJs in a silly way, and challenging them to get into the very same position as the PJs' shape once they're in them.

☆ Check with them. 'Is that all the night-time jobs done?' They'll soon tell you what the next job is and think you're funny for 'forgetting'. If teeth-cleaning is next, why not get to the bathroom by tiptoeing – creep up on those toothbrushes in the beaker; try to catch them having their 'tooth-brush party'. To make tooth-brushing fun, see p.276.

☆ After tooth-brushing it could be time for the night-time wee. See p.280 for playful ways to encourage them to happily complete that job.

☆ When it's time to go to their bedroom, maybe tiptoe back; creep round the door to see if you can spot the soft toys 'jumping on the bed', or something equally playful.

☆ With soft lights on, now's the time to check again that all the night-time jobs have been done. Get them to help you remember. 'PJs on?' 'CHECK',

'Teeth?' 'CHECK, 'Have breakfast?' 'CHE . . . Whaa . . . NO!' They'll love it when you make silly mistakes.

☆ The next night-time job might be to *spritz* (water) any monsters away, or whatever technique you know keeps those pesky pests at bay – if that happens to be an issue with your child.

☆ *Say the day.* This is a gentle way to remember the day. Say one great thing about the day to each other; a special one-to-one quiet conversation.

☆ If there are any worries to share, now's the time to do it. We have used those little worry dolls before (you tell one of them your worry then you then pop it under your pillow to help the worry go during the night). These are particularly good if your little one is prone to feeling anxious; it gets all those worries out there and addressed in a second.

☆ Keep checking in with your little one as to how the list of night-time jobs is going, 'So is that all the night-time jobs done now?' 'We put on our PJs, we cleaned our teeth, we did our *night-time* wee, we told each other our *wows* and our *woes* of the day. Is that it?' 'No! We have to have our story!'

☆ Let your little one pick the story. There are so many lovely picture books to choose from. Do use your local library; you could have a special borrowed-bedtime-book season, for example.

☆ Getting your little one into bed before the *grand finale*, i.e. a story, is a good way to make them happily make that final manoeuvre. You could use a when/then to help with this. '*When* you've got into your bed, *then* we can have our story', or '*When* the cuddly toy you need is in bed and ready, *then* we can start our story'. Make a big thing of storytime; it really should be a special part of the bedtime routine. (See p.228 for tips on making the most out of sharing a book with a little one.)

☆ You could sing them a lullaby. Here are our favourites. We love them because they each have a simple narrative as well as a calming melody:

All the pretty little horses 🎵

Hush-a-bye don't you cry,
Go to sleep-y, little baby.
When you wake you shall have
All the pretty little horses.
Blacks and bays, dapple grays,
Coach and six white horses.
Hush-a-bye don't you cry,
Go to sleep-y, little baby.

Mockingbird 🎵

Hush, little baby, don't say a word,
Papa's gonna buy you a mockingbird

And if that mockingbird won't sing,
Papa's gonna buy you a diamond ring

And if that diamond ring turns brass,
Papa's gonna buy you a looking glass

And if that looking glass gets broke,
Papa's gonna buy you a billy goat

And if that billy goat won't pull,
Papa's gonna buy you a cart and bull

And if that cart and bull turn over,
Papa's gonna buy you a dog named Rover

And if that dog named Rover won't bark
Papa's gonna buy you a horse and cart

And if that horse and cart fall down,
You'll still be the sweetest little baby in town.

☆ All picture books for this age group finish with a happy ending, so when the story is done, or the lullaby has lilted its last, and there have been kisses goodnight, of course, do remind them to think about the story when they shut their eyes. They might get to 'see' it again in their mind's eye if they think carefully enough.

☆ Finally, lights should be turned off, but should a night-light be required this can be left on, glowing reassuringly. (See p.210 to see how to make an owl night-light.)

☆ Returning to your child's room with a small glass of water a couple of minutes later is a good way to check they are doing the last night-time job. 'What is the very last night-time job?' 'To close my eyes and find sweet dreams'.

☆ Sometimes turning their pillow (for extra coolness and comfort) and tucking them in again is the perfect way to get them really still, ready to have sweet dreams and hopefully a long and good night's sleep.

Daily transitions

Whether it's time to leave the house, the park, nursery or a friend's house, or to have lunch, making the transition from one activity to another can be a real pressure point in a young family's day. As toddlers are still grappling with how to control their impulses, asking your child to stop what they are currently doing (and enjoying) is undoubtedly going to be tough. However, using their love of playful rules and rituals, it really is possible to make those transitions clear and tempting to a young child.

☆ Give them plenty of warning that it will soon be time to leave or change activities. Instead of saying how long they've got left in minutes, though, talk in terms of what they've got time to do before you need to go, so perhaps there's time for five more turns on the slide, or there's time to look at three more books, or whatever's relevant for your situation.

☆ Check in with them as you spot they are on their last turn, or book or whatever, and praise them for getting to the 'last one' so nicely.

☆ Help them become interested in the next activity by gently 'selling it'. If it's to get an ice cream or to visit their friend, say, then this shouldn't be too hard. Chat about it as you physically move away from the old activity. Often this is enough to get them happily trotting along with you, listening about how great it's going to be to see their friend, or telling you what ice cream they're going to choose.

☆ If the next activity is rather more mundane, and you're not quite sure how to put a positive spin on 'getting in the car to go home', instead, make the journey there irresistible. You can sing-as-you-go with a march or a skip, for example:

Skip to my Lou *(a skipping song)* ♫

Skip, skip, skip to my Lou, (3x)
Skip to my Lou, my darlin'.

Verse here (repeated 3 times)
Skip to my Lou, my darlin'.

Verses
Fly's in the buttermilk, shoo, fly, shoo
There's a little red wagon, paint it blue
Lost my partner, what'll I do?
Cat's in the cream jar, ooh, ooh, ooh

Or

The grand old Duke of York *(a marching song)* 🎵

Oh, the grand old Duke of York,
He had ten thousand men,
He marched them up to the top of
the hill and he marched
them down again.

And when they were up, they were up
And when they were down they were down.

And when they were only half way up,
They were neither up nor down.

☆ Give them a choice as to whether they hold hands with you or jump all the way to the car. Giving them a choice (between two ways of complying) gives them a sense of some control. And if your toddler refuses to budge, you might ask them if they want to walk to the car or they want a piggy-back. Don't ask a question that can be answered with a 'no', though, or you will definitely get a 'no'!

☆ Set yourselves a challenge. 'Do you think we could hop like frogs all the way to our shoes?', or 'How many giant's footsteps will it take to get to our coats? Let's see'.

☆ My two children used to love the book *We're Going on A Bear Hunt*, so I would often use this to help them get downstairs or out and into the car or whatever. We'd just say it out loud, 'Oh look, a river!' and then we'd splish splash through it. And then, 'Oh look, some grass!' And then swish, swish through that, and we'd be there.

☆ If strapping into the car seat or pushchair is frequently a struggle, make it more playful, instead of a battle of wills. You might see if you could get it done before you count to five, or by the time you've finished a verse of *Twinkle, Twinkle Little Star*. Or make up your own story or rhyme for 'buckling-in time'.

☆ *'Is this astronaut ready to get strapped in to the rocket? It's nearly time to take off. She's getting into her space suit; she's lowering her space helmet; she's putting on her moon-boots. But will she be safely strapped in before the rocket blasts into space? The engines are starting . . . The countdown begins . . . ' and so on*

Or

One, two, buckle straps blue ♫
Three, four, sit down for more
Five, six, strap Sam in quick
Seven, eight, we won't be late
Nine, ten, safely in then

☆ Sometimes, the offer of bringing along a favourite toy can help to make the idea of transition a little more appealing to a young child.

Getting their attention is sometimes the tricky part. They may even develop the talent of being able to shut out your voice altogether. They are not doing this to be 'naughty' – they are simply engrossed in what they're doing and they'll need some help to burst their bubble of bliss. Get their attention in a positive and clear way; don't tell them your instruction or your great idea for transition yet – they won't hear it. Instead:

☆ You might go close to them and say their name along with an ever-so-polite expression to catch their attention, for example, 'Excuse me, Daisy'. Or you might whisper their name and say, 'listen' as if you're going to tell them a fantastic secret.

Or sing-song quietly something like,

> '*Buddy, Buddy, one, two, three* ♫
> *Buddy, Buddy, listen to me*'

☆ If they're charging around you can attract their attention by a short rhythm of claps and/or movement like patting your head, or 'winding up the bobbin'. If you practise this in a game they'll soon know that when they hear the claps, they've to copy your rhythm and movement.

☆ Get down to your child's level whenever possible. Crouch down and tell them clearly what needs to happen; they don't necessarily need to be *looking* at you for this one to work. It's like putting the clutch down, and helps them switch gears to move on to the next activity.

Sometimes, if asking them to make the transition to a new activity makes them angry or frustrated, or if they are over-tired or hungry, then they could well 'lose it' and go over to the dark side. If this happens, then no amount of playful banter and tactics will work. They are obviously dealing with some pretty big emotions, or they are so tired or hungry that a meltdown comes over them with the speed and ferocity of a tidal wave – and there's nothing they can do about it yet. It's all part of being a two- or three-year-old with developing emotional self-control. At this point, they need our help. We need to recognise their anger or upset and acknowledge it verbally, 'I know you don't want to come in for lunch. I know it's a fun game. I know you're sad.' Let them have their big feelings without trying to distract them with tricks and the like, and let them know you're going to help them move on to the next activity. Comfort them; give them time to be with you and to express their frustrations or sadness, but then let them know you will help them leave. Then gently help your child back home to *green-light* behaviour.

Walking along 'nicely'

The desire to get out of the pushchair and 'be free' is a healthy part of normal child development. It can emerge strongly and early in some toddlers – way before their gross motor skills or listening skills are really up to it. In allowing your child to *try* walking along with you, you may discover them to be a slow ambler, with little to no forward momentum, or they might become like a rabbit out of a trap the moment they are given any freedom. Neither situation is acceptable, of course. If they are hoping to walk along 'nicely' on the pavement then it's up to us to help them become experts because, first and foremost, they need to be *safe*.

The answer is practise, practise, practise. The more opportunities we can give our toddler to try out the skills involved in walking along 'nicely', the more confident we will feel about letting them out of their pushchair and being one of the big kids.

Mastering the art of walking along 'nicely' with a grown up is a rather complex process. There are several levels of trust, and so there are several levels of freedom. There must be certain rules at every level to ensure everyone's safety. These include the child being able to:

☆ Listen well
☆ Respond appropriately to the grown up's instructions or reminders
☆ Walk holding on to the pushchair or the grown up's hand when asked
☆ Sometimes walk along next to the grown up without holding hands at an agreed distance
☆ Come straight back to the adult very quickly when asked

To practise, choose somewhere in your neighbourhood, like a paved lane or a pedestrianised street where there aren't too many distracting temptations for your child, and try these exercises to help those walking along 'nicely' skills with positivity and fun.

☆ Hone their listening skills by asking them to hold on to your hand or pushchair alternately every 10–20 seconds as you walk along by saying *Hand* or *Pushchair*! Make it fun by sometimes saying *Hand* twice in a row.

☆ Play *Red Light, Green Light.* Start with them holding your hand or the pushchair. *Red* means stop; *Green* means walk. They'll eventually be able to play this without holding hands. When they get good at this, add *Reverse* for them to come right back and hold your hand; if unpredictable things happen when walking along with your child, it's important that you can trust them to come back to you immediately.

When your child gets reliable with walking along holding your hand, eventually you can let go, telling them you are giving them a chance to walk near you. Let them know that if they get too far away, they will be asked to revert straight back to holding hands.

☆ If they get too much speed up, try saying *Brakes on.* This is a fun way of making them think like Thomas the Tank Engine or similar; they'll not be able to resist playing along and slowing down. There may be sound effects.

☆ Play *Back to me.* This is very useful for when your little one is getting good at walking along without holding hands. As soon as they hear you say '*Back to me!*' they have to come right back to your side. See if they can do this before you've counted to five.

Your child will need gentle reminders of how to behave when walking along. They may understand that they are supposed to walk by you, but they may not have developed that degree of self-control yet. And as much as you may try to instil the dangers of traffic or getting lost, it may really not mean much to your child just yet. So:

☆ Keep reminders and instructions simple and positive. Stating things in a positive way gets them thinking in the right direction. For example, *'Please hold my hand when we cross the road'* rather than *'Why aren't you holding my hand when we cross the road?'* or *'Stay on the pavement'* rather than *'Don't go on the road'*.

If they're pretty good at this whole walking along 'nicely' thing, you may find you can walk a fair way without the pushchair. However, they *will* get tired and will definitely need motivating to carry on after the out-of-the-pushchair novelty has gone. Try the following games to keep them going.

Let's Go!

This simple game involves you taking turns to announce *how* the journey will take place. So for example, it might start with, *Let's march to the next tree*, then, *Now, let's jump to the next corner* and then, *Now, let's trot to that wall.*

Make up a little story about your journey – if it's a route you take often you can be very imaginative with its well-known features. For example, *'Let's see if that little cat is home at no. 47. Ah – she's out on another adventure. Now, let's creep past the giant's garden (the allotment) so as not to wake him. I think I can hear him snoring! Now we're at the Pavement Maze. We have to walk on the cracks to get to the Whispering Tree. Can you hear it? What is it telling us today?'* etc . . .

If you have to walk somewhere on a cold, possibly snowy day, why not use Winnie-the Pooh's motivational hum as you stomp along:

The more it snows (Tiddely pom), ♫
The more it goes (Tiddely pom),
The more it goes (Tiddely pom),
On snowing.

And nobody knows (Tiddely pom),
How cold my toes (Tiddely pom),
How cold my toes (Tiddely pom),
Are growing.

A marching song usually motivates everyone very well. Here's another tune, which might just do the job:

They're changing guard at Buckingham Palace –
Christopher Robin went down with Alice.
Alice is marrying one of the guard.
'A soldier's life is terrible hard,'
Says Alice.

They're changing guard at Buckingham Palace –
Christopher Robin went down with Alice.
We saw a guard in a sentry-box.
'One of the sergeants looks after their socks,'
Says Alice.

Supermarket sweep

Love it or loathe it, it's inevitable that at some stage you'll be taking your little one with you while you shop at the supermarket. Before having children, you may have witnessed some pretty sobering scenes down the aisles of your local shop – whining kids or screaming toddlers, parents yelling and tempers frayed – so you're determined that this won't be you and your little family. But how can we get our children to keep in the *green light* under the bright lights of the supermarket? Here are some playful tips and ideas to make your trip tolerable and, hopefully, even pleasurable.

☆ Good times need good timing. Choose a time of day when you and your children are likely to be at your best. Overtiredness and hunger can factor hugely in determining the success of the supermarket experience. When you and your child are wakeful and with full tummies, that's the optimum time to make that trip.

Trolley tricks. Most young children love to ride in the trolley; if you want your child to be happy in there for a while, think about what the experience might be like for them.

☆ Make it comfortable by popping in a jumper, or the like, as cushioning, and always secure the safety straps.

☆ Give them a job straight away – this will start them off feeling very grown up and wanting to help. Try putting them in charge of the 'shopping list' for a few aisles – an old receipt usually works well. Hand over a crayon so they can 'tick things off' when the items have been placed in the trolley.

☆ Keep them posted with what you're looking for next. Let them look around for it too, and if they spot it 'first', praise them for their great detective work.

☆ Talk about the items as they go into the trolley – chat about who in your family loves apples, how many bananas you need to pick out, that kind of thing. Let them hold the more robust items for a while; 'looking after them'. These can be added to the trolley once the novelty has worn off.

☆ Change your tactic for each aisle to keep their interest. So, down one you could get them to sing a well-known tune. How many times can they sing it before you reach the end? Down another, a later aisle with less fresh stuff perhaps, you could play *Box, Tin, Packet, Bottle*. Just choose one type of packaging per aisle and look carefully for examples of it on the shelves. Say you choose *Bottle* as your first category, your little one could point and call out *'Bottle!'* every time they see one. Choose *Box* as your category for another aisle then every time you or your little one sees a box on the shelf they call out '*Box!*'

☆ Snacks on the home stretch are a great idea; bring something from home. A piece of cut-up apple, a few raisins, a rice cake or cracker could be handed out at intervals as you load up the trolley with the final items; perhaps every time you reach a new aisle.

☆ The checkout queue can be lengthy. Here's where you can give your little one some attention with some favourite songs, or a game like *Mirror Mirror* where they have to try to copy all your moves and facial expressions. (See p.257 for some more one-to-one games.)

☆ While you're loading up the conveyer belt, packing the shopping back in the trolley, and paying, you'll need to pull something out of the bag – literally. It could be a book, a couple of toy cars, a small soft toy and a handkerchief blanket, or any item that's tempting and absorbing for a while. This will work especially well if they haven't seen that particular toy in a while.

Remember to praise your child throughout the supermarket visit; for sitting so well in the trolley, for being such a great help picking out those sausages or for singing so sweetly to get you to the end of an aisle. Nothing sustains the behaviour you want and influences what they're going to do next like a well-timed bit of praise.

Travelling in the car or on the bus

For most young children, travelling on a bus or in the car is an exciting and interesting experience. That is until there's a traffic jam or it just goes on too long. Some parents, however, don't even give it a chance to be interesting; instead they immediately switch on the in-car DVD player, or hand over their iPhone or the like, as if their child needs to be plugged-in to travel. This is, of course, not the case. Even though it's not possible for us to physically play with our children in such situations we can certainly have some vocal and visual fun and games to make everyone's journey interesting, fun and in the *real* world.

Play some simple word games.

Can you spot . . . ?

This game is great for getting everyone looking around and out of the windows at the ever-changing scenery. Youngest goes first usually, and picks something for everyone to look out for. So it could be a shed, or a dog, or a cyclist. Whatever they like. Sometimes it can be a minute or two before someone spots whatever's been chosen.

I went shopping and I bought . . .

This game is superb for giving everyone's memory a good workout. Youngest goes first to choose something to buy at the shops. They then say, 'I went shopping and I bought a cake' or whatever they thought of. The next person has to choose something else to buy but also has to buy the cake. So they might say, 'I went shopping and I bought a cake, and a bicycle.' Carry on shopping and adding to the list. Keep the rounds short to start with – see if you can get to buying, say, six things. Then start again.

Be music reviewers

This one works very well in the car. Choose a CD – perhaps a compilation – and after listening to each song everyone has to say whether they thought it was good, bad or ugly. Everyone decides their favourite tune at the end.

Count Christmas trees

Of course the thing you actually count doesn't have to be Christmas trees. Just decide what you're going to look out for during the journey and stick to it. Steer clear of counting anything that's too abundant

– 'cars', for example – but you could choose '*red* cars' or perhaps 'yellow front doors', or maybe 'people in hats'.

Listen to a story

This is another one for the car, of course. There are some wonderful audio story CDs available, and they can be most absorbing for everyone in the vehicle. We've especially enjoyed *Charlie and the Chocolate Factory* and *Fantastic Mr Fox* by Roald Dahl, and the stories of *Winnie-the-Pooh* by A.A. Milne.

The waiting game; cafes, waiting rooms and train journeys

On *Facebook* recently, someone wrote this as their *status update* whilst on a journey with their young children,

'On the slow train to Reading. Jake is banging the windows and squawking; Kit is seeing how many times he can count to a hundred. Does anyone have some heroin?'

Apart from being very glad I wasn't on that particular slow train to Reading, it got me thinking how sometimes we can steer, unintentionally, right into the 'nightmare' of travelling with children. Why this parent hadn't thought that he or she could, or should, have redirected their children to do something less maddening is quite baffling. But sometimes we are just so close to it, that we feel resigned to it. It seems inevitable that the little 'tikes' are going to cause havoc and run amok.

Of course this is not the case. With some fun and games, waiting for our food to arrive in cafes, or for our name to be called for our appointment in a waiting room, or for the train to reach its destination can be okay. (Check 10-Second Set-ups, p.70, for plenty of ideas for keeping your little one busy while you're waiting.) It can also be more than okay; a great chance to actually engage with your children and enjoy their company, and not at the expense of annoying other cafe customers or passengers either. See p.257 of Stay and Play for some great word games to play with your child in such situations.

If you can, plan ahead and pack a few things to do together during a waiting time:

Paper games

Bring a few pieces of paper and crayons to play:

☆ **Growing pictures:** Make a crazy picture by each taking turns to add one thing to it.

☆ **Three-part people:** For really young children, fold each player's piece of A4 paper into thirds before you begin – the top section is for a head, the middle third is for a body, and the bottom section is for legs (and feet). Each player draws a head, any head, to fill the top third. Then fold the paper down to the first crease to hide it (your little one will definitely need help with this) and then pass the paper around so everyone has someone else's drawing. Each player now draws a body in the middle section, just as they like, and then folds the paper down to hide their drawing. The last section is for the legs. Pass the paper round again and on the newly received paper draw some legs and feet on the bottom third. Hide the leg drawings then pass the folded sheets of paper round one last time before revealing the very silly and mismatched three-part people (or animals or aliens) by unfolding each sheet of paper.

☆ **Don't cross the line:** One player draws two crosses on a piece of A4 paper some distance apart. The next player joins the two crosses with a line. Then they draw two crosses for the next player to join together. The only rule for this is that when joining the crosses you mustn't cross any line that's already drawn. It gets brilliantly spaghetti-like very quickly.

☆ **Fortune tellers and paper planes:** Simple paper-craft will absolutely wow your little one. Make them a paper hat, a boat, a fan, a plane or fortune teller – whatever you know how to make – and let them decorate it, just as they like, with some crayons.

☆ **Portraiture:** Sit opposite each other and try to draw one another. It's quite hard to do without getting the giggles – and that's before you've seen the finished pictures.

☆ **Hand characters:** We used to play endless rounds of this. Draw around someone's hand on the A4 paper. Now take it in turns to transform each digit into a person or animal character. They could all be from a story if you like. For example, each finger could have a character from Little Red Riding Hood; the woodcutter, the grandmother, the wolf and the wolf in grandma's clothes, and the eponymous heroine herself.

What can we make?

We've played this game many, many times; I always try to have a roll of Sellotape in my bag for the very purpose. It's especially good if there's a lot of packaging left on your table from a recent snack. Use the plastic bottles and straws, boxes and containers destined for the bin in a design challenge. Work together to stick that bottle to that box there, and that stirrer to that rolled-up packet there; see what you can make together. We've had spacecrafts, rockets, machines, sculptural objets d'art and palaces created before now.

Look at a book together

You might feel a little self-conscious reading a story out loud to your children in a public place. If that's the case, choose a favourite look-book from your collection for some gentle conversation instead. See p.228 in Stay and Play for some great examples.

Caring, sharing and other social niceties

A child's individual rate of growth and development will determine *how* and *when* their burgeoning social skills will emerge but, whatever our children are doing and wherever they are, they will absorb how the people around them interact socially. Like little sponges they'll soak it all up, so it's vitally important to model all those caring, sharing and social niceties whenever we can, as early as we can. So, if you want your little one to learn manners, always use good manners yourself. If you'd like them to be able to have basic social interactions with peers and grown ups, make sure you are giving those friendly greetings when you meet acquaintances yourself. And if you don't want them to shout at you all the time, then check *your* volume. Here are some more playful ways to work on those social niceties.

Being able to share

Although it's not in their nature to share, toddlers can be taught how to in a fun way.

☆ Try cutting fruit or flapjack into pieces and putting them on one plate for the whole family to share. Gently guide and prompt your little one to share out the fruit, 'One for Daddy, one for Mia, one for you . . . ' giving lots of praise for sharing so well.

☆ If friends come over to play, put favourite toys away if you think your child will be unlikely to want to share those just yet. Leave out items that are to be the shared toys during the playdate.

☆ Toddlers won't always wait till something is free before making a grab for it. It's important to let them know that sharing is a two-way thing; sometimes you do have to wait to get a turn. Help them understand that waiting for the other person to finish playing with the toy is a kind thing to do.

☆ A game of pass-the-parcel (but using a trinket instead of a parcel) is perfect for trying out those waiting-and-taking timings. See p.256 for a great game that involves this skill.

Learning some basic manners

Have a 'let's pretend' tea party full of phrases like *please, thank you* and *you're welcome, excuse me* and *pardon me*. You could get to some very sophisticated manners in the role-play, like always waiting for an invitation before eating or drinking, or helping the host and saying thank you for having me at the end of the party.

Enjoying basic social interactions with grown ups and peers

Play shops. This will encourage all those well-mannered greetings, polite ways to ask for things and the like. Use soft toys as the other customers or friends meeting in the shop and act out introductions. The more they play this, the more they'll be likely to feel comfortable with a real shopping situation, and not dive behind your leg if you bump into a friend.

Learning to wait their turn without tears or pushing in

Play 'let's pretend' fairgrounds or playgrounds with a few soft toys. Work out together how to stop Teddy from pushing into the queue for the roundabout (umbrellas make great roundabouts for soft toys, by the way) and how to get Hetty the Hedgehog off the seesaw when there are so many others waiting to have a turn. They'll soon be able to handle most situations in the playground confidently and courteously.

Getting adult attention without whining, clinging, crying, screaming or throwing things

Learning to not interrupt adults when they're talking is very hard for little ones, especially if their grown up's attention is always hard to get. Teach them the expression '*Excuse me*' as early as you can and practise responding immediately when they do remember to say the right thing. Use this decorous expression to get their attention too.

Being a leader, and sometimes a follower

Play Follow the Leader, swapping over every minute or so, so that everyone gets a turn at being the leader, deciding the actions everyone has to follow.

Being able to listen, to follow a two or three step set of instructions or directions

☆ Try playing Simon Says. You can change the name of the direction-giver, of course, to 'Ben 10' for example, or to the actual name of the caller. Take out the competitive element of the game – i.e. no eliminations – and instead, take it in turns to listen-and-follow, or direct-and-lead. Remember the trick with this game is to ignore the direction if the caller doesn't say 'Simon says' (or 'Ben 10 says'). You can make it a little more sophisticated by the caller saying to do two things in succession, so, for example, they could say, 'Ben 10 says "nod your head then turn around".'

☆ Play Red Light Green Light. This is a great game to develop those essential listening skills for following directions for road safety. See p.300 to see how to play.

And finally . . .

Play is the most important thing your under-five does; it is their special talent, so *always* recognise it, embrace it and above all celebrate it. Know that it's crucial to their development; it's how they're learning everything right now. The hardwiring for *all* their future imagining, thinking and interacting with the world and everything and everyone in it is being laid down *now*. Play is by far the best way to get all that circuitry beautifully connected and working like a dream. It's an amazing time. So enjoy these years when play rules the day in your little one's world.

A play planner for your family favourites

What did we play?	Why did we play it?	
What's the time Mr Wolf?	Kids full of beans I had 5 mins to play We were outside on a grass area	
We made sun-catchers	It was sunny for once, we wanted to make something together	
We went for a walk – they collected leaves in their bucket	We needed some fresh air and had to walk back from nursery	
I set out blocks, fabric scraps and their little Star Wars figures	Thought they might find their flow with this combination of play-things	
Glow-sticks in bath	To make bath-time irresistible	

Which of the 7 Ways to Play did we use?	What time of day?	Notes
Stay and Play	Afternoon	They LOVED this – loads of running and giggles
Make and Take	Morning	Next time do it when baby is napping
Stay and Play	Just before lunch	Pleased I took the bucket with me
Invitation to Play	Morning	Lots of other things got brought into the play. Stayed with it for about 20 mins, before finding something else to do
Sanity Savers	Just before bedtime	Quite an exciting bath with the lights out for a while

What did we play?	Why did we play it?	

Which of the 7 Ways to Play did we use?	What time of day?	Notes

Useful websites and further reading

There are a huge number of magazines, books, websites and blogs featuring everything and anything to do with parenting. From inspiration, ideas and tips, to opinion, warnings and advice, 'Google' any question about any aspect of parenting and you get literally hundreds of suggested links. Of course, sifting through all that information for what's really relevant can be time-consuming, so this section lists my own personal recommendations for further reading, with particular reference to *playful, positive* parenting. It also includes references to some of the books, articles and websites I used when researching this book. Happily, evidence of the parenting-with-play approach seems to be increasingly prevalent in print, and I'm hopeful it will continue to become more widespread in practice. I am proud to be a playful parent. How about you?

Introduction

David Whitebread, *School starting age: the evidence*, University of Cambridge Research, 2013
www.cam.ac.uk/research/discussion/school-starting-age-the-evidence

Graeme Paton, *Nurseries 'should focus on play – not the three-Rs'*, *The Telegraph*, Sept 2013
www.telegraph.co.uk/education/educationnews/10340228/Nurseries-should-focus-on-play-not-the-three-Rs.html

Emily Dugan, *Under-fives need more time to play, say carers as they warn of 'schoolification' of children's early years, The Independent,* July 2013
www.independent.co.uk/news/education/education-news/underfives-need-more-time-to-play-say-carers-as-they-warn-of-schoolification-of-childrens-early-years-8696176.html

Baby's Brain Begins Now: Conception to Age 3
The Urban Child Institute, 2014
www.urbanchildinstitute.org/why-0-3/baby-and-brain

Susie Steiner, *Six-year-olds need to play, The Guardian,* Jan 2013
www.guardian.co.uk/commentisfree/2013/jan/28/six-year-olds-need-to-play

Paula Spencer, *The magic of play,* parenting.com, 2011
www.parenting.com/article/the-magic-of-play

Anna Ranson, *The central importance of play,* Theimaginationtree.com, March 2011
http://theimaginationtree.com/2011/03/central-importance-of-play.html

Creating indoor environments for young children,
Communityplaythings.com, 2013
www.communityplaythings.com/resources/articles/2011/creating-indoor-environments-for-young-children

Jenny Kable, *Be Reggio inspired,* Letthechildrenplay.net, March 2013
www.letthechildrenplay.net/2013/03/be-reggio-inspired-play-materials.html

Hughes, B., *A Playworker's Taxonomy of Play Types,* 2nd edition, PlayLink 2002

Chores: not Bores

Amelia Hill, *Lack of household chores making children less responsible claims survey, The Guardian,* November 2009
www.theguardian.com/lifeandstyle/2009/nov/15/child-development-chores-responsibility

Heike Larson, *Supporting your child's budding independence at home*, LePort Schools, May, 2013
www.leportschools.com/blog/supporting-your-childs-budding-independence-at-home/

Steve Biddulph, *Raising Girls*, Harper, Jan 2013

10-Second Set-ups
Find inspiration and advice from RIE (Resources for Infant Educarers) parenting expert Janet Lansbury at **www.janetlansbury.com**

Young Children and Computers: Some Pros and Cons, Whattoexpect.com
www.whattoexpect.com/toddler/toddler-learning/young-children-and-computers.aspx

Elizabeth Pantley, *Should babies and toddlers watch television?*, Pregnancy.com
www.pregnancy.about.com/od/yourbaby/a/babiesandtv.htm

Catherine Kedjidjian, *Teaching Concepts of Time to Young Children*, Babyzone.com
www.babyzone.com/kids/preparing-for-preschool/teaching-time-concepts_73200

Carla Poole, Susan A. Miller, EdD, and Ellen Booth Church, *Ages & Stages: How Children Develop a Sense of Time*, Scholastic.com
www.scholastic.com/teachers/article/ages-stages-how-children-develop-sense-time

Sue Palmer, *Toxic Childhood: How The Modern World Is Damaging Our Children And What We Can Do About It*, Orion; New edition, Feb 2007

Pamela Druckerman, *French Kids Don't Throw Food*, Black Swan, Jan 2013

Peter Gray, *The play deficit*, Aeon Magazine, 2013
http://aeon.co/magazine/being-human/children-today-are-suffering-a-severe-deficit-of-play/

Invitations to Play

Lots of parent and teacher bloggers regularly share ideas for setting up invitations to play. Here are a few of my favourites:

Jenny Kable, *Let the children play*, **http://www.letthechildrenplay.net/**
Christie Burnett, *Childhood 101*, **http://childhood101.com/**
Anna Ranson, *The Imagination Tree*, **http://theimaginationtree.com/**
Arlee Greenwood, *Small Potatoes*, **www.mysmallpotatoes.com**
Sheryl Cooper, *Teaching 2 and 3 year olds*, **http://www. teaching2and3yearolds.com/**

Ken Finch, *A Parent's Guide to Nature Play*, Greenhearts; Institute for Nature in Childhood, 2009
http://www.greenheartsinc.org/uploads/A_Parents__Guide_to_Nature_Play.pdf

Ashley Phillips, *Going Solo: Independent Play in Toddlers*, *Parents Magazine* 2009
www.parents.com/toddlers-preschoolers/development/social/independent-play-toddlers/?page=2

Deborah Stewart, *An invitation to play tutorial*, Teachpreschool.org, July 2013
www.teachpreschool.org/2012/07/an-invitation-to-play-tutorial/

Kim Row, *There are only two types of toys*, Modernparentsmessykids.com, June 2012
www.modernparentsmessykids.com/2012/06/there-are-only-two-types-of-toys.html

Kristie Lau, *How almost half of preschool children do not play outside each day – and girls are less likely to get fresh air than boys*, *The Daily Mail*, April 2012
www.dailymail.co.uk/femail/article-2125197/How-half-preschool-children-play-outside-day-girls-likely-fresh-air-boys.html

National Wildlife Federation, *Why be out there; health benefits*, nwf.org
www.nwf.org/Be-Out-There/Why-Be-Out-There/Health-Benefits.aspx

Invitations to Create

Guy Claxton and Bill Lucas, *Be Creative*, BBC Books, 2004

Sir Ken Robinson, *Out of our Minds: Learning To Be Creative*, Oxford 2001

Education Scotland, *Fostering creativity*, Journeytoexcellence.org.uk
**www.journeytoexcellence.org.uk/resourcesandcpd/research/summaries/
rsfosteringcreativity.asp**

Shared creative projects aplenty here online at the *Kids Get Arty Linky Party* with Maggy Woodley's website, Red Ted Art
http://www.redtedart.com/kids-get-arty/

Caroline Sharp, *Developing young children's creativity: what can we learn from research?*, NFER Issue 32, Autumn 2004
www.nfer.ac.uk/nfer/publications/55502/55502.pdf

Valerie Strauss, *Top 10 skills children learn from the arts*, The Washington Post, Jan 2013
www.washingtonpost.com/blogs/answer-sheet/wp/2013/01/22/top-10-skills-children-learn-from-the-arts/

Make and Take

Cathy Abraham, *Woodworking with children*, Childcarelounge, 2005
www.childcarelounge.com/activity/wood-working.php

Collaborative *Pinterest* board from the amazing *Kid Blogger Network* has hundreds of make and take ideas
http://www.pinterest.com/playdrmom/kid-blogger-network-activities-crafts/

Katy Ashworth, *If flour + sugar + children = mess, why let them bake?*, BBC News Magazine, Aug 2010
www.bbc.co.uk/news/magazine-10936342

Valerie Deneen, *5 biggest obstacles to crafting with kids*, Innerchildfun, Jan 2013
innerchildfun.com/2013/01/5-biggest-obstacles-to-crafting-with-kids.html

Alissa Marquess, *10 Ways to Guarantee You Will Hate Doing Kids Crafts*, Creativewithkids.com, September 20, 2011
creativewithkids.com/10-way-to-guarantee-you-will-hate-doing-kids-crafts/

Susan Case, *Why Craft? Why Art?*, Kindergarten for parents and teachers, December 2011
kindergartenbasics.blogspot.co.uk/2011/12/why-craft.html

Lots of parent and teacher bloggers regularly share ideas for make and take activities. Here are a couple of my favourites:
Jackie Currie, *Happy Hooligans*, **http://happyhooligans.ca/**
Maggy Woodley, *Red Ted Art*, **http://www.redtedart.com/**

Stay and Play

Melinda Smith, M.A., Bernie DeKoven, Robert Segal, M.A., and Jeanne Segal, Ph.D, *How to play and boost creativity*, Helpguide.org, February 2014. **www.helpguide.org/life/creative_play_fun_games.htm**

Sanity Savers

Anne Stonehouse, *Positive toileting and nappy changing*, National Childcare Accreditation Council Inc, archived resources, 2009
ncac.acecqa.gov.au/educator-resources/factsheets/fdcqa_factsheet_16_ toileting_and_nappy_changing.pdf

James Lehman, MSW, *Temper, Temper: Keeping Your Cool When Kids Push Your Buttons*, Empoweringparents.com
www.empoweringparents.com/How-to-Keep-Cool-When-the-Kids-Push-Your-Buttons.php

Dr Laura Markham's website *AHA! Parenting* has advice aplenty about transforming parenting – and children's behaviour – for the better
www.ahaparenting.com/

The NSPCC website has advice for parents on positive parenting methods for encouraging good behaviour in children, and a downloadable booklet *Encouraging better behaviour: A practical guide to positive parenting.*
http://www.nspcc.org.uk/help-and-advice/for-parents/positive-parenting-tips/encouraging-better-behaviour/better-behaviour_wda96810.html

Index